Praise for *A Small Town Rises*

"*A Small Town Rises* enlarges the landscape of the 1960s civil rights movement by recording the heroism of small-town Shaw, Mississippi. Through the memories of Eddie Short and Mary Sue Gellatly, we discover the dedication and passion that propelled the transformation of a nation. In the process, they discovered a love born in the struggle for social justice that would span decades."
—Dr. Sandra E. Jones, Department of African and African Diasporic Studies, University of Wisconsin, Milwaukee

"Volunteering in Shaw, Mississippi, in the mid-sixties was an epiphany for me. *A Small Town Rises* tells a story of guts, fear, jail, and love. A tale of daring in a time of great danger, the book recounts the activism of a white woman from Oregon and a black sharecropper, two of the unknown heroes working for justice in a small Delta town."
—Dennis Flannigan, Washington State Representative, 2002–2010

"As someone who grew up in Mississippi during the civil rights era, I can confirm that the story authentically captures the time, the place, and the people involved in the struggle. As I read *A Small Town Rises*, I came to admire Mary Sue and Eddie and the courageous residents of Shaw. This story is a fundamental part of the great American story and is one that should be widely read and discussed."
—William "Bill" Blakney, senior deputy, Prosecuting Attorney's Office, King County, Washington (retired)

A Small Town Rises

A Small Town Rises

A Sharecropper and a College
Girl Join the Struggle for Justice
in Shaw, Mississippi

Lee Anna Sherman

Bog Lily Press

Design by Meadowlark Publishing Services
Cover photo: Shaw activists march for voting rights at the Bolivar County Courthouse, Cleveland, Mississippi, February 11, 1965. (Photo by Mary Sue Gellatly; spot color by Richard Hawk)

Published by Bog Lily Press
www.asmalltownrises.com

Manufactured in the United States of America
ISBN 978-1-73447881-5

Published 2020

This book is dedicated to Janie Beatrice Short,
Verna Gellatly, and Molly Sherman Percival,
mothers of another generation
whose choices in life were limited
but who nevertheless persevered with love.

Contents

Prologue

From a distance on Google Earth, the Mississippi-Arkansas border forms a jigsaw pattern, its extravagant curves and swooping oxbows carved by the Mississippi River as it flows from its headwaters in Minnesota toward the Gulf of Mexico. To the east of the great river, some thirty miles inside the Mississippi state line, the town of Shaw appears as a tiny triangle in an endless expanse of farmland. The rectangular patches of cotton and soy contrast sharply with the unfettered wanderings of nature's bayous and streams as they run ribbonlike through the regimented landscape. This clash, visible on the map—free-running waters pushing against the hard, straight lines made by plows to box in nature—mirrors the clash that rocked Shaw in the mid-1960s.

The little town of Shaw sits on some of the world's most fertile land, the Mississippi Delta, whose rich alluvial soils were laid down over eons by the mighty river's muddy floodwaters and those of a parallel river to the east called the Yazoo. Shaw shares this northwest edge of Mississippi with a scattering of other hamlets—Merigold, Mound Bayou, Sunflower, Ruleville—and with the seat of Bolivar County, the relative metropolis of Cleveland, Mississippi, population twelve thousand.

When European settlers arrived on this floodplain in the mid-1800s, the six-thousand-square-mile crescent of deep,

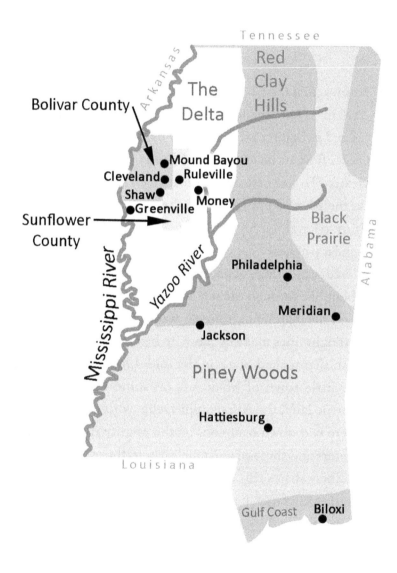

Mississippi

rich bottomland was a wilderness. Its swamps and bayous bristled with catfish, buffalo fish, turtles, and sturgeon. It buzzed with battalions of cicadas and squadrons of dragonflies. Its forests of cypress, ash, cottonwood, oak, hickory, pecan, persimmon, wild plum, and mulberry were home to panthers, wolves, and bears. Ducks by the millions stopped there on their long migrations. Cranes and swans and osprey foraged and hunted in the wildlands then. The Choctaw and Chickasaw Indians and other bands and tribes inhabited the region in the unrecorded time before white settlers arrived.

In this teeming landscape, the white settlers found fertile ground for a lucrative cash crop: cotton. But millions of tons of hardwood forest were in the way of cultivation. At a time when land was cleared not by machine but by muscle, the settlers brought enslaved black men to the task. Marching their captive labor force to the Delta, the settlers set them to hacking down the wilderness with axes. The cotton that would eventually enrich the white settlers was, in turn, planted, weeded, and harvested by enslaved black families.

Within a couple of decades, the Civil War freed American slaves from overt bondage. But planters found new ways to extract black labor. Sharecropping was one of the exploitive tactics Pulitzer Prize–winning journalist Douglas A. Blackmon characterizes as "slavery by another name." King Cotton continued to hold black citizens in economic servitude for a hundred years after emancipation.

When you zoom in further on Google Earth, the tiny triangle of Shaw resolves into a cluster of small roofs and

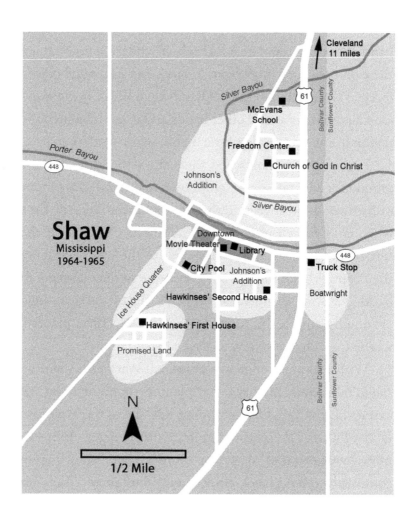

treetops wedged into the angle where U.S. Highway 61 intersects Highway 448, which parallels a lazy waterway known as Porter Bayou. Shaw's footprint at that intersection of fast, noisy traffic and slow, silent water is an apt metaphor for the collision of civil action and cultural inertia that rattled the little town in the 1960s.

This is the story of two civil rights activists, one black, one white, anonymous foot soldiers in the struggle for racial justice in the cotton town of Shaw. A college girl from the North, Mary Sue Gellatly, and a sharecropper from the South, Eddie Short, teamed up with a charismatic black tradesman named Andrew Hawkins to help shake the townspeople out of a long torpor, one that a century of white intimidation and exploitation had lulled black residents into. Hawkins, known around town as a hard-working, brave, and righteous man, laid the groundwork for Shaw's rising starting in about 1962.

He began by holding covert meetings in the living room of his family's modest wood-plank house, with up-and-coming black leaders like Bob Moses, Stokely Carmichael, and Fannie Lou Hamer, to help plan a massive statewide voter-registration campaign. By 1964, the campaign had been christened the Mississippi Summer Project. Quickly nicknamed Freedom Summer, the project was the brainchild of Moses, a twenty-nine-year-old from Harlem who had earned his master's in philosophy from Harvard, and other passionate young visionaries in a powerful coalition of civil rights organizations—CORE, SNCC ("Snick"), the NAACP, the SCLC, and the umbrella that arched over them all, COFO*—that were gaining traction in the civil rights community nationwide.

During the project's planning phase, dissent rocked SNCC's leadership ranks. Moses's idea of enlisting white college kids met fierce resistance among his colleagues. But black Mississippians felt otherwise. "The farmers, and the people who live and work there, welcomed the whole idea," Moses said. "Because they feel that anybody who comes down to help is good."

So Moses's plan prevailed. CORE, SNCC, and COFO would recruit and train some eight hundred northern volunteers, mostly white college students, to come to Mississippi for ten weeks. The volunteers would live in the homes of black residents and collaborate with black activists to teach the fundamentals of voting—registration, polling places, ballots.

Mary Sue was finishing her degree in music at Oregon's Willamette University when she heard about the call for volunteers for the summer project. She had spent the previous summer canvassing black voters in Nashville and had gone to jail for a night with her fellow activists. She resolved to go to Mississippi. For his part, Eddie plunged into activism as soon as he got wind of Hawkins's covert meetings. To him, the coming influx of white volunteers from the North represented a once-unthinkable chink in the armor of southern racism. He was ready to fight for his rights.

Freedom Summer shook loose the latent power of Shaw's

---

* Congress of Racial Equality, Student Nonviolent Coordinating Committee, National Association for the Advancement of Colored People, Southern Christian Leadership Conference, Council of Federated Organizations

black citizenry—power that had been browbeaten and bullied and, for self-preservation, had gone mostly underground in the years since Reconstruction unraveled. But beneath the surface, beyond the scrutiny of the white establishment, that power still bubbled and hummed in Shaw's black community. It lived in church services, where the Holy Spirt had a lively presence. It thrived in family bonds, fierce and proud and enduring. It survived in neighbor-to-neighbor ties, folks lending a hand. The strength of Shaw's collective black power, when uncorked in 1964, blew the lid off the town's status quo in ways nobody could have foreseen.

White supremacists fought back against the rising. Deputies arrested dozens of citizens, some over and over, Mary Sue and Eddie among them. But the power was unstoppable. High school students unionized and staged a protest for better education. Church mothers stood up in mass meetings to speak about racial justice. Families shared their spartan homes with strangers. Elders hosted "freedom schools" in the nooks and crannies of their shacks, where citizens old and young pressed in close to learn the ropes of voting. Black youths staged a public protest, the first ever in Shaw. At segregated public places—a diner, a library, a theater, a park—they asserted their rights to service, rights Congress encoded in the Civil Rights Act that very summer. They even poked at the South's biggest boogeyman—physical mingling of the races—when they conspired to take a dip in the public swimming pool. And in perhaps the most stunning affront to the once-immovable power of King Cotton, black fieldworkers laid down their hoes and dropped their cotton sacks to demand fair wages for chopping and picking.

Freedom Summer had barely gotten off the ground when it grabbed the national spotlight. Three civil rights workers—a black activist from Mississippi and two white activists from New York—disappeared in a Delta town just hours down the road from Shaw. Americans watched FBI agents and corpse-sniffing dogs on their TV screens as CBS anchorman Walter Cronkite and a team of reporters fanned out across Mississippi with their notepads, microphones, and cameras. Six weeks later, the unearthing of the murdered activists' bodies from the Mississippi mud horrified Americans from coast to coast. In the flickering images displayed on millions of cathode-ray tubes, the status quo in Mississippi took a body blow.

Shaw was in the trenches of the seismic changes rocking the Mississippi Delta not only in the summer of 1964 but also for several years afterward. Whites abandoned or even burned down their businesses rather than serve black customers. City workers drained the pool to avoid integration. Displaced fieldworkers and blackballed activists packed their few possessions and headed north to Chicago or Memphis or Detroit. The town's white-power bastion took another hit when Andrew Hawkins and twenty other black residents filed a class-action lawsuit against the city in 1967. The suit, a landmark in civil rights law, brought both victory and tragedy to the little town of Shaw.

From Google Earth's street-level view, the physical evidence of that collision comes into stark focus. On Main Street are the same cracked and buckled sidewalks, shattered storefronts, and charred remains of a movie theater that have sat in the center of Shaw for fifty years. The once-lively downtown, now a forlorn ruin, looks like a crime scene. If you were to sift the forensic clues, you would find evidence of a shameful conspiracy against African Americans, a generations-old tradition of exploitation whose cover was blown when a bunch of idealistic students from up north joined forces with black Mississippians to push for equal access to voting rights in the summer of 1964.

The story begins as the moon rises over the bayou one winter night in 1965 and an act of hate shakes the town.

1

Rumblings

Just like moons and like suns,
With the certainty of tides,
Just like hopes springing high,
Still I'll rise.
—Maya Angelou, from "Still I Rise"

Shaw, Mississippi, February 1965

On the night of February 5, 1965, the little town of Shaw lay still beneath a dome of stars. Its two thousand residents, most of them black, were tucking in their small children, three or four to a bed, while the last embers in their woodstoves turned to ash. Outside, the calls of winter-breeding frogs sounded up and down the bayou, a restless chorus of croaks, clicks, and whistles, the ancient symphony of the Mississippi Delta. Beyond, from horizon to horizon, stretched the cotton fields, hard and cold under the starlight, fallow and waiting.

Whites owned most of the land in the Delta, while blacks chopped the weeds and picked the crops under summer's merciless sun. The miserly wages they earned with their sweat, muscle, skill, and endurance kept them perpetually on the cusp of hunger and in debt to the Boss Man.

Late winter typically brought a respite of sorts to the little Delta town of Shaw, a break from the grinding labor. But without the wages that kept collard greens and cornbread on the table, fieldworkers had to be resourceful or go hungry. During the cool months when Shaw's cotton gins sat dark and still, black residents patched together whatever odd jobs they could find until Earth's orbit carried them around to planting season once more. Then they would rise each morning at first light and, if they lived in town, climb aboard one of the trucks sent by Bolivar County's white planters to pick up workers. If they lived on a plantation, working a small plot of land for the planter, the cotton grew right up to their front porch. Hoes in hand, they would bend to the task of growing Delta cotton, a crop that brought cash receipts of $313 million to Mississippi in 1964—75 percent of the state's total for all crops grown. Whole families of black Mississippians labored "from sun to sun" (sunup to sundown) in the fields of their white overlords.

But if the rhythms of the Delta seemed eternal on this star-filled night in 1965, a closer look would tell a different story. As the Milky Way swarmed across the heavens like a million fireflies, it cast nearly the only light visible in Shaw's drowsy neighborhood called Johnson's Addition, with one exception: a yellow glow shining from the windows of a small, plain wooden church, where a longer-than-usual civil rights meeting was just adjourning. A kind of electricity bristled in the postures of the people as they dispersed into the night. Buttoning their coats against the chill, these descendants of African slaves radiated the power of collective action, of standing firm for a righteous cause, of acting in concert to throw off, once and for all, the boot of racial injustice they and their forebears had endured for generations.

Some of them cradled babies or sleeping toddlers in their arms as they called out their goodbyes, their voices newly emboldened since the civil rights movement had come to Shaw the year before.

"G'night, Nola Mae!"

"Y'all take care, now, Missey."

"See ya in the mornin', Charles, bright 'n' early."

No streetlamps lit their homeward trek on this dark night. In Shaw, street lighting was reserved for white neighborhoods. So, too, were indoor plumbing, paved roads, and telephone service. As the activists made their way along the dirt roads and footpaths that were their familiar avenues of commerce and community, the shadows quickly swallowed them up.

Among the last to leave the church that night were two young civil rights workers who had been challenging the white power structure in Mississippi since the previous summer. Their names were Eddie Short and Mary Sue Gellatly. Eddie was a Delta native, born and bred in Shaw. Mary Sue was new to the Delta, some would say an outsider, a girl whose roots were in the rain-soaked soil of the Pacific Northwest two thousand miles away. As different as they were, they had forged a bond of friendship as they stood together against the clenched hands and tight fists of the planters, politicians, publishers, and business owners who ran the town and the county.

Theirs was an improbable friendship on just about every

level. Eddie was raised in the very marrow of King Cotton. He had Shaw in his blood. Mary Sue, on the other hand, was new to the South, one of about eight hundred college students and recent graduates who in June 1964 had rolled into Mississippi aboard clunky old cars and chartered buses from points north and west—from California and New York, from the Pacific Northwest and New England, from Puget Sound and Cape Cod. Inspired by the ideal of social justice, these young Americans, mostly white, mostly affluent, had volunteered to join black Mississippians in their struggle against discriminatory voting practices in a segregated state that flagrantly flouted the rights of its black citizens. The initiative's formal name was the Mississippi Summer Project, but the project's name had quickly shifted to something punchier, something easier to remember, something that rolled off the tongue: Freedom Summer. The shorthand stuck.

Before Freedom Summer, few of these young northerners had met overt racism face-to-face. By summer's end, all of them had looked it straight in the eye. Mississippi's culture of terror and intimidation against black citizens shocked their consciences. But for black residents, this was their habitat, their day-upon-day waking, their night-after-night sleeping. For Eddie, racism had defined his life in a thousand ways since he was a toddler living in a sharecropper's shack. Watching his mama, Janie Beatrice (known by everyone as Mrs. Janie Bea), cry when her babies died for lack of medical care. Seeing his father, Willie James (known around Shaw as Mr. Willie), flee Shaw after a white man threatened to kill him for joining the NAACP, a civil rights organization formed in 1909 to fight for racial equality and against discrimination.

4

Before Freedom Summer, Eddie had decided to enlist in the Army. He figured if he didn't die in the jungles of Vietnam, he might come back with a bankable skill. But on the morning of his Army physical exam, he woke up with a nasty case of tonsillitis. The recruiter took one look at his inflamed throat and sent him home with instructions to come back when the infection had subsided. Eddie went back to Shaw to get well. The civil rights meetings in Shaw were by then picking up steam, moving out of living rooms into black churches. To pass the time, Eddie would slip into a pew at the Church of God in Christ and listen to Andrew Hawkins from Shaw and Fannie Lou Hamer (pronounced *HAY-mer*) from the neighboring town of Ruleville speak and sing about freedom and justice. A realization took hold in his heart: his fight wasn't in Vietnam but right here in his hometown. He would fight, he decided, or he would die.

Since the early 1960s, black-led sit-ins and boycotts and marches had been disrupting white complacency in Mississippi's neighboring states. Activists that were dubbed the Freedom Riders had tried to integrate buses starting in 1961, and many of them had been jailed and beaten. During a series of protests in Birmingham, Alabama, in the spring of 1963, the police had turned dogs and fire hoses on demonstrators and arrested civil rights leader Dr. Martin Luther King Jr. The August 1963 March for Jobs in Washington, D.C., had drawn a quarter of a million people to mass peacefully on the mall. Mary Sue was among them, a college student who had ridden a yellow school bus with a team of activists from Nashville, where she had spent the summer canvassing black neighborhoods.

On the eve of Freedom Summer, Eddie could feel the tremor of change in his own neighborhood, the black neighborhood where Andrew Hawkins was risking his livelihood, even his life, to stand against injustice, against the indignities of being black in the segregated South. Indignities like casting your eyes downward when passing a white person on the street. Like ordering food at the back door of a diner. Like looking through a chain-link fence at the city swimming pool on a hot summer day, watching white kids splash and laugh.

When the northern volunteers started to show up in towns up and down Mississippi, white resistance rose to a fever pitch. But this time, unlike the past, the timeworn tactics of intimidation and terror—of beating down black rebellion by burning crosses and bombing churches, firing fieldworkers and threatening families, hanging men in trees and dumping their bodies in bayous—would come under scrutiny when northern journalists came south to cover Freedom Summer for mainstream media outlets. And journalists wouldn't be the only ones watching. Religious leaders, members of Congress, civil rights lawyers, and most important, the parents of the volunteers would be keeping a stern eye on Mississippi that summer.

Still, the risks were tangible and terrifying, the outcomes unknown. Just one thing was certain: change was coming to the Delta. There was a prickling in the air, a sensation like a sudden shift in the weather, like storm clouds moving across the landscape heavy with rain. Everyone sensed, somehow knew, that nothing would ever be the same—not for Eddie Short and the other black activists who rose up in Shaw, not for Mary Sue Gellatly and the other northern volunteers who with their southern counterparts waded into the dark waters of Mississippi racism with little more than idealism to buoy them.

THE TWO FREEDOM FIGHTERS were barely out of their teens as they stepped into the civil rights battle. Eddie was twenty-one, Mary Sue twenty-two, when they met in 1964. Age was the only outward similarity between them. He was from the rural South, his skin the color of coffee. She was from the urban North, her skin the color of cream. His ancestors came to America from West Africa forcibly in chains, kidnapped from their ancestral homeland—Ghana, Cameroon, Togo, Ivory Coast—by white slave traders. Her ancestors came from northern Europe, freely, uncoerced, farmers and tradesmen from Great Britain and Scandinavia, seeking a fresh start and a better life. She was six feet tall, he was five foot six. Eddie had a diploma from a segregated high school whose textbooks were handed down, torn and outdated, from the white school across town. She had just graduated from a prestigious private university in the capital city of one of the whitest states in America.

Before the summer of 1964, Mary Sue had never heard of Shaw, Mississippi. For Eddie, Shaw was all he knew. He grew up picking cotton on a white man's plantation. In a two-room shack without plumbing or electricity, his God-fearing mama would stoke up the woodstove until it glowed red and cook cracklin' pork and collard greens "like nobody else," Eddie recalls. But in the winter, when the fields were fallow, Eddie and his siblings often went to bed hungry. Mary Sue grew up in a small house her father had built on a wooded hill above Portland, Oregon. Her blue-collar dad was a steady provider, and her stay-at-home mom was an avid reader who borrowed paintings and piano music from the Multnomah County Library so her children could know Matisse and Mozart on a tight budget. The Gellatlys lived modestly but comfortably.

The outward differences, then, were stark. Eddie was part of the "other America" described in the eponymous 1962 best-selling book by Michael Harrington—poor people living in desperation amidst unprecedented wealth and abundance. Mary Sue was a product of middle-class America, a straight-arrow girl who followed the rules, got good grades, and was headed for a conventional life. But there was something inside her, a kernel of outrage that smoldered in her chest whenever she glimpsed injustice, inhumanity, or indignity inflicted on others. Racism, especially, made her blood boil. She remembers seeing a live performance by black comedian and civil rights activist Dick Gregory in her hometown of Portland. Famous for his satirical commentary on racial injustice in America, Gregory stirred her conscience, his hard truths wrapped in raw humor, like a rock in a snowball. Eddie's blood boiled, too, but his outrage was personal, rising from a lifetime of subjugation and oppression, a culture that robbed him of his wholeness as a human being and thwarted his potential as a man.

It was this, then, that drew these two American youths toward the same light. With unflinching countenance, they stood together in Mississippi in 1964 and 1965. Even when things turned murderous—as they did when three young civil rights workers were kidnapped, murdered, and buried with a backhoe in an earthen dam just hours after leaving a weeklong Freedom Summer training—Eddie and Mary Sue were able to tamp down the fear that could so easily have defeated them. As the hate and brutality played out, the two activists became masters of managing anxiety.

In Shaw, whose population of two thousand was nearly 65 percent black, Mary Sue stood out like a willow tree in a field of wheat. Folks who hadn't met her yet referred to her as the "tall, skinny white girl." People would nod, knowingly, "Yessir, I know the one you mean, that college girl from up north." Eddie admired her grit and doggedness, traits he shared—traits that let him survive a childhood of scarcity, hunger, and grinding labor. He also liked the sincere respect Mary Sue showed to everyone, whether the giggling preteens who would peek through the church windows during late-night meetings or Mrs. Florence "Flossie" Minley, a black landowner and proprietor of a tiny grocery store where Mary Sue often bought a hot pork sandwich for lunch, sometimes topping it off with a slice of Mrs. Minley's sweet potato pie at no extra charge. Eddie noticed that Mary Sue voiced her opinions without ego or arrogance, in keeping with SNCC's mission to empower local leaders, not boss them around. Eddie observed that Mary Sue readily deferred to the wishes of local black activists, never insisting on her own viewpoint.

For her part, Mary Sue admired Eddie's courage and resolve. She shared the assessment of his many friends and large family, who knew him as a stand-up guy, pretty much fearless, often worrying his mama nearly to death with his rebellious spirit. Eddie packed a surprising measure of pride and power into his featherweight body. Every ounce of the one hundred twenty-five pounds he carried on his compact frame was rock solid. As the months unfolded, Mary Sue found Eddie to be uncommonly reliable, both as a coworker and as a friend. One night not long after coming to Shaw, she turned her ankle painfully in a drainage ditch along one of the dark dirt roads. Every evening thereafter, Eddie walked her home after work, an act of chivalry that put him at great risk. In the Mississippi Delta of 1965, a black man who walked with a white woman, especially at night, could be hanging on a rope by morning. Looking back, he shrugged off the danger. "I wanted to keep her safe."

THAT STAR-FILLED FEBRUARY NIGHT as the church deacons switched off the lights and locked the doors, the evening's songs reverberated in the minds of the two activists. The "freedom songs," derived from old Negro spirituals and field hollers (call-and-response chants synchronized with the rhythms of sowing and reaping), echoed the earliest themes of black music in America, the hidden subtexts of resistance to slavery and hope of liberation. Eddie and Mary Sue were especially buoyed, as they always were, by the end-of-meeting ritual: crossing their arms in front of their bodies and joining hands with the men and women on either side, then raising their voices to the rafters as they sang, "Deep in my heart, I do believe, we shall overcome someday," the anthem of the civil rights movement. To their bones, they felt the person-to-person bond, the affirmation of unity, the embodiment of solidarity the ritual symbolized. This time, on this starry night, the aspiration of the anthem seemed closer at hand than ever before.

Outside the church, four or five other young activists lingered as the night deepened. When Mary Sue and Eddie appeared, they all fell in together for the short walk back to project headquarters. It was so dark, they couldn't see each other's faces, much less the ditches and potholes that made walking treacherous on this dirt road. Despite the chill and the potholes and the lateness of the night, their footsteps were light. They were riding a wave of inspiration and energy sparked by the gathering, whose cadence had flowed like a river's—the freshet of freedom songs, the churn of fiery speeches, the deep pools of prayerfulness.

That evening's meeting had been one of the best-attended mass meetings in Shaw, drawing at least sixty black citizens. They knew the risks. The ranks of the Ku Klux Klan, the white terrorist group whose hooded members had been burning crosses and lynching blacks in the South for more than a hundred years, had swelled to ten thousand in Mississippi in 1964, a reaction to the growing strength of civil rights activism throughout the South. On April 24, the Klan set fire to sixty-one crosses simultaneously across Mississippi. Then, over the summer, twenty black churches were torched in retribution for hosting civil rights meetings—meetings just like the one they had attended that very night. They knew that local informants were ready to rat out a neighbor for a few bucks or an extra bucket of molasses. They knew, too, that if anyone at the meeting got beaten or turned up dead in the bayou, the perpetrators would not be held to account in this state where the cops and the courts not only turned a blind eye to white-on-black violence but also were often complicit in the crime.

What the meeting goers *didn't* know that night was that a gang of local white supremacists was gathering on a remote road, unseen in the darkness. While the activists stood shoulder-to-shoulder in the small wooden church singing chorus after chorus of "This little light of mine, I'm gonna let it shine"—a children's folk song that had become another anthem of the civil rights movement—they were unaware that the gang members were at that moment loading the makings of a Molotov cocktail into a dusty pickup truck. As the civil rights meeting broke up and the people headed home, the gang skulked in the shadows, waiting, biding their time.

Shaw might have seemed sleepy and peaceful, but that outward tranquility had been bought over the years by intimidation and fear. The threat of violence, like an evil wind, had long been blowing through town and its surrounding plantations, a constant reminder to keep your eyes cast down and your demeanor submissive if you were black. When Freedom Summer threatened to supplant intimidation with electoral power, to give voice to Bolivar County's black majority at the ballot box, the foul winds of racism whirled up with new fury. Klansmen dusted off their pointy hoods. They cleaned their guns. They sent their spies into the churches and pool halls and juke joints to finger activists and their sympathizers.

As Eddie, Mary Sue, and their companions walked along the dark dirt road on that star-filled night, trying to keep the excitement out of their voices so as not to disturb sleeping neighbors, their conversation mingled with the winter songs of frogs in Shaw's bayous, the big Porter and the little Silver—marshy streams that flowed through town, sluggish but determined. To local residents, Porter Bayou was just "the bayou," a landmark by which they navigated day to day, the defining characteristic of Shaw's geography. It was a watery demarcation between the places where people traded and where they lived.

To the south of the bayou was a cluster of white-owned businesses—Rubenstein's Dry Goods, Ross Dry Goods, Seligman's Dry Goods, Piggly Wiggly, Chung Lee Grocery, Five & Ten Cent Store, P.M. Bennett Furniture, Dixie Tobacco & Candy Wholesalers, Langston Insurance, Union Planter Bank, two black barbershops, one white barbershop, and three doctors' offices. Shaw's best-known physician, Doc Peeler, accepted black patients, but like every other service in Jim Crow Mississippi, his clinic was split into two sections, one for "colored" people and one for white people. The two-block commercial district, everyone called downtown. To the north and south of downtown was Johnson's Addition, the black neighborhood where the church hosted mass meetings several times a week.

After walking a few blocks down the dark road, the young workers turned in at a small white wooden house, freshly painted. They bounded up the creaky steps and once inside flipped the switch that lit up the front room's single bare lightbulb. The house, owned by a black resident Eddie remembers only as Mrs. Lee, was the local headquarters of SNCC. They called it the Freedom Center. It was the hub of activism in Shaw.

Eddie was making everyone laugh with his wisecracks. Humor was one of his many survival skills, the ability to laugh in the face of danger that is shared by soldiers in situations that seem anything but funny. As the author of *Deep Survival: Who Lives, Who Dies, and Why,* Laurence Gonzales, writes, "Foxhole humor is well known among soldiers and is an essential ingredient for survival anywhere." Eddie perched on one of the rickety donated chairs while Mary Sue, calm and methodical as usual, checked for messages from SNCC's Jackson headquarters. As the only two staff members at the Shaw headquarters that winter, each earned living expenses of $9.64 a week. The stipend, which amounted to $38.56 per month, was bare bones even at a time when the average American renter paid $115 a month for housing. It lent extra irony to the local newspaper's assertion that northern activists—whom the editor characterized as "invaders," "hate mongers," "beatniks," and "communists"—were "paid agitators" motivated by "financial gain."

Despite the late hour, the civil rights workers quickly got down to business, talking over what they'd learned about the next day's action on voting rights violations. Frank Davis, a Bolivar County activist from nearby Rosedale, the so-called Delta City of Brotherly Love, had stood up in church that evening and electrified the crowd with big news: corrupt elections officials had been subpoenaed by Congress to testify about illegal tactics to block the black vote. They would be forced, finally, to defend the unlawful poll taxes and phony literacy tests they were using to deprive black voters of their rights as citizens.

According to Davis, the very next day up the road in Cleveland, Mississippi, black citizens would show up in droves to sign affidavits testifying to their own thwarted attempts to register. The residents of Shaw had stood up, one by one, in the church and vowed to participate. Mary Sue and Eddie had offered to drive people to Cleveland in the 1956 Chevy station wagon that had been donated to SNCC by a supporter in Staten Island, New York, and driven to Shaw in a choking cloud of burning oil by a volunteer from Tacoma, Washington, named Dennis Flannigan.

As the young civil rights workers excitedly talked over the new developments, their conversation stalled in midsentence. They sat still, their ears alert to the noise of an engine coming toward them from down the dark dirt road, probably a pickup truck. The sound got louder until it was right outside the Freedom Center. In a frenzy of honking, its engine gunning aggressively, the truck roared past and disappeared down the road.

The workers, frozen to their chairs, stared at each other in mute confusion. The whole commotion had lasted maybe half a minute. One of the workers jumped up from his perch and looked out the window. "Our car's on fire!" he shouted.

They all ran outside. Just feet from the house, the Chevy wagon sat engulfed in a white-hot ball of flame. Mary Sue grabbed her camera and snapped some photos to document the crime. Her eyes scanned the shadows, which seemed to deepen around her as the Chevy burned. She shivered. Then she shook off her uneasiness and, in keeping with her characteristic devotion to duty, reverted from shaken activist to clear-headed project director in barely more than a blink of her brown eyes.

Running into the center, she picked up the phone and dialed SNCC headquarters on the WATS line. Civil rights groups like SNCC could not only save money using WATS

(Wide Area Telephone Service, an early version of low-cost, direct-dial, long-distance phone service) but also dodge the eavesdropping phone operators who might listen in and tip off other whites. Waiting for the Jackson office to pick up the phone, her mind flashed back to the photos she had seen just a few weeks earlier of the burnt-out shell of the blue Ford station wagon the three volunteers had been driving when they disappeared in June 1964. She thought, too, of the WATS reports she had read from the other SNCC project sites. Towns across Mississippi had experienced car bombings, church arsons, and even murder since the project had launched the previous summer.

Intimidation was a way of life for civil rights workers in the South. The so-called night riders—Klan-affiliated white men skulking around town shouting obscenities from pickup trucks outfitted with shotguns—were nothing new for Eddie and Mary Sue. Over the months, men in pickups had circled the Freedom Center over and over, spewing their venom with taunts such as "Nigger lover!" and "Yankees go home!" But this was the first violent act aimed directly at Shaw's civil rights workers and volunteers. Eddie and Mary Sue sensed that the risks had increased by several orders of magnitude that night.

Mary Sue knew there was no point in calling the police in this white-controlled town. Even if the cops came, which was not guaranteed, no legitimate investigation would be launched, no perpetrator arrested. City officials, including the police, had a vested interest in protecting white dominance on the Delta.

By the time the fire had burned out, the car was nothing

but a smoking carcass of blackened steel. The Chevy had been the activists' only means of travel beyond the cramped confines of Shaw's city limits. It was essential to their work, getting out to neighboring plantations where potential black voters lived under the suspicious eyes of their white bosses, men who would fire a laborer (or worse) for exercising their rights—attending a meeting, trying to vote, even speaking to a known activist. These simple acts of citizenship were rocking the boat of exploitation that kept Delta cotton farms afloat. Cars were out of reach financially for most rural black Mississippians, the lack of wheels being just another in a long string of barriers to voting. The Chevy wagon would have carried black citizens the eleven-mile stretch from Shaw to Cleveland, where civil rights lawyers would take their sworn statements about voting rights violations in Bolivar County.

Without the Chevy, the workers felt stymied. The fire-bombers had achieved their immediate aim: to silence witnesses who wished to testify in Cleveland the next day. Their broader goal was to hurl a warning along with the firebomb ("Watch out. Next time someone could get hurt").

THE MORNING AFTER THE car bombing, Mary Sue and Eddie arrived early at the Freedom Center. The burnt-out metal skeleton smoldered beside the house like an apparition, a raw symbol of the rage their work had ignited in the white community. One by one, the other activists trickled into the center. Together, they huddled to discuss their plight. With no SNCC wheels to help carry Shaw's black citizens to Cleveland to give their affidavits about voter suppression, they wondered if anyone would show up. They felt stuck, as if ankle-deep in the slick, greasy ooze that local people called buckshot mud.

And then the cars started coming. Overnight, word of the firebombing had spread through the little town, friend to friend, neighbor to neighbor, until everyone knew what had happened and what was at stake. At eight o'clock sharp, as the morning sun topped the cypress trees along the bayou, vehicles began pulling up in front of the Freedom Center. People showed up who had never dared to step up before. At the steering wheels of those cars were the handful of Shaw's black residents who owned vehicles—not many, but enough. Mary Sue and Eddie stood on the porch, watching in stunned gratitude.

Then, in a hail of cheers, everyone piled into the unexpected vehicles. Taking care to obey the speed limit and avoid any other infraction that might draw the attention of police, the activists set out on Highway 61.

At the deposition, black citizens from Shaw and the rest of Bolivar County bore witness to the ways they had been barred from voting and the harassment they had suffered. Mary Sue filed the following report to SNCC headquarters in Jackson on February 22, 1965:

Depositions were held in a Negro church in Cleveland with both friendly and unfriendly witnesses appearing in the same session. Mrs. Walter Lewis, the registrar, refused to say whether or not she is a member of the KKK, WCC [White Citizens' Council], or any auxiliary they may have. She was very proud to be able to prove that she had failed a white man on the voter registration test. The words "niggra and nigger" were used by the opposition in spite of frequent objections, and they addressed several friendly Negro witnesses by their first names (but they didn't answer). The depositions made a powerful impact on the community. The people really spread the word of what had happened.

A rental house dubbed the Freedom Center headquartered Shaw's civil rights workers and volunteers in 1964 and 1965. (Photo by Mary Sue Gellatly)

Eddie Short (center with glasses) meets with local activists (from left) Jimmy Johnson, Nola Mae Coleman, and Aaron German at the Freedom Center. (Photo by Mary Sue Gellatly)

Mary Sue Gellatly (far side of table) meets with local activists. (Photo courtesy of Mary Sue Short)

A local woman speaks during a mass meeting at Shaw's Church of God in Christ. (Photo by Wallace Roberts)

Mrs. Flossie Minley (right) stands in front of her grocery store with Mrs. Leona Stoltz, a member of the Waukesha chapter of the Women's International League for Peace and Freedom who visited Shaw to deliver school supplies and clothing. (Photo courtesy of Mary Sue Short)

SNCC coworkers Eddie and Mary Sue collaborate on voting rights issues in Shaw. (Photo courtesy of Eddie and Mary Sue Short)

The '56 Chevy station wagon civil rights activists in Shaw were depending on was firebombed by white supremacists on February 5, 1965. (Photo by Mary Sue Gellatly)

By the morning of February 6, 1965, the Chevy was a hunk of charred metal. (Photo by Mary Sue Gellatly)

2

Stirrings

The mid-sixties were a turning point
in the southern struggle for human rights.
—Julian Bond, in *Letters from Mississippi*

Shaw, Mississippi, late summer 1964

Eddie's memory of the day he met Mary Sue hasn't lost a single pixel of detail in the intervening years. Something about that moment, about the young woman who strode into his life on that late-August morning in 1964, lodged in his mind like a cocklebur clings to a wool coat. Fifty years later, he can call up the memory in high definition: the waste-no-time pace of her gait, the take-no-prisoners look in her eyes, even the color and style of the schoolgirlish outfit she wore, incongruous on a young woman of such obvious self-assurance. The moment wasn't only remarkable for who Mary Sue was. It was remarkable, too, for what she represented: Shaw was now clearly mapped onto the larger world.

It was a typical morning at the Freedom Center. Eddie was standing in the back room—more of a walk-in closet, really—churning out fliers on a hand-crank mimeograph machine. This portable printing technology was in wide use by schools, churches, and offices in the days before Xerox, but the machines weren't merely mundane tools for, say, copying pop quizzes for fifth-graders. First patented in the United States by Thomas Edison in the 1870s, mimeo machines had played a historical role in the hands of underground freedom fighters in Europe resisting Hitler's occupying forces during World War II. Cheap, small, and portable, about the size of a carry-on suitcase, a mimeo machine could be hidden in an attic or a cellar and used to roll out pages that would keep fighters informed about covert actions and bolster the spirits of resisters. The mimeograph as subversive messaging medium seems quaint from the vantage point of today's digital technologies—fiber-optic cables crisscrossing the seafloor, satellites spinning across the skies, laptop computers in every satchel, miniaturized hard drives in every hip pocket. But its vital role in subterfuge against the racist Nazi invaders gave the mimeograph the perfect pedigree for black resistance to white supremacy in the American South.

The castor-oil-based ink gave off a distinctive smell as Eddie cranked. The process wasn't flawless. He often had to stop and tinker with the balky machine, which had already been well worn when it was donated to the Freedom Summer project. Eddie's daddy had passed along to his son his knack with machinery, and Eddie kept that old mimeo machine going long past its natural lifespan.

While he worked, he listened to the banter of the volunteers in the front room as they made plans for the next day's voter-registration drive. Clustered around a hand-drawn map, they were divvying up routes for canvassing. They decided that some of the volunteers would head out from the center, in

Johnson's Addition, into black neighborhoods up and down the bayou and west of Highway 61—small districts with names like Boatwright and Ice House Quarter and Promised Land. There, the doors they would knock on belonged mostly to people who worked in the fields or survived in whatever niche they could fill or create: cutting hair in the kitchen for fifty cents; mixing cocktails in a backroom juke joint while patrons danced to the R&B licks of Sam Cooke and the Four Tops; scrubbing floors and washing clothes for white landowners; operating a tiny store where customers could buy staples or get a slice of sweet potato pie to go.

This was true not only in Shaw but all across the Delta. In the neighboring town of Ruleville, Fannie Lou Hamer and her husband, Perry, nicknamed Pap, supplemented their wages as sharecroppers by running "her late father's juke joint, from which they sold bootleg liquor," according to Chana Kai Lee in her 1999 book *For Freedom's Sake: The Life of Fannie Lou Hamer.* They fished, too, and Pap hunted squirrels and raccoons. Fannie Lou even sold insurance for a time. Such on-the-side enterprises helped stave off hunger, especially in winter when the cottonfields were fallow. But the road to riches they weren't. "Despite all their efforts, they remained poor," Lee concluded, a statement that applied to most black Mississippians in those days.

The other volunteers would drive to the surrounding plantations. After scouting for signs of the Boss Man, they would tap quietly at the shacks of sharecroppers to persuade them to risk their jobs, their bodily well-being, even their lives, to exercise their rights as American citizens. The volunteers knew that few doors would open wide to them. Mostly, people would peer out through a narrow crack and in hushed voices tell the volunteers, "Thank y'all for stoppin' by, but we got no need for no votin'. You go on now."

The right to vote—the most fundamental civic right granted to a citizen of a democracy—was denied to Mississippi's black citizens starting in the nineteenth century through discriminatory election laws written by white legislators to exclude freed slaves from politics and, by extension, from power. A so-called literacy clause had been encoded in Mississippi's 1890 constitution requiring would-be voters to read or interpret a section of the state constitution chosen at the caprice of county elections officials. In 1964, the literacy clause was still being enforced by white elections officials to keep black citizens out of the voting booth. Poll taxes—fees collected from people trying to register to vote—were illegal but widespread, levied at the whim of elections officials. For sharecroppers and other laborers scraping by on meager wages, even a small poll tax could block their participation at the polls.

An even higher hurdle was the policy of local white newspapers of printing the names of all citizens who registered, or tried to register, to vote. A would-be black voter knew that if his or her name turned up in the local paper as one who desired to exercise the franchise, the Boss Man might fire him or her. It's what happened, famously, to Fannie Lou Hammer, the sharecropper who lost her job for trying to vote. She turned a national spotlight on her plight when she started stepping up to the microphone, telling her story all over the South and then in Washington, D.C.

In the Deep South of the mid-1960s, then, fear of white

retaliation was a powerful deterrent to black voters, whose numbers had been plummeting since the end of Reconstruction. In 1880, a decade and a half after the Civil War won freedom for America's slaves, more than 130,000 black Mississippians were registered to vote. The next decade and a half, however, saw aggressive and systematic intimidation and discrimination toward blacks who tried to register at courthouses across the state. At the three-month-long 1890 constitutional convention in Jackson, the delegation conspired to disenfranchise the state's black citizens, who made up 58 percent of the state's population. Each session began, cynically, with a prayer led by the Reverend Irvin Miller, grand master of the Masons of Mississippi. Discussion by the delegates followed. Delegate George P. Melchior, a Bolivar County planter, captured the spirit of the proceedings when he declared, "It is the manifest intention of this Convention to secure to the State of Mississippi, 'white supremacy.'" By 1896, black voter numbers had plunged by nearly 90 percent, down to about 16,000.

"As of 1901, nearly every African American had been effectively stripped of all elective rights ... in virtually every southern state.... In Mississippi, only those who were able to pay a poll tax of up to $3 and who could, according to the voting registrar's personal assessment, read or understand any clause of the [state constitution] could register," according to Douglas A. Blackmon in his 2009 book, *Slavery by Another Name*.

EDDIE CRANKED THE HANDLE on the mimeo machine with arms muscled from a lifetime of physical labor. An aura of energy, taut and unflagging, emanated from the cramped room where he worked, sweating in the Delta heat. People who knew him described an inner knot of doggedness in Eddie, a tangible determination, that was contagious to those around him.

As the fliers piled up on the table beside Eddie, he happened to glance out the window. What he saw was unusual enough to make him stop midcrank. Striding down the road in his direction was a young woman with pale skin and chin-length light-brown hair, traits scarcely ever seen in Johnson's Addition, the largest black neighborhood in the segregated town. Even in her flat shoes, she was taller than Eddie by a full six inches. And there was something else, a steeliness in her step, a resolute posture in her slender figure, that suggested to Eddie a character staunch beyond her years.

When she reached the path to the Freedom Center, she turned in.

"Okay," Eddie thought, "this must be the new project director they sent over from Hattiesburg."

Not wanting her to see him staring, he went back to his mimeo machine, pretending to be 100 percent absorbed in his job. In her knee-length brown-plaid skirt, its stitch-down pleats swishing side to side, she stepped lightly up the stairs and let herself in. She greeted the volunteers by name.

"Hi, George. Morning, Aaron."

George Shelton and Aaron German were two of Shaw's most stalwart volunteers, locals who had been at Eddie's side since the early days of Freedom Summer. George, known around town as Buddy Boy, was nineteen years old, big, with a prematurely receding hairline. He gave the impression of a gentle giant, wearing a mild expression on his soft features.

But when Buddy Boy stood up at mass meetings to speak, there was nothing wishy-washy about his convictions. He would voice his views with a clarity that got people's attention. Aaron, age seventeen, was another of Shaw's all-in freedom fighters. He was slender, with prominent cheekbones, a small goatee, and large eyes in his angular face. Like Eddie, he loved to laugh. But his sense of humor was more subdued, a little bit tentative, perhaps, in contrast to Eddie's more boisterous nature. Aaron, who was president of Shaw's chapter of the Mississippi Student Union—a statewide organization of politically active black high school students—looked up to Eddie and often sought his counsel.

Eddie stopped cranking mimeos and stood there feeling a little awkward. Aaron realized Eddie hadn't yet met the young woman in the plaid skirt. Juggling two jobs to help feed his mama and siblings, Eddie hadn't made it to the Freedom Center for a couple of days.

"This is Mary Sue, our new project director," Aaron said.

Mary Sue had spent Freedom Summer volunteering in Hattiesburg. When the project ended in mid-August and most of the Freedom Summer volunteers headed home, she and a handful of other northern volunteers reupped, choosing to continue their work in Mississippi as part of a scaled-down follow-up to Freedom Summer. She joined SNCC as a paid staff member. Her new posting: the little town of Shaw.

"Hi, Eddie," she answered, briefly looking into his eyes.

"Hi," he said, looking back at her from behind black-rimmed glasses in the style made famous by rock 'n' roll icon Buddy Holly.

She sat down at the Freedom Center's makeshift desk, a

wobbly card table shared by all the volunteers. As Mary Sue turned her attention to sorting through a stack of papers, Eddie cranked the mimeo machine back up. Fliers piled up beside him once more. In spite of himself, he cast sidelong glances in her direction as he spun the handle, watching her without appearing to watch. It was the way he sized up everyone and everything around him. Reading signs of disrespect or danger in the faces, voices, and postures of others was a survival skill for Eddie, heightened after black teenager Emmett Till was murdered less than fifty miles away when Eddie was eleven.

As Mary Sue got down to work, Eddie noticed that she took charge without any hint of bossiness. The volunteers followed her lead, seeming to trust the clarity she projected. She conveyed, above all, a sense of purpose. Later, as he got to know her, he learned that that purposefulness imbued everything she had tackled in her twenty-two years, whether earning top grades, volunteering for social justice in Nashville and village infrastructure projects in South Korea during college breaks, mastering Bach concertos on a pipe organ, or with the same fast, nimble fingers, picking beans and strawberries to pay for music lessons.

Looking back five decades later at that hot August day, Mary Sue confesses that she has no memory of meeting the man who would soon alter her life forever. On that day, every strand of her DNA was aligned with her mission: to get black Mississippians to the voting booth.

Only gradually did Eddie come into clear focus for her. It happened over the next few months as they worked long days at the Freedom Center, attended mass meetings at the church, sang freedom songs (she in a rich alto, he in a sonorous tenor), and got arrested, booked, jailed, and released. They were coworkers first, then companions who looked out for each other, then friends who unwound on Saturday nights with other activists, dancing and sipping cocktails at Club DeLisa or another of Shaw's neighborhood juke joints. Those Saturday nights were a chance to slough off the weight of the week, if only for a few hours. They were not unlike R&R for soldiers after being pinned down for days by enemy fire, or shore leave for sailors freed from the confines of a battleship.

Eddie and Mary Sue worked in what amounted to a war zone. Pledged to SNCC's policy of nonviolence, they were unarmed foot soldiers whose enemies, hiding in the sheep's clothing of southern tradition, were armed to the teeth. Theirs may have been a battle for lofty ideals—social justice, equality for all, human dignity—but the bullets of the white resistance were solid lead. It was probably inevitable that Mary Sue and Eddie would bond in the same way military comrades bond on the battlefield. It took a long time for them to recognize that such a bond cannot be broken.

"SHE'S CUTE," EDDIE THOUGHT to himself as he cranked away at the mimeograph. This thought, this reaction, plays out a million times a day across the globe as young men and young women of all social classes and nationalities see and meet each other. Even Martin Ginsburg, the late husband of U.S. Supreme Court justice Ruth Bader Ginsburg, reveals in the documentary *The Notorious RBG* that those exact words, "She's cute," popped into his mind when at age eighteen he first met seventeen-year-old Ruth Bader.

For Martin Ginsburg, "she's cute" led to courtship, love, and marriage. But for Eddie, that thought elicited a rote reproach, a subconscious warning. It was like the time when as a toddler he had gotten too close to the family's red-hot woodstove. His grandma, after the umpteenth verbal warning, had swatted him with a diaper that happened to be close at hand. It stung. The lesson stuck. A similar reflex kicked in after Eddie first met Mary Sue. His second thought, coming a nanosecond after his first, was, "Whoa, are you crazy, man?" This was the reflex of a black man imbued with the white man's credo in the American South: don't go near a white woman if you value your life. Many young men fear rejection when showing interest in a young woman. Few, however, have to fear for their lives.

For Eddie, his momentary attraction to Mary Sue instantly collided with the facts. It wasn't just that she was tall, six feet, while he was five foot six, although his proud bearing—head held high, shoulders squared up—gave the illusion of greater stature. For another thing, she was a college girl, having just earned her bachelor's degree in music from Willamette University in the Pacific Northwest, a place he'd never seen and couldn't even imagine. He had a diploma, having graduated from McEvans, Shaw's black school, despite picking cotton from an age when white children would be in kindergarten reciting nursery rhymes. But college was not even a pipe dream for the sharecropper's son who was working two jobs to keep food on the table for his younger siblings and ailing mother. It wasn't that Eddie was intimidated by Mary Sue's academic credentials. It was snobbery he couldn't stomach. As he surreptitiously watched Mary Sue on their first day together in the Freedom Center, his antennas were out for conceit, for any sign that she was looking down on Shaw's black citizens.

Differences in height or education could, of course, be overcome. But in Mississippi in 1964, there was one taboo that no one could surmount: interracial mixing, or miscegenation. Marriage between blacks and whites was prohibited by law. But the prohibition went much farther than that. For simply being friendly to a white woman or casting an appreciative glance in her direction, black men were beaten up or run out of town. And those were the lucky ones. The threat of lynching—of being murdered by white terrorists—was all too real. Thousands of black people, mostly men, were lynched in the South in the eight-plus decades between 1882 and 1968. Mississippi held the record for number of race-based murders, having lynched more black individuals—539—than any other state.

The KKK and other white terrorist groups considered it nothing less than a sacred duty to punish romance and sex between the races, especially between black men and white women. As stated in a Klan document titled *Kloran: Klan in Action: Constitution,* discovered in Alabama in 1984 by renowned civil rights lawyer Morris Dees and his investigators, "the chastity of the mother, wife, sister, and daughter was imperiled" and "the very blood of the Caucasian race was seriously threatened with everlasting contamination" when slaves were freed at the end of the Civil War. White women's "sacred persons," the Klan constitution declared, "were placed in jeopardy to the licentious longings of lust-crazed beasts in human form."

Mary Sue had arrived in Mississippi earlier that summer with little personal experience of southern racist culture. That culture was rooted in centuries of slavery and then, after emancipation, the broken promises of Reconstruction. The "forty acres and a mule" promised to each freed family unit by General William Tecumseh Sherman in 1865 remained a mirage, systematized through the relentless exploitation, intimidation, and segregation of black citizens. As a child growing up in the North, she hadn't come face-to-face with "Jim Crow," the discriminatory laws passed in Mississippi, Tennessee, Alabama, Georgia, and other southern states that heaped humiliation on blacks in the form of apartheid—the institutionalized separation of the races usually associated with South Africa but just as real, just as viciously enforced, in the United States. The Jim Crow laws forced blacks to use separate bathrooms and water fountains. They allowed shopkeepers and restaurateurs—even hospitals—to turn blacks away without service.

She had canvassed black voters in Nashville the year before. But it wasn't until Freedom Summer that Mary Sue entered ground zero of American racism.

EXACTLY ONE DECADE BEFORE Freedom Summer, black citizens in the South had won a legal victory that had given them new impetus to rise and claim their rights. The catalyst was *Brown v. Board of Education*, a landmark of U.S. jurisprudence whose various short-form monikers *(Brown, Brown v. Board)* are household words in America today. The 1954 Supreme Court decision overturning the "separate-but-equal" justification for segregated schools energized and mobilized black activists by giving them the legal footing to challenge Jim Crow. They formed local voting associations to register black voters. Young blacks, many of them still in high school, began to stage sit-ins and walkouts in their communities.

But the decision was a double-edged sword. It energized white resistance at least as much as it energized black activism. As black journalist Simeon Booker writes in his 2013 memoir, *Shocking the Conscience: A Reporter's Account of the Civil Rights Movement,* "Although the Supreme Court's decision required only the desegregation of public schools, and not other public places such as restaurants and restrooms, Southern whites were worried that it signaled a threat to all racial segregation—and white supremacy."

Mississippi's white leadership reacted to *Brown* with outrage, declaring that they would not be pushed around by the "federals." On March 29, 1956, they created an official, taxpayer-funded, in-house spy agency called the Mississippi State Sovereignty Commission and gave it broad powers and a budget to "maintain the sovereignty [meaning autonomy or self-rule] of the State of Mississippi." In practice, the commission was given free rein to maintain segregation at all costs and to use taxpayers' dollars to spy on activists.

In Shaw, a charismatic local leader in his mid-forties named Andrew Hawkins stepped up to push against injustice, inspiring young people and adults alike to challenge the status quo. Hawkins worked in construction and had a reputation as a skilled tradesman, one who was adept at reading blueprints, a carpenter and master plumber. Like so many black civil rights leaders, he was a man of faith. He served as a deacon at the Mount Tabor Baptist Church in Shaw, which Eddie grew up attending. For Eddie and other youths in Shaw, this forty-six-year-old father of four, handsome and proud in bearing, stalwart for family, fierce in faith, unshakeable in conviction, offered a role model for manhood.

Hawkins had long chafed at the inequities he saw in city government, public accommodations, school administration, job opportunities, public works, and law enforcement. With skills in carpentry, wiring, and plumbing, he worked mostly for white residents and contractors for the obvious reason that they were the ones who could afford to pay for construction projects and repairs—indeed, whites had indoor plumbing and electricity in their homes, while most blacks did not. He was not naïve. He knew the risks to his livelihood when he began organizing for racial justice in Shaw.

His daughter Glory was twelve years old in 1962 when Hawkins started hosting civil rights meetings in their home. Charismatic young black leaders who were gaining a national profile—people like SNCC field secretary Bob Moses from Harlem; Delta project director Stokely Carmichael, originally from Trinidad; and John Lewis from rural Alabama—were connecting with local black leaders in Mississippi to lay the groundwork for the statewide voter-registration campaign that became Freedom Summer. In the Delta, decorated military veteran Amzie Moore of Cleveland, sharecropper Fannie Lou Hamer of Ruleville, and Andrew Hawkins of Shaw were among the most prominent grassroots activists. They traveled from town to town, talking with local activists or would-be activists who were willing to stand up to the white establishment. Eddie got wind of these secret meetings. Knowing that Hawkins, a man he knew and admired, was part of a growing groundswell of dissent in Mississippi planted in Eddie the seeds of his own activism.

The next year, 1963, Glory's daddy was elected to chair the local chapter of the NAACP, considered by the white resistance to be a subversive organization because of its equality-for-all mission and its pull-no-punches messaging. A poster printed in 1956 as part of an NAACP membership drive, for instance, bore the headline "Stamp Out Mississippi-ism!" along with a headstone engraved with the names of four black males lynched in 1955. His taking a leadership position with the NAACP, Hawkins knew, would stir the pot of white hatred in Shaw. But by then, he was all in.

As the summer of 1964 drew near, he and his wife, Mary Lou, known around town as Mae Lou, prepared their house to accommodate several of the Freedom Summer volunteers who soon would be rolling into town. As word of Hawkins's bold and blatant civil rights activism leaked out, white contractors and customers dropped him. "Somebody found out Daddy was in civil rights," Glory Hawkins-Scott recalled fifty years later. "He was fired from construction work, so he went out on his own." This was inevitable in a very small town where the White Citizens' Council, which had sprung up in reaction to *Brown* and was dedicated to defending segregation come hell or high water, was paying off informants to betray their neighbors. Blackballed by his white customers, Hawkins suffered financially for daring to cast off the expected persona of the southern black man, passive and compliant, and rocking the boat of white dominance in Mississippi.

But it wasn't just whites who looked askance at Hawkins's activism. Some of Shaw's black citizens saw it as a danger to their own well-being, like a virus that could infect anyone who got too close. Fearful for their safety and their livelihoods, afraid of being tarred with the civil rights brush that had made Andrew a pariah among whites, some black residents shunned the Hawkins family, even the children. Glory still remembers, fifty years later, the sting of her black neighbors' fear, her hurt feelings when parents of longtime playmates forbade them to socialize with Glory and her siblings, saying, "You can't play with the civil rights workers' children no more."

Glory's mother, Mae Lou, was a firebrand in Shaw. "Mama, she was short, about four foot ten inches tall," Glory says. "She'd tell ya what she think. She didn't take no mess. She didn't care how big you were, what color you were." One story that quickly made its way around town was the time George Waxman, chief of police in Shaw, allegedly slapped Mae Lou. "She grabbed his pistol and whipped him with it," Glory reports. "She fed all the kids in the neighborhood, but she whupped your butt if you messed up."

Her parents were strict with her and her siblings—two sisters and one brother. "We had to go to church every night," she remembers. "We had to walk because we had no car. The church was out past the bogue. We'd be so tired and sleepy."

In 1967, Andrew and Mae Lou would make civil rights history when they led a class-action lawsuit against the town of Shaw for its discriminatory practices in the allocation of city funds for sewers, street paving, electricity, and other services deemed essential in America in the 1960s. But in the end, the family would pay a heavy price for their high-visibility challenge to Jim Crow, for their leadership in the landmark lawsuit, which they eventually won on appeal.

Soon after the court decision, Mae Lou was fatally shot by a local policeman. Then, several years later, three family members—Glory's brother, Andrew Hawkins Junior, and two of Glory's young children, Bernadette and Mary Yvette—burned to death when their home was firebombed in the wake of their legal victory.

When the U.S. Congress and the U.S. Supreme Court took bold action against Jim Crow, white Mississippians deeply resented what they saw as an intrusion on their sovereignty as a state. To clamp down on unrest, plantation owners hired local spies to inform them about their workers' activities. If a grower got word that one of his sharecroppers or field hands had attended a civil rights meeting, he would threaten him or her with firing. Black citizens who were spotted at the courthouse trying to register risked the same fate. One sure way to keep tabs on black workers was the collusion between growers and white newspaper publishers. They were thick as thieves. Publishers would print the name of any citizen who registered—or even tried to register—in the pages of the local paper.

Fannie Lou Hamer is the most famous sharecropper tossed off her plantation for exercising her rights. She began picking cotton with her family on W. D. Marlow's plantation starting at age six in 1923. But over the years, Fannie Lou— who had been stricken with polio as a young child—struggled to keep up with the grueling field labor. She did, however, have an ace in the hole: her reading and writing skills. Soon after she married sharecropper Perry "Pap" Hamer in 1944, W. D. Marlow assigned her to the important job of timekeeper, which "involved maintaining records on working hours, the number of bales picked by each fieldworker, and the amount of pay due each person," explains Chana Kai Lee in her book *For Freedom's Sake*. Fannie Lou was "a recognized leader among her people," Lee notes. "She had earned this reputation by being a fair timekeeper who often jeopardized her own relationship to the boss in her secret efforts to ensure fair returns for other sharecroppers."

On August 31, 1962, two years before Freedom Summer, forty-four-year-old Fannie Lou traveled from her home in Ruleville to Indianola, the seat of Sunflower County, to, as she expressed it, "register to become a first-class citizen." Marlow got wind of it instantly. He was incensed that his reliable, highly skilled, steady worker had taken this step. In his mind, Fannie Lou had committed sedition by trying to claim her voting rights. He knew that as a respected member of the black community, she would inspire others by her example. Black registrations would gain momentum, like a snowball tumbling down a mountain, getting bigger and weightier and faster. In the black-majority Delta, the entrenchment of white power would lose its hundred-year grip.

To Marlow's way of thinking, Fannie Lou Hamer was pushing the snowball that threatened to break loose his position at the pinnacle of power as a planter in Mississippi. That vaunted position must have seemed precarious in a way it never had before. As he stood looking down from his privileged perch, he probably felt himself beginning to teeter. This worker of his, this black sharecropper, this woman of color, had ambitions to stand beside him as a "first-class citizen."

The sense of teetering scared and angered him. Even before Fannie Lou got home from the courthouse, Marlow had stormed over to the Hamer house looking for her. When she got home, her family warned her that the Boss Man had come by "raisin' a lotta Cain." Before she could blink, the grower was standing on her front porch. "We're not ready for this in Mississippi!" he railed at her. Fannie Lou looked at him, this man who held her livelihood in his hands. "Well, Mr. Marlow, I didn't register for you, I was tryin' to register for myself," she answered. Marlow probably couldn't believe what he was hearing with his own ears. A black sharecropper speaking her mind to a white grower? Fannie Lou's brazen comeback represented a revolution right there in Ruleville on that hot August day.

For a moment, he must have felt unsteady on his feet. Then, remembering his status as a landowner and a cotton grower, he retorted: "We're not going to have this in Mississippi, and you'll have to go back down and withdraw. I'm lookin' for your answer, yah or nay." She stood there and looked at him, saying no more. Then Mr. Marlow ratcheted up his threatening tone. "I'll give you till end o' mornin.' If you don't go down and withdraw, you will have to leave. And if you do go down and withdraw, dependin' on how I feel, you *still* might have to leave."

If Fannie Lou had any thought of withdrawing her registration, it dissolved as she considered Marlow's offer: don't withdraw, get fired; withdraw, and very likely still get fired. "I had to leave that same night," Fannie Lou testified on August 22, 1964, before the Credentials Committee at the Democratic National Convention in Atlantic City as it considered which of two rival delegations from Mississippi to seat.

If Marlow's firing of Fannie Lou Hamer was meant to intimidate other blacks and keep them from registering to vote, it backfired. Freed from her labors in the cotton fields, Hamer became a full-time activist. Her story had first burst onto the national stage in 1963 after she was arrested for sitting at a lunch counter in the "white only" section of the Greyhound bus depot in Winona, Mississippi, and brutally beaten in the county jail there on her way home from a voting registration workshop in South Carolina. Thereafter, her face and voice would resonate throughout the civil rights movement, inspiring millions just as she had inspired Eddie to stand up in Shaw.

IN THE FRACTIOUS DECADE of the 1960s, Mississippi "emerged as the fortress of southern white racism," according to the 2018 NBC documentary *Hope and Fury*, directed by Rachel Dretzin and Phil Bertelsen. The *Washington Post* went even further when Dorothy Gilliam, the paper's first black woman reporter, called out Mississippi as "the South Africa of America," according to the same documentary. So when Freedom Summer activists, including Mary Sue, finished their training in Ohio and rolled into the former Confederate state of Mississippi, they entered the place Freedom Summer director Bob Moses called "the middle of the iceberg" of American racism.

Skilled tradesman Andrew Hawkins (second from left) led Shaw's local civil rights movement. (Photo by Mary Sue Gellatly)

Bob Moses, SNCC's field secretary in Mississippi, was a regular presence among the frontline activists during Freedom Summer. (Photo by Wallace Roberts)

Three Shaw girls—from left to right, Ann Lewis, Patricia
Greenwood, and Ann's sister, Gail Lewis—read together at
the Freedom Center. (Photo by Mary Sue Gellatly)

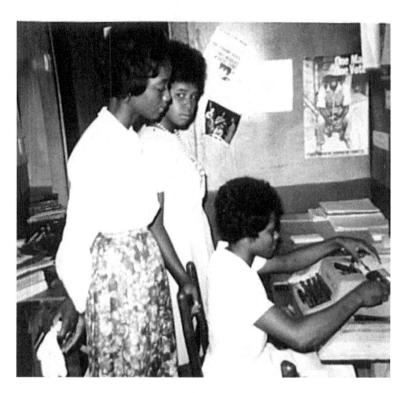

Teenage activists (from left) Ruby Richard, Betty Lane,
and Betty Smith volunteer at the Freedom Center in Shaw.
(Photo by Mary Sue Gellatly)

3

Arrivals

Don't call me the brave one for going
No, don't pin a medal to my name
For even if there was any choice to make
I'd be going down just the same
—Phil Ochs, "Going Down to Mississippi"

Mississippi, summer 1964

The South simmered in triple-digit temperatures, the air thick and sticky, when caravans of chartered buses and a few private cars started rolling south from Ohio toward Mississippi. From the two back-to-back Freedom Summer training sessions in Ohio starting in mid-June, twin cadres of northern college students headed toward the Magnolia State, a week apart, four hundred or so in each wave. The first cadre would focus on voter registration. The second cadre, Mary Sue's, would help organize and operate community centers and freedom schools, teaching citizenship and black history to kids and adults across Mississippi. Between late June when the first cadre arrived in Mississippi and early July when the second cadre rolled in, eight hundred students stepped off buses into the withering heat and the racial tensions of nearly thirty Mississippi towns.

From U.S. Highway 55, Mississippi's main north-south arterial, the volunteer-filled buses veered off to the four corners of the state, unloading students in twos and threes and fours. Mary Sue's bus headed to the Piney Woods region, where the Natchez Indians had once thrived among stands of longleaf pine, a tree prized for timber and wood fiber. It dropped off volunteers at Canton and Harmony and Hattiesburg, the town where Mary Sue disembarked and would help set up and run a freedom school stocked with donated books about black history and information on civil rights, including voting laws and procedures. Mary Sue would spend the next six weeks in Hattiesburg, while Eddie worked with the volunteers assigned to Shaw.

Other buses traveled eastward to the Red Clay Hills, whose warm-toned soils had been scoured and gouged over eons into a labyrinth of gullies and ravines. Volunteers stepped off the bus in Philadelphia and the nearby town of Meridian, where the three missing civil rights workers were last seen alive. Continuing south, the buses headed to Mississippi's Gulf Coast region, where Biloxi and Gulfport sat at the state's southernmost tip, the estuary where the Mississippi River braided into the Gulf of Mexico, a pastiche of swamps and salt-grass marshes and mangroves, a watery Eden where people drew their sustenance from shrimp and snapper, black drum and blue crab, catfish and crawfish. Biloxi was the site of several "wade-ins" in the late 1950s and early 1960s, organized by local black physician and civil rights leader Dr. Gilbert Mason to protest segregation of the city's public beaches.

One Greyhound veered west into the Delta, the flat-as-a-pancake floodplain where cottonfields seemed to stretch on forever, stopping at midsized cities like Indianola and Cleveland and small towns like Tchula and Batesville, Greenville and Ruleville. It rumbled along Highway 61 and downshifted in a noisy grinding of gears before pulling off the road onto the shoulder in a choking cloud of dust and diesel fumes and parking beside a greasy-spoon diner and gas station in the little town of Shaw known as the Truck Stop. Gathered outside the wooden structure, a small crowd of townsfolk waited in anticipation. They watched curiously to see who would step off the bus into the Delta heat, wondering what this Greyhound cavalry of young Americans, many still in their teens, would bring to their quiet corner of Mississippi.

One onlooker that day was a teenager named Mary McWilliams. Her mother, who was active in Shaw's civil rights movement, had urged her, "Go along now, Mary. You go meet that bus." This event—white college kids from up north coming to live with black families while working on civil rights in Shaw—was surely something to take note of, Mary's mother told her. "This is history in the making." And so it came to be that Mary McWilliams was an eyewitness to history that day as a handful of young people not much older than she stepped down into the dust and the heat.

The townsfolk, white and black, were anticipating the students' arrival. Everyone was nervous, but for different reasons. After getting wind of the Mississippi Summer Project, whites braced for the northern influx by hog-tying free speech and pumping up fear. Police forces beefed up their ranks and brought in military-style gear—armored trucks, machine guns. Ignoring the U.S. Constitution and flouting federal civil rights laws, legislators passed their own laws and ordinances in the statehouse, county courthouses, and city halls in clear violation of constitutional protections for free speech and equal treatment, including bans on public demonstrations and protests.

Activists faced arrest, jail time, fines, expulsion from school, and often firings by their employers when they disregarded laws that restricted their rights to gather together and speak their truths. In 1964 and 1965, Mississippi law was upside-down: police threw people in jail for breaking unconstitutional laws, while people went to jail for exercising lawful rights.

WHEN THE YOUNG MEN and women from northern and western states stepped onto Mississippi soil for the first time and looked around, clutching their satchels and duffel bags, their faces must have betrayed some uncertainty, maybe some wariness. They had come from San Francisco and Seattle and Portland on the West Coast, from midwestern cities like Chicago and Pittsburgh, and from Boston and New York City on the Eastern Seaboard. Mississippi might as well have been rural India or the indigenous wilds of northwest Alaska for all the cultural similarities it bore to the cities they had come from.

If they were afraid after the lectures and role playing of their training in Ohio, they quickly had a flesh-and-blood reason to recast their fears, to put them into the context of actual black lives. As local black citizens folded the volunteers into their towns and their homes with hugs and handshakes and expressions of gratitude, a certain truth hit the students like the hard, cold spray of a firehose: at summer's end, they would melt back into the dappled quads and lofty lecture halls of college campuses, return to comfy homes in quiet suburbs or plush apartments in upscale urban neighborhoods, while their black hosts and comrades would stay behind, their jobs in jeopardy, their lives imperiled by their decision to resist the injustices that had infected their communities for generations.

It was against this hard truth that the northern students gauged their own risks. Most of them were children of privilege from some of the nation's most prestigious universities—Yale, Harvard, Berkeley, Stanford, Brown, and Johns Hopkins, among others. Some—Barney Frank and Jerry Brown, for example—would rise to national prominence in the years to come. That elite demographic was no accident. By recruiting affluent white students, Bob Moses figured, the Mississippi Summer Project would accrue two big pluses. First, it would keep a lid on white hate groups itching to lynch, torch, and otherwise terrorize civil rights activists. Second, it would switch on the high beams, illuminating southern racism for a new sector of American society, one that had never seen a whites-only water fountain or heard a man called nigger to his face.

The optics would speak volumes: eight hundred promising white kids—high-minded, studious, earnest, brave—joining black leaders and local activists in a righteous cause. Moses was pretty sure the nation at large would no longer have the luxury of looking away. As he remarked in an interview with James Atwater published in the *Saturday Evening Post* in July 1964, "These students bring the rest of the country with them. They're from good schools and their parents are influential. The interest of the country is awakened and when that happens, the government responds to that issue."

Moses was right. As the volunteers rolled into Mississippi, religious leaders and elected officials across the northern states and along the two coastlines formed a virtual army of vigilance. Worried parents waited impatiently for letters from their children and reported concerns to law enforcement. President Johnson directed FBI director J. Edgar Hoover to send in undercover FBI agents to keep an eye on the volunteers.

And then three civil rights workers who had driven away from the orientation in Ohio in a blue Ford station wagon headed for Mississippi's Neshoba County disappeared on June 21. Just as the first cadre of Freedom Summer volunteers rode into Mississippi, the eyes of the whole nation turned, stunned and appalled, toward ground zero of racial animus in America. Millions of Americans born to white privilege were, finally, paying attention to the plight of their southern black brethren.

Across Mississippi, Freedom Summer uncorked a frothing, sputtering geyser of fury in the local press and among white hate groups, including the Klan and the White Citizens' Council, a powerful network of white supremacists who used every tactic under the sun to resist integration. "We are now in the midst of the 'long, hot summer' agitation which was promised to the innocent people of Mississippi by the savage blacks and their communist masters," proclaimed the July 1964 issue of the *Klan Ledger*, the official publication of the

White Knights of the Ku Klux Klan of Mississippi. The pages of local newspapers crackled with hateful invective from a white citizenry seething with indignation toward the northern "invaders" who were challenging their system of apartheid.

Yet black residents were ready to put the volunteers at ease. Pushing down their doubts as best they could, they threw open their arms and embraced the newcomers like long-lost sisters and brothers from another mother. Black families across the state, including the Hawkins family in Shaw, had carried in extra beds and sometimes slept on sofas and floors so the volunteers could room in their homes. Eddie was ready, too, for the northern influx after months of anticipation and preparation. The countless hours he had spent in mass meetings, absorbing the inspired words of leaders like Hamer and Carmichael and Andrew Hawkins as they geared up for Freedom Summer, were about to bear fruit.

And though he was grateful for the arrival of these much-anticipated white volunteers, Eddie was uncertain about their motives. Would they try to take over the movement? Would they be appalled by the poverty and deprivation in Shaw's black neighborhoods? Would they respect local black leaders and activists who had been laying the groundwork for Freedom Summer in Shaw? Despite his mixed feelings, Eddie knew this was just about the biggest thing that had happened to his hometown, the only place he really knew.

THE VANGUARD OF SHAW's volunteers and SNCC staffers arrived in Shaw that sweltering June not only by bus but also by car. One was Wallace "Wally" Roberts, the freedom school coordinator for Bolivar County and director of Shaw's freedom school. He roomed in the Hawkins family home along with three other volunteers, including a girl from the University of Chicago named Heather Tobis. Another volunteer in Shaw that summer was Fred Winn, a carpenter and lawyer's son from the San Francisco Bay Area who had come to Shaw after spending his first week volunteering in nearby Ruleville. Winn was "appalled by the squalor of Shaw," according to journalist Bruce Watson in his 2010 book, *Freedom Summer: The Savage Season That Made Mississippi Burn and Made America a Democracy.* "There he met children with bellies swollen by hunger and visited fetid shacks tilted and sinking into the soil."

Another Shaw arrival was Robert Hargreaves, a graduate student in poultry management at Michigan State, who was assigned to teach at Shaw's freedom school. He pitched in that first week to fix up the Freedom Center, which he described as a "one-room shack." Years later, he gave a statement to the Civil Rights Movement Veterans website hosted by Tougaloo College. "I had a long conversation with two local black teachers. Since we were planning to teach a basic civics course, I asked what was being taught in the schools. They told me they would be immediately fired if they ever tried to teach the U.S. Constitution!" Hargreaves later worked in Vietnam as an agricultural volunteer, helping villagers raise chickens, pigs, and grapes. "The war was on, but I felt safer in Vietnam than I ever did in Mississippi," he said.

Law student Len Edwards, son of California congressman Don Edwards, was also assigned to Bolivar County. Len and a trio of other volunteers from the first cadre trained in Ohio—three young men dressed neatly in slacks and cotton dress shirts, one young woman in a summery, floral-print dress—set out for the Delta first thing in the morning after their training ended. It was June 20, a seminal day in the history of Freedom Summer. That day, Mary Sue arrived in Ohio with the second cadre of trainees. That day, too, three young men from the first cohort—Michael "Mickey" Schwerner, James Chaney, and Andrew Goodman—waved goodbye to their fellow activists and drove toward Mississippi's Neshoba County in a blue Ford station wagon. As Edwards and his companions breezed south in Len's 1960 Corvair, the top rolled down, the hot wind in their faces, singing freedom songs to shake off the disquieting lessons of their training—don't go anywhere alone, don't stand in front of a lit window at night, avoid riding in cars with both black and white passengers—they couldn't have known or even imagined that Schwerner, Chaney, and Goodman were about to vanish into thin air.

A few hours after turning onto Highway 61 from Memphis, they pulled into the hamlet of Ruleville, population about two thousand, where they were warmly greeted by local activists. Within minutes, as they were talking with sharecropper Pap Hamer, Fannie Lou's husband, a police truck with a large dog in the back cruised up beside them. The four volunteers instantly forgot all their training—like the directive to ask, "Are we under arrest?" if cops tried to detain them—and meekly complied with the officer's command to come with him. "The mayor wants to talk to you," the cop said. Later, when Edwards was on camera being interviewed by a CBS reporter, he confessed, "I was scared." The clean-cut young man, looking like the boy next door in his shirt and tie, told the reporter, a little bit sheepishly, "My knees were shaking."

At the mayor's office, the young activists listened for the next forty-five minutes as Charles Dorrough laid out his concerns for the northern activists, along with his hope that nothing bad would happen to them on his watch. "He knows that Ruleville is the center of a lot of attention this summer," Edwards told the CBS reporter as the cameras rolled, confirming Bob Moses's belief that caravans of white college kids pouring in from the North would, for the first time, shine a national spotlight on Mississippi's shameful racial realities.

A week after Len Edwards's foursome arrived in Ruleville, Dennis "Denny" Flannigan from Tacoma, Washington, rolled into town in a white four-door sedan driven by *Look* magazine editor Christopher Wren and photographer Thomas Koeniges after an eighteen-hour drive south from Ohio. Dennis was the Freedom Summer communications director for the Delta towns of Shaw, Ruleville, and Cleveland, plus Mound Bayou and Rosedale, as Eddie remembers it. He helped coordinate news coverage for media outlets like *Look*. Another of his duties was raising money for the summer project, including bail money for volunteers who were jailed for their civil rights actions—money that would eventually help spring Mary Sue and Eddie from the Bolivar County jail more than once.

Dennis's proximity to *Look*'s editor meant he was on hand for an early photo shoot in Ruleville. His young face, bright and unblemished, shows up in Wren's September 8, 1964, article in *Look* titled "Mississippi: The Attack on Bigotry." His image was captured, too, in footage of a mass meeting in a black church in Walter Cronkite's CBS News special report "The Search in Mississippi." TV viewers across America watched as Dennis and other white volunteers stood shoulder-to-shoulder with their young black comrades, crowded into pews on a steamy summer day, clapping and singing, marking the rhythm with their feet, their faces full of the righteousness of their cause. As quickly as the group coalesced, as unified as they appeared, TV viewers might have been surprised to learn that this was the first black-church experience for most of the white students.

If Dennis and the other Freedom Summer volunteers had any doubts about the seriousness of the threats their trainers had warned them about, those doubts dissolved almost as soon as they set foot on Delta soil. "I've been in [the Delta] six days now and experienced everything—including murder," wrote Dennis to a friend in Tacoma. The murder had occurred just the day before. As Dennis explained, an unarmed mentally ill black man was gunned down by a white highway patrolman in a hamlet called Doddsville right next door to Ruleville.

Doddsville had an especially repugnant place in the history of Mississippi racism. The hometown of the notorious segregationist and plantation owner U.S. Senator James Eastland, Doddsville was described by black civil rights leader Charlie McLaurin as a place "where many years ago the burning of Negroes was a Sunday spectacle." McLaurin, who had been attempting to register black voters in Ruleville and the surrounding Sunflower County since 1962, was the SNCC coordinator who welcomed Dennis and Len and the other volunteers to Ruleville and warned them of the risks they faced. In a report to SNCC headquarters (as recounted by Kay Mills in her 2007 book *This Little Light of Mine: The Life of Fannie Lou Hamer*), McLaurin noted that Doddsville was a place "where whites young and old delighted at this evil which killed the spirit of the old Negroes and set the stage of the place-fixing of the young ones not yet born."

Next came a firebombing right in the heart of Ruleville. "Less dramatic than the killing, but for us more intimidating, was the bombing of the church where we hold our [civil rights] meetings, William Chapel, Thursday morning," wrote Dennis. "A Molotov cocktail was thrown against the front of the church and started a fire. Fortunately, it failed to ignite eight plastic bags filled with kerosene placed around the chapel.... The FBI refused to collect the bottle used in the bomb for possible fingerprint evidence."

Sham investigations were the norm in white-on-black violence in the Delta, as the Freedom Summer volunteers were learning. Mississippi in the mid-1960s was the Wild West, with white vigilantes committing heinous crimes against their black neighbors and experiencing few or no consequences from law enforcement. Indeed, many police and sheriff's deputies were in cahoots with terrorist organizations like the Klan, and many were members of their local chapter of the White Citizens' Council. In 1964, no white person had ever been convicted of killing a black person in Mississippi, not even when there were eyewitnesses. Not even when there were confessions. But that summer, with the safety of hundreds of privileged white kids at stake, law enforcement had to at least pretend to solve bias crimes like the church fire in Ruleville.

IN HIS NEXT LETTER home, Dennis wrote: "I am now in Shaw, Mississippi, setting up a new project." He described arranging to rent Mrs. Lee's tiny house—two months for a total of thirty dollars—where the volunteers would establish their Freedom Center and begin stocking a library, outfitting an all-purpose office space and classroom, and organizing voter-registration drives. He ended his letter with a plea for donations to support the Shaw project—money for utilities (phone and gas), vitamins (kids, he said, are "undervita-mined"), books, paper, finger paints, crayons, pencils, softballs and mitts, clothes, food, and just about anything else a school could use. Flannigan would later score the '56 Chevy station wagon used by the Freedom Center from a donor on New York's Staten Island and drive it to Shaw.

One night soon after Dennis arrived in Shaw, an "old, old man" held a meeting for the volunteers in his house. Twenty people—black residents and a few white volun-teers—scrunched into the small, sparsely furnished space. Some stood against the walls. Others sat on the wood-plank floor. Wind leaked through the unpainted slats. To Dennis it seemed as if the tiny one-room house might come apart in a strong gust.

The old man, whose name was Miller Lark, stood up and looked at the faces around him. In a voice quavering with age, he asked the people to bow their heads in prayer. He asked the Lord for protection and blessings on the young activists from the North. And then he led the people in song, Gospel music known by heart in this pious community of churchgoers (inside the one-square-mile city limits, eight churches graced the town), hymns inflected with the shape-note tradition in which the South was steeped. Low notes vibrated in the floorboards. High notes floated to the rafters, dancing and dipping under the roofline like swallows plying the sky. As he stood there, scrunched tightly with the other activists, Dennis closed his eyes and let the music wash over him.

"It was like being in heaven's choir," he says.

For Dennis, the meeting in the house of the old man was an epiphany—not the religious kind, exactly, but more of a sociological kind. The black people of Shaw, as poor as they were, shared with the young white strangers whatever they could of shelter and food. Material goods were, in Dennis's mind, the least of their gifts. As improbable as it may seem, these black citizens whose rights and dignity had been crushed over and over by their white neighbors were willing to trust the motives of a bunch of privileged white college kids who had rolled in from who-knows-where.

"They gave us their music and their hearts," Dennis says, the night of prayer and song still bright in his memory. "It was one of those moments when you realize that the desperate are more generous than the affluent." It was a moment he would take with him into his life as a social justice advocate and eventually into four terms as the state representative for District 27 in the Washington Legislature.

FREEDOM SUMMER WAS A poke at the hornet's nest of white supremacy in Bolivar County. In Shaw, that poke unleashed parades of gun-fitted pickup trucks and torrents of profanity directed at the little Freedom Center on the eve of its opening in early July 1964. These spasms of hate and intimidation signaled the project's perceived threat to white dominance in Mississippi.

On Saturday night, July 11, several volunteers were sitting in the cramped office with Freedom Summer staff member Heather Tobis, talking over last-minute details for Monday's opening. In the suffocating heat, they had opened the windows and the front door of the tiny wooden house hoping for a breath of air. The thrumming of cicadas, thousands of them hidden in the shadowy cypress trees along the bayous, filled the humid night air, vibrating with a kind of restless urgency.

Then, in a burst of breathless energy, a black kid from Shaw came running through the door, looking terrified. The young boy, "stuttering, trembling," as Bruce Watson describes the incident in his book *Freedom Summer*, told them that "he'd just been offered $400 to blow up the building."

Before the volunteers could absorb his words, another disturbance became audible, at first a faint hum in the background of the insects' calls. The workers switched off the lights and listened. They could just make out the rumbling of engines, getting louder and closer to the Freedom Center. Finally, they were able to see a caravan of a half dozen dusty cars and pickup trucks approaching along the dark dirt road. White men, some wearing military-style helmets, were hanging out the truck windows, shouting obscenities and throwing bottles. The workers hastily shut the windows and door and lay down on the floor as they had been trained to do. Never stand in front of a window at night, they had been taught during their SNCC training in Ohio. Years later, Tobis recalled, "We stayed on the floor of the center, with a phone line open to the Jackson office, wondering if violence would break out."

And then the summer sky lit up with sheets of lightning. As the storm crackled across the Delta in growls of thunder and shards of hot, white light, the night riders scattered.

Volunteer Wally Roberts was there that night. In a letter dated July 13, 1964, Roberts gave his firsthand account of what happened after the black teenager ran in with news of a possible bombing:

> All of us immediately moved into a back room and shut off the lights. Guards were posted on the roof and sides of the house. Calls were made to the Jackson headquarters of COFO, the FBI in Greenwood and the local police ... [who] told us that police cars had already been posted on the roads leading into our section of "Niggertown." ... The windows facing the street were barricaded with boxes of books to prevent bombs from being thrown through them. Water buckets were filled, a hose connected and one fire extinguisher readied. Almost constant contact was being maintained with Jackson.
>
> When it appeared that the FBI was not going to show up, Len Edwards, a project member from neighboring Ruleville over for the night and son of Congressman Donald Edwards of California, called his father in Washington. Because of Representative Edwards' pressure, the Washington FBI headquarters dispatched two agents from Memphis. They arrived here at 1:30 A.M. and took statements from Sam

Thomas, the man [or boy] to whom the offer was made, the project director, and Len Edwards. Thomas gave the FBI the names of the four men who offered him the money and a good case can be made against them.

In the morning after the lightning storm, Eddie and the other volunteers demonstrated their imperviousness to intimidation. They gathered at the Freedom Center and headed out to canvass Shaw's black neighborhoods. There was Johnson's Addition, a triangle of small houses just north of downtown Shaw, where the Freedom Center stood, and including a small cluster of homes south of Porter Bayou. There was Boatwright, a tiny huddle of houses to the south. There was Ice House Quarter, a strip along an unpaved road to the west. And there was Promised Land, where Andrew Hawkins and his family had lived before moving to a home in Johnson's Addition. Knocking on doors up and down the dirt roads of Shaw, mimeographed fliers in hand, the volunteers worked the clusters of black homes over the coming days.

IN THOSE FIRST FEW days, the editor and publisher of the *Bolivar Commercial* weekly newspaper, Clifton L. Langford, tried to downplay the threat. He wrote that Mississippi was proud to be America's "last bulwark of conservatism." His rhetoric would have readers think that Freedom Summer had hit the state with nothing more than a faint *plink*, like a pebble hitting a windshield. That chip in the status quo, he suggested, was just a minor irritant to those in the driver's seat of state policy and administration—the white sheriffs, growers, business owners, newspaper publishers, civic leaders, and politicians. On July 2, 1964, the editorial pages of the *Bolivar Commercial* dismissed the project as a "long summer 'binge' of stirring up racial unrest." Langford went on:

> The much-heralded invasion of Mississippi by students and paid agitators is in full swing with hundreds arriving daily. They are from all sections of the country and there are many among them undoubtedly sincere in their thinking that they are contributing to the elevation of the Negroes in the state of Mississippi. But … there are many among the invaders who are nothing more than moronic in their desire to upset the lives and habits of Mississippians. There are beatnik types among the invaders, dressed in the beatnik uniform of tennis shoes, blue jeans, shirt tail sticking out, long hair hanging down over their ears and generally giving the appearance of non-conformists.

But within weeks, the *plink* on Mississippi's windshield began to sound more like a *thwack* as Langford and his cronies watched a web of hairline cracks begin to spread from that initial chip, marring their accustomed line of sight. Their black citizens, once so outwardly compliant, were, at least in some towns, showing up at elections offices in numbers unprecedented since Reconstruction. They were out in their neighborhoods knocking on doors, passing out literature, and attending freedom schools to learn the ropes of voting.

Meanwhile, passage of the Civil Rights Act, signed into

law by President Lyndon Johnson on July 2, just as the second cohort of Freedom Summer volunteers was arriving, further fanned the flames of racism in Mississippi. The act outlawed segregation and discrimination in jobs, public accommodations, education, and voting. It was widely reviled by white southerners. Clifton Langford called the Civil Rights Act "one of the most repugnant pieces of legislation ever written by Congress." He urged his readers to resist federal civil rights laws, which he saw as a gross violation of Mississippi's sovereignty. "Mississippi is just one step away from being taken over by the Federals," Langford blustered soon after the law was passed.

As the summer wore on, the newspaper became an ever-shriller echo chamber for white alarmists. The Freedom Summer students whom Langford had disparaged as "beatniks" and "non-conformists" were now branded as "communists" and "infiltrators" promoting "foreign ideologies." On July 16, 1964, under the headline "Trouble Arrives," he fulminated:

> For many weeks Mississippi has been the gathering place of "missionaries" from all parts of the United States. They have invaded our state and set up schools to teach Negroes to register and vote. Today (Thursday), … the City of Cleveland will see and feel the impact of carloads of "freedom" riders. Among the invaders will be Bolivar County Negroes who have been attending these schools and also "white niggers" who have been the teachers along with some Northern "niggers." (They) will picket the Court House and

attempt to register those who they have been teaching.
... The "Freedom" people will come to Cleveland from
Mound Bayou and Shaw.

The day of which he wrote was Freedom Day, July 16,
the first of many so-named days organized by the Freedom
Summer activists. The goal was to register black voters en
masse at county courthouses across the state. Journalist Bruce
Watson describes the scene at the Bolivar County Courthouse
in Cleveland. Across the street, he wrote, "stood three dozen
deputies with shotguns—Sheriff Charlie Capps's 'massive
firepower'—keeping angry whites at a safe distance. At 11:00
a.m. a crop duster veered from nearby fields to buzz the
treetops."

In the same column, Langford went on to say, "As long as
we can remember, the white and colored citizens of Mound
Bayou and Shaw have lived together peacefully with both
races being able to solve their differences and making economic progress." Whether this statement was a deliberate lie
or just a convenient delusion, the U.S. Census for 1960 gave a
very different picture. That year, blacks in Mississippi earned
an annual income of $606 on average, only 29 percent of the
average annual income of Mississippi's whites, $2,023. Only
one-third of black homes in Mississippi, whether owned or
rented, "could be classified as being in sound condition," noted
a SNCC report summarizing the 1960 Census in Mississippi.
"The others have been classified as either deteriorating or
dilapidated. Of the homes in rural areas, over 75 percent are
without any piped water at all and over 90 percent of these
rural homes had no flush toilets, no bathtub and no shower."

On July 23, Langford fumed in the *Bolivar Commercial*: "Last Thursday the people of Cleveland were treated to one of the most insulting sights ever witnessed in our fine city. A group of agitators from over the country came to 'demonstrate' against our customs and educate us in the ways of what they call 'modern Americanism.' ... They are the most malcontent, dirty, brain-washed group of society misfits we have ever seen."

MEANWHILE, FREEDOM SUMMER ACTIVISTS were organizing a parallel political party called the Mississippi Freedom Democratic Party (MFDP) to challenge the state's all-white Democratic Party delegation at the Democratic National Convention in August. In the early months of Freedom Summer, Bob Moses led the creation of this audacious new party, which was symbolic, conceived as a poke in the eye of the regular party's all-white representation. But Moses hoped it would go beyond symbolism to become a catalyst for real change, to give Mississippi's disenfranchised black citizens an equal voice in elections.

As Moses explained at Stanford University in April 1964:

We're going to go to the National Democratic Convention in Atlantic City and challenge the regular Mississippi delegation. We're going to ask the national Democratic Party that they unseat that delegation, that they seat our people in its place, and that they make real structural change, or the beginning of a structural change within their party.... We're carrying on within the state what we call a "Freedom Registration." ... We don't have any questions which will make people interpret some section of the Constitution. We're making it as simple as we possibly can. We want to register upwards of 300,000 to 400,000 Negroes around the state of Mississippi. To dispel, at least, once and for all, the argument that the reason Negroes don't register is because they're apathetic.... With the freedom registration, we also have freedom candidates.... The idea is to begin to develop again, within the people, the Negro people and some white people in the state, a different conception of their politics, and to begin to see if we can evolve a political organization in Mississippi.

On August 20, after regular party delegates to the convention agreed to seat only two black delegates from the MFDP among the mainstream party's delegation, Langford wrote: "Mississippi has no need to bow and scrape to a bunch of politicians who have and are using our state as a stepping stone to curry favor with negro voters in the North and East. This is no time to beg for crumbs from a table occupied by gluttonous jackals who have no love for Mississippians and whose only desire is to further embarrass us nationally."

White Mississippians watched all this with growing alarm. By reflex, they doubled down on their go-to strategy: terrorizing black citizens. The Klan dusted off their ghoulish disguises—white sheets and hoods with eyeholes—and out in their sheds and garages started stockpiling wooden crosses, handheld torches, and cans of gasoline. Members of the White Citizens' Council (many of whom were also Klansmen) hatched plots over drinks and dinner at their country clubs and fraternal organizations. Sheriffs and their deputies trolled the streets, hunting for activists to arrest on flimsy charges. White men with shotguns drove their pickups in caravans, circling civil rights headquarters, black churches, and the homes of known activists.

As IF TO PUT an exclamation point on Bolivar County's white fury, a fiery cross appeared one night in the yard of a black farmer near Shaw, one of the few black landowners in Bolivar County who had managed to hang on to his land despite discriminatory lending by local banks. The farmer's offense— the thing that sparked the ire of the Klan—was his family connection to a civil rights activist. Volunteer Wally Roberts submitted this report to Jackson headquarters via WATS line on August 8, 1964:

> There was a crass [cross] burning the night of August 6 on the farm of Mr. Mack Carter, 6 miles from Shaw. Mr. Carter is the brother-in-law of Ernestine Bryant, one of the 13 civil rights workers who was arrested on August 4 for distributing leaflets without a permit. The police of Shaw told Carter's son that they knew all about Ernestine's activities and that there wasn't anything that she didn't know about. He also said that when the white volunteers leave there will be no telling what will happen to Ernestine.

Threats like this had been lobbed at Mississippi's black citizens for a century. But this time, the reaction in Promised Land and Ice House Quarter and Boatwright was different. This time, the residents of Johnson's Addition and sharecroppers' shacks sensed the tremors of change in the fertile Delta soil because in that moment, the summer of 1964, black Mississippians had an army at their backs: hundreds of northern college kids standing behind them as witnesses and allies. Each one of those white volunteers had, in turn, parents, pastors, and political leaders back home keeping a watchful eye on events down south.

Even though Ernestine Bryant and twelve other civil rights workers, Eddie Short among them, were arrested on August 4, as mentioned by Wally Roberts in his report, the black residents of Shaw had begun to believe that just maybe they could throw off injustices that had seemed immutable only months before, injustices that had felt like "just the way things are." By the time the cross was ignited on Mack Carter's farm, more than a handful of Shaw's black citizens were all in for freedom. By registering to vote, by protesting downtown, by going to jail, Shaw's bravest were at last facing down the hooded hoodlums and the crooked cops and the night-riding racists.

By the end of Freedom Summer, the power structure in Shaw was beginning to shift, if only by inches. For the first time, the traditional hierarchy—in which all rights, privileges, and authority were concentrated in white hands—looked vulnerable. The groundwork had been laid for the unlikely duo of a six-foot-tall, skinny-as-a-rail, white-skinned college girl from urban Oregon and a five-foot-six, strong-as-a-bodybuilder, brown-skinned sharecropper from rural Mississippi to work beside other black citizens of Shaw to achieve unthinkable gains. Nothing would ever be the same in Shaw.

A Freedom Summer volunteer knocks on doors in one of
Shaw's black neighborhoods to encourage people to register
to vote. (Photo courtesy of Dennis Flannigan)

Freedom Summer volunteer Dennis Flannigan from Tacoma, Washington, was hosted by Lucy Mae O'Quinn (shown here) and her family in Shaw. (Photo courtesy of Dennis Flannigan)

Dennis Flannigan works on Freedom Summer communications at the Freedom Center in Shaw, 1964. (Photo courtesy of Dennis Flannigan)

4

Vanishings

I'm sick and tired of going to the funerals of black men
who have been murdered by white men.
—Dave Dennis, civil rights activist

Ohio and Mississippi, June 1964

On a sleepy Saturday morning in southwest Ohio, the first and second cohort of Freedom Summer trainees passed each other like ships in the night. It was June 20, the only moment that summer when all eight hundred volunteers would be at the same place on the map simultaneously.

The two groups converged on the campus of the Western College for Women in Oxford, Ohio, not far from Cincinnati. The first four hundred volunteers were heading out, a week of training in nonviolent resistance under their belts, a week in which they had been hammered with warnings about the racial hatred and incipient violence awaiting them in Mississippi. The second four hundred were arriving from towns and cities across the country to begin their own weeklong orientation. Those heading out and those heading in churned with worry. It was not unlike the worry of the enlistee arriving at bootcamp. Can I hack it? Will I survive?

The first cohort piling into chartered buses and a few private cars with their belongings and their trepidation en route to their assignments in Mississippi included University of Chicago student Heather Tobis. Her destination was the tiny cotton town of Shaw, where she would spend the summer canvassing voters and setting up a freedom school with a small band of volunteers assigned to the Delta towns of Ruleville, Shaw, and Cleveland. Mary Sue Gellatly, meanwhile, was stepping off a Greyhound bus, her blue-gray satchel in hand. Her hometown of Portland, Oregon, was thirty-six grinding highway hours behind her as she strode across campus on her long legs and checked into her dorm.

The serene surroundings belied the raw lessons to come. By week's end, Mary Sue would have been teargassed in a classroom, harassed by a trainer role-playing a white supremacist, and taught to curl up on the floor in a fetal position in order to survive kicks and blows from police batons. That was the planned part, the Freedom Summer training curriculum. Then there was the unplanned part—the gut punch of proximity to murder.

THE MORNING AFTER HER arrival, Mary Sue had a small knot of nervousness in her stomach as she and the other student volunteers gathered in a large classroom for their first training session. One by one, prominent civil rights leaders including Stokely Carmichael, Bob Moses, Fannie Lou Hamer, Lawrence Guyot, Ivanhoe Donaldson, and Dave Dennis stepped to the microphone at the lectern and laid out the realities of race relations in Mississippi. They told their personal stories of jailings and beatings. Some had been shot.

Soft-spoken Bob Moses, director of the Freedom Summer project, stood up and looked at the earnest young men and women seated before him. Serious and intense by nature, Moses knew the idealism that drove these college kids. Idealism was good. But he wanted to disabuse them quickly of any naivete that might blind them to the very real, very raw dangers ahead. He also wanted to plant the idea that freedom and liberty "for all" actually means for all—that allowing racial oppression to keep its grip in Mississippi, even in the hidden backwaters of the Delta, was an affront to everyone in the United States.

"Don't come to Mississippi this summer to save the Mississippi Negro," Moses told them, his eyes scanning the mostly white faces in the crowded room. "Only come if you understand, really understand, that his freedom and yours are one." Maybe, he said, they wouldn't sign up many people to vote. Maybe not many folks would come to freedom schools. "Maybe," he said, "all we're going to do is live through this summer. In Mississippi, that will be so much!"

The next day, Monday, June 22, Mary Sue, refreshed from her sleep and energized by yesterday's training, was one of the first volunteers to arrive at the classroom. The leaders were huddled in front, talking quietly among themselves. Mary Sue watched them as the other students filed in and filled the seats around her. "Something's wrong," she thought. "Something has changed since yesterday." There was a somber tone in their low voices. She couldn't hear the words, but their faces were grim. They leant toward each another, heads bowed as if in prayer.

After all four hundred student volunteers had arrived and

were seated, one of the leaders stepped to the microphone and looked out at the expectant faces. Certain details of that moment are unclear for Mary Sue as she looks back now. She doesn't remember which leader spoke first that morning. She doesn't recall the exact words. But she remembers the quiet intake of breath that rippled through the room as the students heard the news: three twenty-something men in the vanguard of the Freedom Summer project had gone missing the day before, Sunday, June 21.

Just two days earlier, James Chaney, Andrew Goodman, and Michael "Mickey" Schwerner had been in that very Ohio classroom as participants in Freedom Summer's first-cohort training. Both Chaney, twenty-one years old, a black activist native to Meridian, Mississippi, and Schwerner, a twenty-four-year-old Jewish social worker from New York, were staff members of CORE. They were seasoned civil rights workers who had been organizing black people in Mississippi's Neshoba County in the Red Clay Hills region before taking a week off to join the training effort in Ohio. Andrew Goodman was, like Schwerner, a Jewish kid from New York. At twenty-three, he was a neophyte in civil rights who would make his first acquaintance with the Jim Crow South on their trip together to Mississippi.

Revved up and inspired by their week in Ohio, the three young men climbed into a CORE-owned dark-blue 1963 Ford station wagon on Saturday morning as the second cohort, Mary Sue's group, was arriving on campus. Looking back on it later, when Mary Sue thought about the proximity in time between her arrival and their departure, she shivered.

In the hushed classroom, the leaders' voices, so self-assured the day before, were now chinked with uncertainty. The facts so far were sketchy. On Saturday, the three workers had driven from Ohio straight through to Neshoba County, a ten-hour, seven-hundred-mile trip, to investigate the fire-bombing of a black church that had links to Chaney's and Schwerner's civil rights activism. They slept in Meridian that night, fueled up in the morning, and then pointed the blue Ford toward the town of Longdale, site of the arson, where Mount Zion Methodist Church was still smoldering on that Sunday, June 21. By that afternoon, the three had vanished. When they failed to show up at COFO headquarters in the town of Meridian by 4 p.m. as expected, their fellow volunteers waited less than an hour before reporting them missing.

Mickey Schwerner's wife, Rita, whom Mary Sue remembers as "tiny and forceful," stepped to the microphone in Ohio. The signs were ominous, she told the students. Any hope that the three young men would be found alive was fading by the hour.

Mary Sue absorbed the news with two minds. She knew this shattering development had everything to do with her as a freshly minted civil rights worker heading into Mississippi. The disappearance made the danger horrifyingly real. Still, she never questioned whether she was willing to step into the maelstrom. Mississippi was still an abstraction for her. She had yet to see this place with her own eyes, a place notorious for its savage treatment of blacks, for its whites' death grip on power, for its hooded terrorists carrying ropes and guns and Holy Bibles under their white robes, Klansmen whose numbers included "many fundamentalist preachers," as journalist and novelist William Bradford Huie noted in his 1965 book, *Three Lives for Mississippi*.

Reserved and introspective, she had an instinct to hold her thoughts and feelings inside. So it was that in this moment, true to her nature, she absorbed the news and then tucked it away to think over later. How could she process it anyway, this girl from the city of forested hills whose population was 98 percent white, this girl who had studied music on a peaceful campus where skipping chapel on Tuesdays was viewed as an edgy show of dissent?

As the trainees took in the news that morning in Ohio, a pall settled over the classroom. The leaders were blunt. They offered no false assurances that the workers would be found alive. They gave the students a chance to reconsider, to drop out of the project with no loss of face. No one would blame them for making that choice, the leaders assured them.

Meanwhile, news reports of the workers' disappearance flashed across the nation. Frantic parents called their children and begged them to come home. A few students left, but very few—fewer, in fact, than you could count on one hand. After all, signing up for Freedom Summer in the first place had taken a beefy measure of bravery. Turning tail was inconsistent with the moral ground they stood on. Mary Sue's response was to double down on her determination to fight. As she saw it, the three lost workers gave her another big reason to go south. If they were dead, as the SNCC leaders feared, they were just the latest victims of a brutal, centuries-old system that had to be obliterated. It never crossed her mind to succumb to intimidation and fear.

In Portland, Mary Sue's parents saw the breaking news on TV. On June 25, CBS anchorman Walter Cronkite—his trimmed mustache and white button-down shirt giving him the reassuring father-knows-best persona trusted by millions of viewers—looked into the camera and somberly informed Americans about the massive search for the missing workers by hundreds of FBI agents and U.S. Navy sailors. Harold and Verna Gellatly sat side-by-side watching the coverage. There was an Ozzie and Harriet aura to the couple, who were as neatly coiffed and conservatively dressed as the popular TV couple of the era—Harold, square-jawed with a manly chin, Verna with fine features set pleasantly in a narrow face. Their relationship wasn't as harmonious as their outward demeanor might suggest. Harold, who carried on with more than one woman outside his marriage, could be dismissive, even disrespectful, of Verna's wishes and opinions. But in that moment, watching sailors pore over military maps and comb swampy thickets for the bodies of three missing workers, their bond was inviolable. As they heard Andrew Goodman's mother make an anguished "plea to all parents everywhere," they shared an identical sense of déjà vu, a familiar dread from six years before. That's when they had lost their oldest son, Dick, to a fevered, pain-wracked death overseas. "I don't think Dad and Mama ever got over it," Mary Sue said decades later.

The CBS News special report, "The Search in Mississippi," aired just two days before Mary Sue would finish her training in Ohio. The Gellatlys absorbed the chilling news about the missing activists in full knowledge that their daughter was about to head into the danger zone. Risks that had seemed amorphous when Mary Sue signed up for Freedom Summer while still in Oregon now took on a new reality. If they could barely imagine the fate of the three missing activists, they were stricken with dread as they contemplated such a fate for their girl.

Harold and Verna knew Mary Sue's steely will, her immoveable spirit, her refusal to stand on the sidelines when there was righteous work to be done, her commitment to finish whatever she started. They had stood by anxiously when after her sophomore year at Willamette University she had gone overseas to do manual labor as a volunteer in Korea, the very place where Dick had died. They had held their tongues when she had joined a voter registration effort in Nashville, Tennessee, the summer after her junior year and had been arrested with several other civil rights volunteers.

Having watched their daughter's always single-minded, often stubborn adherence to challenging tasks over the years, Verna and Harold Gellatly held out little hope that she would change her mind about heading to Mississippi. But on the last day of her SNCC training—the day before she would board a bus for Mississippi—they felt duty bound, as her parents, to at least broach the subject. On the night before Mary Sue was scheduled to set out for Hattiesburg, they sat across from one another at their kitchen table and made a long-distance call on the family's rotary-dial phone.

Holding the receiver a few inches from his ear so Verna could hear Mary Sue's voice, Harold did most of the talking, as he usually did. He told her there would be no shame in backing out and coming home. It wasn't too late. Perhaps, he ventured to suggest, this struggle wasn't really her struggle. Maybe it made no sense for her, a girl from Oregon, to put her life on the line down there among the bayous and cotton fields and Jim Crow laws of Mississippi. Mary Sue listened. She recognized the love behind their words. This was, after all, the frugal couple of modest means who had taken out a loan to help pay her tuition at Willamette, a prestigious private university in Oregon's capital city of Salem.

She heard her parents out. And then she said, "I can't come home now, Dad and Mama. I've got a job to do."

The next morning, after a restless night in her dorm-room bunk, Mary Sue put on a blouse and a knee-length skirt, packed her satchel, choked down a few bites of breakfast in the dining hall, and joined the other SNCC workers on the bus headed south. As she watched the unfamiliar landscape roll past her window, the constants of her life in the North-west—the small house on Canby Street, the chameleon-like moods of Mount Hood, the music building at Willamette University where she had practiced the sacred notes of Bach preludes, the gothic church whose magnificent pipe organ had seemed to reverberate toward heaven on the day she performed her senior recital—felt to Mary Sue like snatches of long-ago dreams, half remembered.

The volunteers talked quietly among themselves as the bus pushed southward through Indiana, Kentucky, and Tennessee, their voices and thoughts merging with the monotonous whir of rubber on asphalt. About fifteen hours after leaving Ohio, someone said, "Hey, look!" The chatter stopped as the volunteers leaned across the seats and aisles to get a better view. The road sign read, WELCOME TO MISSISSIPPI. A few bursts of nervous laughter broke the silence. Their biggest takeaway from their week-long training in Ohio was that they most certainly would *not* be welcome in Mississippi, not by whites, anyway.

As the bus rolled along the highway toward the medium-sized town of Hattiesburg in Forrest County, her Freedom Summer assignment, Mary Sue felt a low, steady fear creep into her heart. She would carry that fear for years to come.

THE YEAR 1964 WAS when Americans were introduced to Diet Pepsi, Lucky Charms, and eight-track tapes. The Beatles had taken hold in the souls of America's youth like some potent elixir. Schoolgirls carried their pocket-sized transistor radios tuned to Top 10 stations everywhere they went, saved their allowances to buy 45-rpm vinyl records, and collected Beatles trading cards in bubblegum packs. Most Americans alive in 1964 still remember the heart-throbbing, breath-stopping moment on Sunday night, February 9, when John, Paul, George, and Ringo made their TV debut, performing "I Wanna Hold Your Hand" on Ed Sullivan's weekly variety show as 74 million viewers watched.

Other top-rated shows that year included *The Beverly Hillbillies*, *The Addams Family*, *Gilligan's Island*, *Gunsmoke*, and *Bonanza*. In the mid-sixties, however, TV served a bigger, more transformative role in American life than as a medium for celebrity performances, goofball sitcoms, and commercials for Tide and Alka-Seltzer. Also playing out on millions of cathode ray tubes was a cultural rift tearing at the fabric of the nation. Traditional norms about sex, marriage, patriotism, materialism, and faith were butting up against a youthful counterculture bent on upending those traditions. While millions of viewers watched the saccharine-sweet sitcom

Leave It to Beaver (featuring June Cleaver, a blonde-coiffed, frilly-aproned mom, and Ward Cleaver, a wise, preternaturally patient dad who wore a necktie at the dinner table), tens of thousands of college kids were wearing long hair and love beads, protesting in the streets, burning draft cards, forming communes and co-ops, experimenting with drugs—rejecting the Cleavers' version of American life and everything else the establishment held sacred.

In a weird juxtaposition—call it sitcoms versus sit-ins— the *CBS Evening News* at six o'clock crashed into *Gilligan's Island* at seven thirty and *The Addams Family* at eight thirty on ABC. Walter Cronkite would report on existential threats: the Cold War, which could annihilate the planet; the Vietnam War, which pitted American soldiers against the Vietcong abroad and their civilian agemates at home; the civil rights movement, which forced Americans to confront racism. Dr. Martin Luther King Jr. was raising his singular voice against the South's backward attitudes even as the nation at large was advancing on multiple fronts—medicine (vaccines for polio and other diseases), space exploration (humans in orbit, satellites, spacecraft on the moon), technology (computer code and memory chips), consumer protection (seatbelts and tobacco warning labels).

When Cronkite signed off at six thirty, Americans turned the channel. Switching off the images of a nation churning with existential angst, civil unrest, and racial turmoil, families gathered around the antics of Gomez and Morticia on *The Addams Family* and the hapless castaways on *Gilligan's Island*. The ghoulish Addamses, "a satirical inversion of the ideal twentieth-century family" as Wikipedia puts it, were a poke at the Ward-and-June-Cleaver version of the American family that nonetheless retained the comfy 1950s nuclear-family structure (mom, dad, two kids, and a crazy-but-beloved uncle). And being vicariously marooned on a tropical island with the Skipper, Gilligan, and the other castaways, all of them white and middle-class or above, offered viewers a comforting respite from the social disintegration shown so graphically on the evening news.

Nowhere was the queasiness over change more vertiginous than in the South. For a hundred years, whites in Mississippi had carried on as if the Civil War had not liberated black citizens, setting up a legal and social system that ensured their continued subjugation and exploitation. Now, flickering blue screens in nearly every American home became portals into southern white terrorism and apartheid, mostly hidden from view behind a cloak of invisibility whose public face was the cherished "way of life" based on tradition and hospitality served up with a drawl and a clap on the back and a fat cigar. Now, from the most distant city or suburb, Americans witnessed their black brethren reaching for their rights in Birmingham and Selma, often answered by a policeman's baton to the skull or a German shepherd's teeth to the leg. They heard the righteous oratory of Dr. King arguing that racial injustice was a stain on the conscience of America, that Jim Crow could not stand. Even the Beatles weighed in. In September 1964 they refused to perform at Florida's Gator Bowl unless the venue agreed to integrate black and white ticketholders. The venue caved. The Beatles played.

However, the rushing American mainstream had, by and large, detoured around Mississippi. And if the state of

Mississippi had been bypassed, the Delta region was an even more forgotten backwater. It was as if the Delta stood in the crook of an oxbow, an ancient meander that had flowed away from the river's mainstem, long cut off from the big currents of commerce and politics, removed from the trends and opportunities and debates and decisions that were roiling the society at large.

In 1964, 90 percent of American families owned a TV. But in Promised Land and the other black neighborhoods of Shaw, TVs were mostly absent. National news reached the citizens in dribs and drabs, usually by word of mouth in what passed for social media at the time. The faster things moved forward in the wider world, the more out-of-touch rural Mississippi became—that is, until the events of Freedom Summer took a Roto-Rooter to the long-clogged pipelines of communication. The efforts of twenty-something activists, black and white, northern and southern, working for justice turned on the information spigot. News flowed into eyes and ears where it hadn't flown before. As national news of black activism and civil disobedience washed over towns like Shaw—places where enforced poverty and relentless intimidation had kept black citizens cut off from their black brethren—the strength of solidarity girded their efforts. They felt the wind of a righteous army at their backs.

IT WAS AGAINST THIS backdrop that Mary Sue arrived in Hattiesburg, her first posting as a SNCC volunteer. A town of thirty-five thousand in Mississippi's Piney Woods region, Hattiesburg lay less than ninety miles south, via Highway 59, of Meridian, where the missing workers were last seen.

In ticks on the odometer, Hattiesburg was more than two thousand miles from Portland. But by any other measure—history, culture, social structure, economics, race, power—Hattiesburg might as well have been in another country. Mary Sue's letters home often bore the scrawled sarcasm, "the foreign country of Mississippi" on the return address. Certainly, Oregon had its own legacy of racial animus and discrimination. But racial bias in Oregon by the mid-1960s tended to hide behind a veneer of tolerance. In Mississippi, bias stood up and shouted from every corner. As Mary Sue stepped off the bus in Mississippi that June afternoon, racial injustice was as perceptible to her as the suffocating summer heat.

She and a volunteer named Virginia "Jinny" Glass from California's Pomona College were met at the bus by the McCullims, an older black couple who were to be their hosts for the summer. Instantly wrapped in hospitality, Mary Sue and Jinny were shown to a spare bedroom that had stood empty since the couple's children had grown up and moved away.

Tight quarters were nothing new for Mary Sue. She had shared a room with her two brothers until she was thirteen, when her parents had moved her bed to a corner of the living room. Tight space aside, the Gellatlys had running water, a flush toilet, and electric lights, amenities most Americans took for granted in the 1960s. In Mississippi, on the other hand, interior plumbing was absent for 90 percent of rural black families, according to the 1960 U.S. Census. The McCullims, who lived three miles outside Hattiesburg in a tiny outpost called Palmers Crossing, were among those who made do without modern conveniences. The couple did, however, have a hand pump in the yard, which set them apart from the 75 percent of rural black Mississippians who had no access to water at all. They opened their bare-bones home to the northern students because they believed in the promise of freedom.

In her diary, Jinny wrote: "Mrs. McCullim is so thrilled about the freedom schools and all. 'We was sure waiting for you,' she says. And when I asked her what she thought would happen when the Civil Righters go, she said, 'We's prepared for anything. Yes, sa, we'll fight!'"

At the McCullims's, Mary Sue and Jinny pitched in on household chores, including pumping and hauling water. The outhouse was unpleasant. But Mary Sue was too focused on her mission—setting up and running a community center for teaching adult literacy—to waste energy fussing about the rustic bathroom facilities. One of her first tasks was to sew curtains for the community center in Palmers Crossing. She had lugged her portable Singer sewing machine all the way from Oregon and soon saw a use for it when the leaders at her Freedom Summer training warned the volunteers to cover windows, especially at night, to avoid the prying eyes (and shotguns) of prowling white supremacists. The blue-and-white-striped denim curtains were pretty. They dressed up the place, made it homier. Mostly, though, they made it more impervious to terrorism.

THE DAYS WERE LONG, the work intense. So when the Fourth of July rolled around, Mary Sue was grateful for the big fish fry hosted by local black farmer and civil rights leader Vernon

Dahmer (pronounced *DAY-mer*) and his wife, Ellie. Along with about sixty other summer volunteers, she arrived at the Dahmers' two-hundred-acre property in a festive mood. Tables were loaded with soul food—black-eyed peas, sautéed collard greens, fried catfish, white cornbread. Sitting on the grass under an old shade tree, Mary Sue strummed a guitar as freedom songs flowed spontaneously through the gathering.

Partway through the fish fry, Mr. Dahmer, whose antennae for white thuggery were always up, noticed a pickup truck with a gun in the rack and a white man at the wheel cruising slowly by. Then it went by again. While the picnickers ate and sang and talked unaware, Dahmer and one of his grown sons, a Marine home on leave, quietly went into the house. When they came out, they each held a rifle. They stood on the porch, casually holding their firearms, as the pickup truck passed the farm one more time. Mary Sue learned later that before the fish fry, Dahmer had stationed several armed friends along the road in case of trouble.

"Mississippi was armed to the teeth," Mary Sue recalled years later. "Every home had at least one gun for hunting, and people weren't hesitant to use them to protect themselves and their families." Though no shots were fired that day, the absence of the still-missing civil rights workers was a sorrowful subtext to the festivities. It had been two weeks, and still no sign of the three young men had been found. Their dark-blue Ford station wagon had turned up, burned to a cinder in a snake-filled swamp. Even as Mary Sue sat on the grass, her legs tucked beneath her, and played the borrowed guitar, she felt the weight of their disappearance. Though she hadn't met them, she knew her arrival in Ohio on June 20 had coincided closely with their departure on the same day. She knew the three young men had vanished in the Red Clay Hills just an hour and a half down the highway from the Dahmers' farm. And even though she pushed the thought away, she knew that she, too, could go missing on a dark road or in a mosquito-infested bayou.

What she couldn't have imagined as she sat under the hot Mississippi sun was that Vernon Dahmer, host of the fish fry, would die at the hands of the Ku Klux Klan just a year and a half later.

THE DAHMERS OWNED A small store on their property. Mr. Dahmer long had championed the rights of his fellow black citizens. In the 1950s, he worked with Medgar Evers to launch a youth chapter of the NAACP in Hattiesburg and served as Forrest County's NAACP president. After Congress passed the Voting Rights Act of 1965 to buttress the rights of black voters in the South, Dahmer announced on the local radio station that he would pay the poll tax for anyone who couldn't afford it. Local elections officials were still charging a two-dollar poll tax in violation of federal law. White Mississippians generally scorned federal laws, especially laws aimed at protecting the rights of black residents. Despite *Brown v. Board of Education*, Mississippi had brazenly maintained its separate white and black schools.

Dahmer's radio announcement hit the airwaves on January 9, 1966. In the darkest hours of the night on January 10, the Dahmers were jolted from their sleep as two carloads of white men sped along the dirt road toward their quiet farmhouse and adjacent store, lobbing bottles full of gasoline stuffed with flaming rags, twelve of them, through the windows of the wooden structures. The house was already engulfed as Dahmer, shouting for Ellie and the three kids then living at home to flee out the back door, stood in front firing his shotgun at the thugs even as flames leapt around him. Little Bettie Dahmer, ten years old at the time, testified at trial that she remembered seeing her father afterward, sitting outside "with his skin hanging from his arms," the *New York Times* reported in a follow-up story in 1998. Vernon Dahmer died the next day, his lungs seared by the flames.

The mastermind of the Dahmer firebombing turned out to be the same person who had plotted the abduction of James Chaney, Andrew Goodman, and Michael Schwerner. His name was Samuel Bowers. He proudly bore the title of Imperial Wizard of the White Knights of the Ku Klux Klan.

EXACTLY A MONTH AFTER the fish fry, on August 4, 1964, news reached the Hattiesburg summer project office that the bodies of the three missing workers had been found. Over the next few weeks, as witnesses came forward, the story of the civil rights workers' fate unfolded. Chaney, a black resident of Meridian, and his two white companions, New Yorkers Michael Schwerner and Andrew Goodman, had been driving along Highway 19 toward Meridian after spending seven hours in custody for a trumped-up traffic stop. Since they hadn't been granted access to a phone from the jail, none of their colleagues or family members knew they had been locked up. It was after 10 p.m. and dark when they were released. On the instructions of Imperial Wizard Bowers, a band of KKK-affiliated white supremacists, several of whom were sheriff's deputies, followed the blue Ford station wagon, eventually forcing them to pull over and abducting them. The white supremacists took the men to a secluded county road and after beating Chaney severely, shot them all.

An informant—a highway patrolman from Meridian—eventually led authorities to the ironically named Old Jolly Farm owned by one of the killers. The three bodies lay buried there in an earthen dam. The autopsy added to the horror of the murder when the medical examiner found fragments of red clay in Andrew Goodman's lungs and grasped in his fists. It appeared that Goodman had survived the shooting only to be buried alive in the Mississippi mud.

The massive search for the missing youths yielded other secrets from the murky waters of Mississippi's swamps. While dragging local bayous for the missing workers, searchers discovered the bodies of eight anonymous black males, some with hands bound or feet "chopped off," in the words of Freedom Summer volunteer Heather Tobis Booth in her foreword to a 2014 collection of writings called *Freedom Summer*.

When news reached Hattiesburg that the three corpses had been unearthed, Mary Sue had the sensation of falling from a great height and landing hard on her back. She felt as if the wind had been knocked out of her. She couldn't breathe.

As chilling as the news was, Mary Sue's sorrow and outrage quickly eclipsed her fear. To cave in to worries about her own safety seemed petty and cowardly in comparison to the atrocities and indignities black Mississippians faced every day of their lives. And so she put aside her fears and prepared to push on. Her overriding reaction to the news of the murders was defiance. A freedom song bubbled up in her mind, "We'll never turn back." Those notes, those lyrics, became a mental refrain, whenever fear threatened to undercut her courage.

The vicious resistance of white Mississippians to racial justice had shown itself in the starkest terms. The resistance was hateful, it was cruel, and it was relentless. Well, she thought, the summer project's drive toward social justice could meet, *would* meet, that relentlessness head-on. She believed, as she had heard professed by Mohandas K. Gandhi and Dr. Martin Luther King Jr., that cruelty and hatred could be defeated with civil disobedience and peaceful perseverance.

IT WASN'T ONLY COLLEGE students or recent graduates like Mary Sue who kicked up the ire of Mississippi's old guard. Equally alarming to the white resistance were the civil rights lawyers who were deployed to Mississippi to have the backs of the volunteers and local activists in court. The Lawyers Constitutional Defense Committee (LCDC) of the American Civil Liberties Union (ACLU) was the main source of legal assistance to the Freedom Summer volunteers.

One civil rights lawyer who cut his teeth on the events of Freedom Summer was Jacob Tanzer, a native northwesterner like Mary Sue and Dennis Flannigan. Starting when Jacob was ten, his family lived just across town from Mary Sue's family in Portland, the Gellatlys on the west side of the Willamette River and the Tanzers on the east side. Tanzer, a Grant High School graduate, eventually married Elaine Rhine, a Wilson High School grad in the same class as Mary Sue's brother Bill. "Mary Sue was a year or two older and much more tuned in than I was," said Rhine, founder of

Portland's popular chain of hip, innovative eateries, Elephant's Delicatessen. "I heard through the grapevine that she had gone to Mississippi and was really impressed."

After law school at the University of Oregon, Tanzer practiced in Portland for a few years. But he felt drawn to bigger issues on a larger stage. In 1962, he joined the U.S. Department of Justice in Washington, D.C., under Attorney General Robert Kennedy. The following year, he volunteered as a marshal on the National Mall when a quarter million people gathered for the 1963 March on Washington, which Mary Sue joined with a group of young voting rights activists from Nashville. They never met, but metaphorically brushed shoulders once again.

The next thing Tanzer knew, he was called upon to play a pivotal role in American civil rights history. In 1964, he was chosen by the Justice Department's Civil Rights Division to interview potential witnesses in the murders of Schwerner, Chaney, and Goodman. "Our task," he wrote years later in an unpublished memoir, "was to augment the FBI's work. We were to turn frightened people into grand jury witnesses, to organize and present the case to the grand jury, and, if possible, to return indictments." And so in late summer 1964, while Mary Sue was in Hattiesburg, he and a team of young prosecutors ventured into the farms and towns and backroads of Neshoba County, Mississippi, the place where three young men had vanished into the night.

Tanzer's memoir about the months he spent as a twenty-nine-year-old prosecutor interviewing witnesses in Mississippi in the late summer and early fall of 1964 portrays an anachronistic South, a place stuck in a brutal past, a tableau of hidebound roles and rules, written and unwritten, ossified by centuries of racial bias and exploitation:

> I met cotton farmers, share-croppers and labor-ers, often in the hot sun of Mississippi in August, sometimes in their homes. I talked with farmhands who had been in jail with Schwerner, Chaney and Goodman. I talked to church elders. We drove the red clay farm roads to find them. Sheriff's cars cruised by, keeping track of us and whom we were talking to. There were other vehicles, but most of them were pickup trucks. They all had gun racks and there were always guns in the racks.... We were careful not to be found alone in Neshoba County after dark.

For Tanzer, coming to Neshoba County felt like stepping into a vintage photograph. He writes evocatively about his sense of a world that stood still.

> It was early twilight and the light was changing. Except for our presence, what we saw had probably not changed for over a century. All around us was cotton plantation, green rows with white puffs against the hills. The twilight sun cast a reddish light, made more intense by the red dust stirred all day from the red clay earth. It was the end of the picking day. As we drove toward the highway, we came upon a wooden horse-drawn cart, perhaps ten feet long, piled high

with long gray bags of raw cotton, slowly making its way to the gin to be weighed.... Black pickers, men and women, adults and kids, most of them with white or red bandannas around their heads, sat on the edges of the cart and on top of the bags. They were chatting, laughing and singing ... old work songs and spirituals.... As the sun lowered toward the horizon and twilight turned to dusk, the golden, reddish cast intensified. It was magical, unreal, as if the Twentieth Century had never reached this corner of the world. Not even the Industrial Revolution had reached it.

When Tanzer died in 2018, the *Oregonian* called him "a lion of the legal profession," his prominence in Oregon crowned by his appointment to the Oregon Supreme Court in 1980.

MARY SUE GOT UP the morning after the civil rights workers' bodies were found filled with new conviction and deeper admiration for the black men, women, and children of Hattiesburg and Palmers Crossing, who were reaching for their rights even as white men with shotguns patrolled the streets, slinging racial slurs and sowing fear. She didn't have to look farther than her host mother, Mrs. McCullim, to find a fearless soldier in the fight for justice. Mrs. McCullim, whose children were grown and gone, would come home from her job cleaning white folks' houses, her feet swollen and her back aching. She was getting old, and she was tired. But more than anything else, she wanted to cast her vote in elections. Over and over, she studied for the voter registration test, which she took again and again at the courthouse in Hattiesburg, only to be told that she had failed to pass.

Shortly after Mary Sue and Jinny arrived, Mrs. McCullim confided to them that she had recently tried to register again and then waited more than a month to get the results, as required by elections registrar Theron Lynd, whose predecessor Luther Cox liked to ask black would-be voters to estimate the "number of bubbles in a bar of soap." Lynd, who admired Cox's methods, had posted a notice at the courthouse, declaring: "Applications for registration must be completely filled out without any assistance or suggestions of any person or memorandum. After ten days, applicants' names and addresses are published for two consecutive weeks in the newspaper. They cannot be ruled on for fourteen days after the second publication. Therefore it can take as long as thirty-three days before we can give you an answer as to your application being accepted or rejected. Your indulgence is appreciated." It was signed "The Registrar." Aside from Lynd's arbitrary delays and discriminatory administration and scoring of voter registration tests, actions that were in themselves illegal under federal law, his policy of publishing the names of would-be voters in the local newspaper had the clear intent of intimidation. Black citizens who sought the vote risked being fired, beaten, even lynched.

But the tide was turning. As Freedom Summer unfolded, Theron Lynd would come under investigation by the U.S. Department of Justice for discriminating against the black citizens of Forrest County.

Mary Sue (left) and fellow Freedom Summer volunteer Jinny Glass from Pomona College shared a room at the McCullim home in Palmers Crossing just outside Hattiesburg. (Photo courtesy of Mary Sue Short)

Mr. and Mrs. Steve McCullim hosted Mary Sue and Jinny Glass in their Palmers Crossing home. (Photo by Mary Sue Gellatly)

Mary Sue plays guitar as Freedom Summer volunteers and local activists sing during a July 4, 1964, fish fry at the Forrest County farm of black civil rights leader Vernon Dahmer. (Photo by Herbert Randall)

A roadside marker in Neshoba County memorializes the triple murder that sparked national outrage at the start of Freedom Summer. (Photo by Lee Anna Sherman)

5

Reckonings

Isn't it awful not to be able to go to a public library
and get an interesting book
Without being put out and given a hateful look?
—Edith Moore, student poet,
McComb Freedom School

Shaw, Mississippi, summer 1964

When the Freedom Summer activists rolled into Shaw in late June 1964, their mission was threefold: to register voters, to open a freedom school, and to establish a community center. Johnson's Addition soon rang with the sounds of construction—the *whirr* of saws slicing wooden planks, the *thwack* of hammers driving nails. Sounds that signified building in a town where stagnation had been the status quo, sounds of newness in a place where the old ways had been so long entrenched. Bookshelves were going in at the Freedom Center, built by volunteer carpenter Fred Winn, assisted by young black people. Books donated by supporters in the North were waiting in boxes. In a town where black citizens were excluded from the public library, to have a houseful of books just for them would be like a moon landing.

"The three-thousand-volume library at the Freedom Center in Shaw is one of the most successful in Mississippi," Dennis Flannigan noted in a letter to Dave Purchase of the Tacoma Friends of Mississippi Volunteers in early July 1964. Shaw's freedom school was off to a promising start, it seemed. But when children failed to show up, the volunteers learned that an unforeseen catch was sabotaging their plans. In Shaw, as elsewhere in the cotton-growing region of the Delta, black children were not on summer vacation as their white neighbors were. They were in school, sweltering in classrooms without air conditioning in the town's segregated school. That's because the white school board, to ensure growers would have all the human hands they needed to tend and harvest their crops, dictated that black children would attend school in "split sessions" coinciding with the growing season. (Except for the occasional poor white sharecropper's kids, white children were exempt from fieldwork in cotton country.)

Summer volunteer Wally Roberts, who was in charge of Shaw's freedom school, described the progression of events in his personal memoirs:

> Once we were set up and ready to start (the Freedom School) … we discovered that in this part of Mississippi, the students had no summer vacation because they were given a month vacation in the spring to chop cotton (weed the new plants) and then another month of "vacation" in the fall when they were needed to pick the cotton. What this meant for us was that after a full day of regular classes in an un-airconditioned school in the torrid heat of July and

August, the students were not about to attend another school after 3 P.M., even if it was a Freedom School.

At first, we were at a loss about what to do, but the students themselves solved that problem by coming to us and saying, "Look, we appreciate what you want to do, but what we want you to do is to help us become Freedom Fighters. We want to go on picket lines and do protests. Teach us how to do that." We were in a quandary because we had been instructed by the SNCC staff not to let the kids get involved in these kinds of activities because they were so dangerous, especially in the Delta, and because there were not enough experienced SNCC staff members to help out. We discussed this all with Staughton Lynd, the director of the Freedom Schools for the state, and with Stokley [sic] Carmichael, who was the SNCC staff person in charge of the Delta, and they both agreed we should go ahead, train the students in nonviolent protest tactics, work out a protest strategy with them, and go from there.

So that's what they did, according to Roberts. They asked the county board of supervisors for a permit to distribute pamphlets outside the courthouse in Cleveland, urging people to register to vote. Their request was denied, as they expected. Then, on August 4, most of the freedom school teachers and a dozen students picketed outside the courthouse in protest of the permit denial and voting rights discrimination. Said Roberts, "We also passed out the leaflets, which guaranteed our arrest."

The kids were delighted to get arrested—it was kind of like a graduation ceremony. Stokley [sic], who had come to observe but had done nothing illegal, was recognized by the police and was also arrested. He was furious.

As we were being photographed and fingerprinted, [Sheriff] Capps asked me, "Well, Wallace, are you happy now?" I said nothing, but thought, "I won't be happy until there's a black man wearing that badge of yours." (The county was 66 percent black, and got a black sheriff in the 1980s. Today, almost every elected office in the county is held by an African American.)

We were in jail for only 24 hours and then released and the charges dropped. We were released quickly because we volunteers all used our one phone call from jail to call our Congressmen or the television network news programs, and similar places to tell them what happened. Capps soon began to get telephone calls from Washington and television reporters in New York, and he quickly caved in.

After we were released from jail, we found that support in the community for what we had done had increased significantly, so we stopped education at the Freedom Schools and began to hold mass meetings around the county and going door-to-door to register members for the Mississippi Freedom Democratic Party.... By the end of the Summer Project in the third week of August, local leaders had begun to emerge and take responsibility for guiding the civil rights work in Bolivar County. Our work was done, and Charlie Capps had done his part.

Eddie was among the marchers arrested in Cleveland that day. The terrifying and exhilarating march ended with cops rounding up the protesters, charging them with violating ordinances against leafletting and parading in the street without a permit.

Eddie's first night in jail initiated him into the ranks of hardcore activism. Marching down the street in full view of white policemen had stirred in him a heady sense of freedom, wrapped though it was in existential dread. When he walked out of jail the next morning still alive, unscathed, the Delta air seemed somehow sweeter, the sun somehow brighter, whetting his appetite for more action. He was ready to join ranks with other local black activists to shake up this sleepy corner of the Delta, the risks be damned.

In the Delta, the schooling of black children took a back-seat to the profits of white landowners. So kids like Eddie and his siblings spent the months of spring chopping weeds, the months of fall picking cotton, and while the cotton matured on its stalks in the fields, the months of summer sitting in stifling classrooms to make up for the instructional time lost. Meanwhile, their white agemates "roamed the hills with an adventurous spirit," to borrow the sentimental language of the *Bolivar Commercial*'s editor, Clifton Langford.

SHAW WAS BUILT ON cotton. Its huddle of houses and shops drew their sustenance from the surrounding acres of cotton fields, thousands of them, stretching from horizon to horizon across Bolivar and Sunflower Counties. The town's main cotton gin—one of four or five gins dotted around Shaw where seeds were separated from the cotton fibers—was the biggest structure in Shaw, crouching like a giant green many-legged insect just a few blocks southwest of Main Street. The gin—a word meaning "machine" or "engine" originating from Middle English via Old French—was a symbol of Mississippi's number one industry, an industry that employed two-thirds of Shaw's black residents, Eddie's family of sharecroppers among them. "Cotton," Eddie noted, "grew right up to our back door."

Bogues and bayous and rows of trees divided the fields into a patchwork that from a distance looked bucolic, a peaceful scene of life lived close to the land, of prosperity wrested from the deep, rich soil. But that scene, so pastoral, so idyllic when perceived, say, from the window of a car whirring by on Highway 61, was only skin deep. Close-up, it dissolved like a pixilated photograph to reveal two parallel worlds, a white world of comfort and opportunity beside a black world of poverty and oppression. Freedom Summer, as conceived by the leaders of SNCC, was all about altering the dynamics of that bifurcated system by empowering Mississippi's black citizens through civic education and access to the ballot box, leading in turn to access to all levels of government—local, state, and national—as jurors and candidates for public office. "SNCC and other organizations fought white terror and helped create a willingness to risk danger in order to register to vote," noted one of SNCC's early leaders, Julian Bond, who later served in the U.S. Congress and chaired the NAACP.

Ruleville and Shaw were two peas in a pod, as towns go.

Just ten miles apart in adjacent counties, both towns were gripped by the demands of King Cotton, the rules set by the planters, enforced by the cops, and reinforced in segregated schools where black children mostly learned how to play their predetermined roles in the command performance staged and directed by the white establishment. Bolivar County, where Shaw resides, is a chunky rectangle bumping up against the Mississippi River on its western edge. Sunflower County, home of Ruleville, sits to its east, its long, skinny shape reminiscent of the nine-foot-long bags cotton pickers dragged through the fields at harvest time.

Today, tourists who visit the Delta have come to know that portion of Highway 61—a 1,400-mile ribbon of blacktop that runs between New Orleans to Minnesota—as the Blues Highway, named for storied black musicians like Muddy Waters, Bessie Smith, and B.B. King who performed in little clubs and juke joints along the 250-mile stretch running north to Memphis and south to Vicksburg, Mississippi, during their heyday in the 1950s and 1960s. Driving past Shaw today, if you noticed it at all, you would see a town just like a hundred other towns that fed the cotton-dominated economy of the Delta—clusters of small houses, little churches, a couple of schools, a diner and a tavern, a Dollar General store. If you turned off the highway at the faded blue sign that reads SHAW: A SMALL TOWN WITH A BIG WELCOME, you would soon come upon the ruins of the town's once-vibrant commercial district.

Those ruins are the downside of the events of that summer. When President Johnson put his pen to the Civil Rights Act of 1964, signing it into law on July 2, the news hit the South like a cluster bomb. Suddenly, white hoteliers, restaurateurs, and clothiers faced federal criminal charges if they refused service to black customers.

That same week, Freedom Summer rolled in on a fleet of chartered buses. This second domino crashed down like a barrage of bomblets battering the fields of cotton. To the white resistance, their beloved South hadn't been under such siege since Appomattox. Northern volunteers like Mary Sue were the visible spearhead of the movement. But black organizers like Bob Moses, Stokely Carmichael, and Fannie Lou Hamer were the project masterminds. And local black citizens like Eddie were the spear's shaft, strong and straight, made of the mettle inherent in people who survive brutality and bondage by drawing deeply on fortitude and faith. They would be there long after the white volunteers went home at summer's end. It was their fight to wage, and theirs to win.

The twin anti-racism dominoes—new federal laws and an army of freedom fighters from the North—touched off a chain reaction of change. Some of those changes brought collateral damage to Bolivar County and the town of Shaw, whose white business owners and cotton growers never really expected black citizens to rock the boat of the Jim Crow tradition or, more to the point, to stare unflinching into the eyes of white power. Before Johnson's handwriting was dry on the new legislation, Shaw's shops began to be shuttered by their white owners. The new law was a frontal assault on Jim Crow. Overnight, the owners of hotels and theaters and diners faced criminal charges if they shut their doors to black customers.

BY THE TIME SHAW'S Freedom Center opened its doors, Eddie was becoming a central figure in the local civil rights struggle—that is, whenever he could break away from his multiple and overlapping seasonal jobs. One job was a night shift of twelve to sixteen hours at the Martin Grain Elevator, filling, stitching, and stacking 120-pound bags of grain for sixty-five cents an hour. He drove a tractor as a hired hand for Mrs. Minley, who was by then managing her forty-acre cotton patch single-handedly. He made quilts (a skill he had learned from his daddy) on a treadle sewing machine for Mrs. Evie Nola, a black woman who ran a boarding house in the neighborhood. She paid him three dollars per quilt. Odd jobs like painting houses and washing windows for white folks filled the gaps in Eddie's work life.

"You had to work when you could," Eddie says.

For the first few weeks that summer, he and the other young black activists deferred to the volunteers' agenda, steering clear of direct confrontation with Jim Crow and sticking instead to voter registration. The Freedom Summer leadership had drummed into the trainees an avoidance of direct action. Much too risky, they said. So for Eddie, who was chomping at the bit to speed forward at a full gallop, the first influx of volunteers was disappointing.

Eddie's tolerance for marginalization—for being shut out of white-owned stores and restaurants as well as city-run facilities funded by taxes, like the public swimming pool and the library downtown—was running out. He was ready to confront apartheid head-on, to challenge restaurants that forced him to walk around to the back to get served, businesses where his money was welcome but not his presence.

Working on voter registration, no matter how crucial it was in the big picture, had begun to feel like dipping his toes in the edge of an ocean. He was ready to brave the dark waters, swim against the riptide of racism until his strength failed and his will gave out.

Before the summer volunteers arrived, Eddie had made his first public foray into direct action against racism in Shaw when he and several of his fellow activists marched down the town's main street carrying signs in support of black citizens like Andrew Hawkins who wanted to run for local offices. Hawkins had tried to run for mayor in 1960, but he was caught in the Catch-22 of black participation in the Jim Crow South. Elections officials had rejected his attempts to register to vote, and only registered voters could run for office. Of this first-ever public demonstration by black citizens in the town of Shaw, Eddie said, "It was only a minor success, but at least no shots were fired."

The march, as small as it was, whetted Eddie's appetite for bigger things. As the summer wore on, the progress being made by Shaw's little band of Freedom Summer volunteers seemed as slow as the sluggish waters of Porter and Silver Bayous. He wanted to bring to Shaw the same high-profile actions making headlines in other towns and cities across the South. Just over the state line in Alabama, sit-ins at lunch counters and boycotts of city buses had been getting nationwide news coverage. But the risks, argued the summer project leaders, were too real and too raw.

MISSISSIPPI WAS, AFTER ALL, the place where fourteen-year-old Emmett Till of Chicago had been savagely murdered in

1955 when Eddie was eleven, an atrocity that had seared itself into the national consciousness and forever changed Eddie's sense of himself as a young black male. It had happened in the Delta hamlet of Money, where Emmett was visiting relatives for the summer. Carolyn Bryant, wife of the proprietor of a small grocery store and gas station in Money, accused Emmett of "insulting" her when he and his cousin bought candy at the store. (Fifty years later, Carolyn recanted her story.) In retribution, Roy Bryant and his half brother, J. W. Milam, kidnapped Emmett in the middle of the night, sadistically tortured him, shot him in the head, and threw him into the Tallahatchie River with a seventy-pound cotton gin fan strung with barbed wire around his neck.

Emmett's mama, Mamie, insisted on an open-casket funeral. She wanted the world to see what the killers had done to her son. *Jet* magazine's publication of photographs of the teenager's mutilated body shocked the nation. Black reporter Simeon Booker, who had written up the Till story for *Jet*, describes the boy's body in his memoir, *Shocking the Conscience*: "The body … looked as if someone had set about to destroy any vestige of its humanity. The tongue was swollen and grossly distended from the mouth. The left eyeball had been gouged out, and the right eyeball was hanging from the socket, held only by an optic nerve…. A bullet hole was apparent on the right side of the head."

For Eddie and other young black males in the Deep South, Emmett Till's murder was more than an outrage. It was a warning, dire and personal. Eddie could close his eyes and imagine his own ruined face on the boy who lay in that casket.

By age eleven, then, Eddie was all too aware of the potential consequences of not heeding the warnings from his mama about what could happen to a black person who failed to, as he says, "treat white people like royalty, like they still owned us." Over time, he developed a sixth sense, an almost preternatural ability to assess character and detect threat from a few external clues: the twitch of an eyebrow, a glance between strangers, the clench of a white man's jaw. As journalist Timothy B. Tyson observed in his 2017 best seller, *The Blood of Emmett Till,* "For black youth across the country … the Till lynching became a decisive moment in the development of their consciousness around race."

So Eddie was part of what SNCC activist Joyce Ladner called "the Emmett Till generation." Just as every American who was alive at the time remembers the exact moment in 1963 when they got news of the assassination of President Kennedy, so every young civil rights activist "knew where they were when they saw pictures of Emmett Till's body," said Charles McDew, who chaired SNCC from 1961 to 1963.

The Freedom Summer volunteers had been trained to avoid "direct action"—that is, challenging Jim Crow laws and customs with the sit-ins, boycotts, and protests that had captured headlines across the nation. But at the same time, the volunteers were instructed to follow the lead of local black activists, letting them set the agenda in their own communities. As one of those local black activists, Eddie was restless, impatient, and ready to jump headlong into the fray. He was itching to claim his rightful place as a man and an American citizen.

So one day at lunchtime, Eddie and six or seven other young black activists met up at the Freedom Center and headed out on foot, walking the quarter mile to Highway 61. Their destination that day was the small diner inside the local gas station and bus stop, known by everyone simply as the Truck Stop. For their personal safety, black people who had grown up in the area followed the unwritten code at such white-owned places, walking around back to the take-out counter to get burgers or fried catfish sandwiches instead of eating inside. But with the Civil Rights Act freshly enacted, Eddie and his posse felt the tide turning. Their fight suddenly seemed bigger than their hometown by miles. Their allies suddenly took on stature beyond even the Freedom Summer leaders, as brilliant and unflinching and single-minded as they were. Knowing that the Congress and the president had given the full weight of federal law to the cause of racial justice was empowerment on steroids for Eddie and his fellow activists. They were ready to confront the age-old customs head-on in Shaw.

The Truck Stop sold bus tickets as well as food. Since few black residents could afford cars, this was their jumping-off point to Cleveland or Memphis, or to St. Paul or Chicago up north. Plenty of poor white folks, too, depended on buses. But at the Truck Stop, white passengers got first-class treatment. After buying a ticket, they were welcome to sit inside, sheltered from the sun, the rain, the bugs, and the dust. A black passenger, on the other hand, had to wait beside the highway, subject to the sun, the rain, the bugs, and the dust.

Eddie never imagined at the time that less than a year later, he would be back at the Truck Stop buying his own ticket north after all his local job prospects vanished in the wake of his civil rights activism. More unimaginable still, he would one day bring his own sons to eat a meal in this once-segregated diner.

The young men were nervous as they walked up to the low wooden building. They knew they were about to look generations of oppression in the eye and say, in essence, "Go to hell." They had no idea what would happen, whether they would be ignored or chased off, arrested or beaten up. Fear was as familiar to them—to all blacks in the Deep South—as lightning on a hot summer day just before a squall. But they were emboldened by the highly publicized actions of black activists across the South who were staging sit-ins at Woolworth's lunch counters. While their numbers were small in the town of Shaw, Eddie felt the solidarity of a million black Americans at his back. And so they choked down their fear and squared their shoulders, ready to assault generations of racist practices by attempting the simple act of ordering food under a public roof and then sitting down at a table to eat it.

With Eddie in the lead, the posse ignored the hand-lettered signs designating the restrooms and water fountains as "white" or "colored." They walked through the front door, sticking close together, drawing courage from their shared resolve. They sat down at one of the long, bare tables. They studied the menu posted on a plastic reader board above the window where the cook would set plates of food and the waitress would grab and serve them. And then they waited. And they waited. The handful of white customers forked angrily at their potato salad and cast dirty looks at the young people. "If looks could kill," Eddie said decades later, "we would have been dead."

The middle-aged waitress, a stout white woman with a flip hairdo and a flowery pink dress, ignored them, a frown etched on her face as she busied herself at the counter. Ten minutes went by. Then twenty. When it was clear that the young black men were going to hold their ground, she finally snatched a pencil from behind her ear and stood before them with a pad of order forms. Her ruby-red painted lips, which had been pursed tightly together ever since the activists walked in, finally parted. "What'll ya'll have?"

"A cheeseburger and Orange Crush," Eddie said, his words almost sticking in his throat. As she wrote down his order and then the others, one by one, the activists stayed outwardly cool even as their minds were racing with shock and excitement. As the waitress slapped down the filled-out order form in front of the cook, the activists avoided looking at each other, afraid they would betray their astonishment at what was happening. When she set their plates brusquely before them and they began to eat, they could sense a fracture opening up in their small corner of the Jim Crow South. If they could get served inside the Truck Stop, what else could they accomplish? What other mountains could they move with the force of their will?

By the time they finished their meal, Eddie felt as if he and his posse had driven the slim end of a wedge into the fissure that was forming in the racist edifice upon which Bolivar County had built its economy, walling off its black citizens from opportunity and prosperity and dignity. Though the fissure that widened when Eddie ordered a thirty-five-cent burger and a ten-cent Orange Crush at a lowly diner along Route 61 was only a hairline crack that day, he felt compelled to keep going. He would hammer on the edifice of injustice in his hometown till it cracked open and gave way. As the first blacks ever served inside the diner on Route 61, they knew as they paid for their meals and walked out the door that the waitress's scowl had no power now. Eddie would never again willingly go to the back of the building, the back of the line, the back of the bus.

EDDIE AND HIS FRIENDS, buoyed by their successful sit-in at the diner, were ready to strike another blow at apartheid in Shaw. So along with his fellow activists James "Jimmy" Johnson Jr. and Willie Wright, Eddie set his sights on the one-room public library downtown, which despite its taxpayer funding base was open only to whites. With them were Freedom Summer volunteers Grace Morton and Mel Fahnestock. Several other members of the Mississippi Student Union (the organization of politically active black high school students) went along as witnesses.

One of the students who joined the library action was a girl named Ruby Richard. Like Eddie, she had started picking cotton as a young child. When Freedom Summer came to Shaw, Ruby joined the student union, was elected chair of the Action Committee, and started going to mass meetings. It was at one of those meetings at Parker's Chapel, an African Methodist Episcopalian church, that she met Fannie Lou Hamer. "Mrs. Hamer was so warm and loving and funny," Ruby said many years later. "She could make you laugh.

When she walked in, the atmosphere changed."

A time or two when Fannie Lou Hamer was delayed on her way to a meeting in Shaw, she would give Ruby a call at the Freedom Center. "She'd tell me: 'Baby, just get the meeting started. I'll be there.'" So seventeen-year-old Ruby would stand up in the chapel and raise her voice in a song for freedom, clapping out the rhythm with hands that had been pricked a thousand times by thorns on cotton bolls.

When Eddie, Jimmy, and Willie sauntered into the library and casually spread out around the book-filled room, scanning titles, the librarian stood there as if struck to stone. When she recovered her senses, she began sputtering and fussing, preaching about the proper care of books and the observance of due dates. Despite the librarian's undisguised disapproval of giving black youths access to reading materials, each of the young activists calmly chose a book and carried it to the checkout counter. The librarian stamped the books one after another, her impotent fury expressed in the loud pounding of her rubber stamp.

In the meantime, the Shaw Police Department had been informed of the invasion of the public library by three black youths. When the activists left the building holding their books, four armed officers were waiting on the street outside. In a bald-faced display of intimidation, the policemen followed the young people, tailing some of them all the way back to their homes. Eddie carried his book to the Freedom Center. No word was spoken between the police and the activists. But when white cops armed with guns tailed black youths armed only with library books, the message needed no words.

EDDIE AND HIS CORPS of student activists soon began scanning their world for the next chance to take a stand. It turned out to be right in front of them, a place they passed every time they went downtown: Liar's Park. Yet another public space maintained by tax dollars, Liar's Park got its name from all the boasting, tall tales, and fish stories that emanated from the white men who gathered around a table under a wooden shelter to play dominoes beside the bayou. One day as Eddie and his sidekicks rounded a corner and saw the shelter sitting empty, they decided spontaneously to have a seat on the green wooden benches and see what would happen. They hung out for an afternoon, talking and laughing and appearing relaxed, as though this were an everyday thing. But inside, they were nervous, wondering if someone would come along and hassle them or bust them. Nothing happened. So a couple of days later, they showed up again and occupied the benches under the wooden shelter. Again, nothing happened to them. The consequences, as it turned out, were indirect: the white men never again returned to Liar's Park, leaving the black community free to "sit in the shade and shoot the breeze," in Eddie's words.

The bus stop, the library, the park—all of these actions to integrate Shaw were victories for Eddie and his fellow activists. As the Liar's Park fallout showed, whites were sensing a shift in the balance of power. The equilibrium long maintained by brutality and economic bondage was tottering, pushed by the inexorable human drive for dignity and justice. When blacks like Eddie stepped up and stood their ground, backed by the new Civil Rights Act, southern whites felt the dizzying sensation of once-solid ground heaving under their feet.

Rather than stay and adjust to their new reality, many whites took flight. Eddie had succeeded in giving blacks access to the park, but integration still eluded the town. Overnight, it seemed, Liar's Park switched from a white space to a black space. It was a new twist on segregation, Jim Crow turned upside down. The same thing was happening in other southern towns. Newly won access for blacks, it turned out, often had the unintended consequence of causing white owners to close shop and move away to avoid integration.

This was exactly what happened with Eddie's next effort to integrate Shaw. It showed the hardening resistance to the idea of blacks and whites sharing public places. One night, he and his friends decided to integrate the movie theater, where blacks were restricted to a small, creaky balcony with a separate entrance. Eddie recalls: "The movie cost white people thirty-five cents. Even though it was cheaper for us, twenty-five cents for a ticket, we were tired of having to sit in the crummy balcony on wooden benches while the white people sat downstairs on cushioned seats." On this particular night, Eddie and about twenty young black activists gathered at the Freedom Center and walked the few blocks to the theater. "I stepped up to the front, showed my thirty-five cents to the ticket lady, and told her I wanted a ticket for downstairs," Eddie says. "She called the owner over. He asked me why I wanted to pay more and sit downstairs. I told him that's what I wanted."

Knowing that LBJ had just signed the Civil Rights Act banning discrimination at public businesses, the owner surely knew he would be on thin ice if he turned the black activists away. So he nodded to the ticket lady, giving his assent. The activists each paid their thirty-five cents and walked down the aisle of the main auditorium. They sat together on the cushioned seats down front. The heads of the white moviegoers who were already seated swiveled, and their mouths gaped. "They got up and left, making negative comments on their way out," Eddie says. His group sat through *Blue Hawaii*, a musical romantic comedy starring Elvis Presley, all the while wondering if they would be ordered to move up to the "colored" section in the balcony. When nothing happened, they went home with a sense of victory. It seemed that they had successfully broken down another barrier in Shaw.

As it turned out, the unheard-of seating of black youths in the "white" section of the theater was the landing of an asteroid in the little town of Shaw. That very night as Eddie and his posse were sleeping, the theater went up in flames. Nobody still alive in Shaw today thinks the timing of the fire was a coincidence. To this day, there is no movie theater in Shaw, Mississippi.

There is no public swimming pool in Shaw, either. About the same time the theater burned down, word got out that Eddie and his fellow activists were eyeing the city pool as their next target for integration. The pool was a small oasis of cool aquamarine water that glistened invitingly down near Shaw's central cotton gin. Eddie had grown up seeing white kids with freckled noses and sunburned shoulders splashing and diving and taking swimming lessons inside the chain-link fence that kept him and his buddies on the outside looking in. But before the young activists could finalize their plans to head downtown in their cut-offs (none of them owned a pair of swim trunks) and take a dip in the taxpayer-supported pool, city officials pulled the plug, literally. They drained the pool, leaving a gaping concrete hole that gradually, over the following months and years, filled up with dirt and weeds. Eventually, the city filled it in.

During the middle decades of the 1900s, while white kids were learning to swim in America's city or suburban pools, Eddie and his friends were taking their chances in the rivers and bayous that crisscrossed the Delta. Having been excluded from public pools over the years, most black citizens in the 1960s did not know how to swim. Still, the cool waters flowing across the Mississippi River floodplain beckoned children of all colors on sweltering midsummer afternoons.

One day when Eddie was a kid, even after Janie Bea gave him her sternest look and said "No!" in her most uncompromising voice, he and his pals snuck off for an afternoon of "mud crawling." Trying to stay camouflaged by the foliage choking the banks of the bayou, they headed to an old wooden train trestle in Johnson's Addition. Hanging from the bottom of the trestle, the boys dropped into the slow-flowing stream oozing with mud and came up sputtering and laughing, caked in layers of cooling silt.

Then one of the boys hissed, "Missus Janie Bea! Missus Janie Bea comin'!" Eddie froze in place and listened. When he heard his mama calling, he knew from the tone of her voice she was furious. "Eddie Short! Where you be, Eddie Short? I got the switch and I gonna whup you whenever I find you, Eddie Short!"

Missus Janie Bea was not to be trifled with. As he heard

his mama get closer, Eddie pulled himself up on the timbers beneath the trestle and flattened himself against the rough boards, tucking his legs onto the rafters. But Janie Bea knew her wayward son was near. Shaw's instant neighbor-to-neighbor network had telegraphed the mud-crawling caper within minutes of Eddie's first splash into the muck. She marched up and down the trestle, scanning the bayou, flicking the switch she carried in her hand, until she noticed a tiny movement below her through the chinks in the wood. "I see you, Eddie Short!" she yelled. She marched him home in a torrent of scolds and a hail of blows from the switch.

Janie Bea had lost two babies in their infancy and a third as a toddler, a consequence of having no money to pay for prenatal care or well-baby checkups or adequate food. When her babies got sick, she cared for them as best she could. When they died, their small bodies were laid to rest in the churchyard of the Green Grove Missionary Baptist Church. She was not alone in the sorrow of burying babies. The SNCC report on the 1960 U.S. Census stated, "It takes no statistical genius to understand what the figures reflect: In Mississippi, the chances of a Negro baby dying within the first year of life are at best twice those of a white baby."

Janie Bea worried night and day about her remaining children, knowing as she did the dangers they faced growing up in the Delta. She had taught them to step off the sidewalk when a white person came along, to show subservience by looking at the ground, never meeting the eye of a white citizen who might interpret that look as defiance or insolence. Emmett Till's murder for supposedly flirting with a white woman had become the nightmarish emblem of all Janie Bea feared for her sons, especially Eddie because of the proud bearing and willfulness he so often showed to the world.

Aside from white violence, drowning was one of Eddie's mama's deepest dreads. She and everyone else in Shaw knew someone who had drowned, usually more than one someone. Glory Hawkins, the daughter of Andrew and Mae Lou Hawkins, knew a boy named Tyrone who drowned. And fifty years later, thinking back, she recalled another victim. "Missus Daisy's Johnny B, he had cat eyes, real light, pretty, a cousin of Eddie's," she said. "He drowned a little before Tyrone."

In the dog days of late summer 1964, soon after Mary Sue was reassigned to Shaw from Hattiesburg, something happened that highlighted the disparity in access to swimming skills. As Glory Hawkins-Scott tells it, "One day, a bunch of us went out to the bogue," a shallow reach of the river labeled Bogue Hasty on topographic maps where young people could cool off splashing and wading under the canopy of shade trees. Suddenly, a note of alarm cut through the banter and laughter of the group. Everyone looked up. Out in the river they saw arms thrashing frantically. Amos Jewett was in trouble. "He went down," Glory recalls. Mary Sue was hanging out at the bogue that day with Glory and the rest of the local young people. When Mary Sue saw Amos struggling to stay above water, she dove in. Like most of her friends in Portland, she had taken swimming lessons, which she paid for with her berry-picking earnings. She had gone on to earn a junior lifesaving certificate and even joined the swim team in high school. And so that day on the bogue, seeing Amos Jewett's panicked splashing after he slipped into a deep hole beyond the reach of his friends, she swam out and saved the teenager. "He'd o' been a goner," Glory says, shaking her head and looking into the distance, as if the near-drowning haunted her still.

So for Janie Bea, the mental image of one of her kids slipping beneath the surface of a river and never coming up made her ailing heart race dangerously. She did her best to teach her children to avoid white anger by behaving submissively, but she was unable to teach them to be safe in the water. She herself had never learned to swim, nor had her husband, Willie, nor any of her brothers. So when Eddie disobeyed her command to stay out of the bayou, all she could do was invoke the fear of God and the hickory switch.

Shaw's whites-only swimming pool and the consequent drownings of black children who never learned to swim was not a problem unique to Shaw or the Delta or even the American South. It was an issue nationwide, says Jeff Wiltse in his book *Contested Waters: A Social History of Swimming in America*. "When federal courts desegregated municipal pools in the late 1940s and early 1950s, white swimmers generally abandoned municipal pools," he wrote.

Shaw, tucked into the backwaters of the Mississippi Delta, defied the new Civil Rights Act to integrate public accommodations until word leaked out that Eddie and other young black activists were planning to take a dip in the city pool. Shaw's town fathers were not about to let that happen. At its core, explains Jeff Wiltse in a 2007 interview with Michel Martin on National Public Radio, keeping blacks and whites apart in pools grew out of southerners' horror of racial mixing—that men and women swimming together, exposing bare arms and bare legs in torso-hugging bathing suits, would stir lustful emotions across racial lines. This in turn would lead to interracial dating, sex, marriage, and procreation.

There was nothing more sacred in white southern mythology than the virtue of white women and, by extension, the purity of the white race. Whites viewed black men in particular as a threat to this vaunted virtue and purity. "Public officials did not want black men having the opportunity to interact with white women at such visually and physically intimate public spaces," Wiltse told Martin during their radio interview.

A 2006 article in the *New York Times* ("Unearthing a Town Pool, and Not for Whites Only") reiterated this theme. It described how the whites-only public pool in the Mississippi cotton mill town of Stonewall was, like the pool in Shaw, filled in when the townspeople could no longer hold off the inevitability of integration. Stonewall, named in honor of Confederate general Stonewall Jackson, is just a stone's throw from Meridian, where the three civil rights workers were murdered in June 1964. "In the fearful cosmos of the segregationist South, the integrated swimming pool occupied a special place: race-mixing carried to an intimate level," according to the article. It quoted one of Stonewall's former mayors, Ardell Covington: "People just didn't want to mingle that close." It also quoted Leslie B. McLemore, a political scientist at Jackson State University: "Black folk and white people swimming together was just absolutely part of this 'black men getting close to white women' idea."

ON THE DAY THAT Eddie and his group crossed the highway and walked into the Truck Stop, sat down on the cracked vinyl stools, and boldly placed their orders for burgers and sodas, the white townsfolks frothed with impotent rage, impotent because the world was watching through the window opened by the Freedom Summer project. Impotent because Congress had acted, laws had been passed. White-on-black terrorism in rural Mississippi towns like Shaw had been a fact of life for decades, hidden from the wider world behind a curtain of obscurity and indifference. Now the cover was blown.

When, the following week, Eddie and his team bought movie tickets and took their seats in the whites-only section in front, the owner gaped in helpless fury. And when word got around that Eddie's group of activists was making plans to take a dip in the city swimming pool, the town leaders were apoplectic, blaming the "northern invaders" like Mary Sue, who were stirring up unrest among their contented black citizens.

But by then the writing on the wall was indelible. When Shaw's white residents realized that Shaw's black community was rising up, the shops began to close, one by one. The theater was burned down. City workers drained the swimming pool dry and secured its chain-link fence with a giant padlock. Blacks had won the right to sit and swim and eat beside their white neighbors, only to watch those public places be locked up or burned down or drained dry. Today, if you stood in downtown Shaw contemplating Main Street's two blocks of ruination, you might be reminded of the rubble of war.

Still, what arose from that rubble was human dignity. If Shaw lost physical facilities, it won spiritual renewal. What happened in Shaw—starting in the early sixties when civil rights leaders and local black citizens started meeting secretly, and helped along by the infusion of energy from Freedom Summer—was nothing less than the uprising of an oppressed people. Eddie was on the front lines of that uprising.

The men of Shaw sing freedom songs at the freedom school in the home of Reverend and Mrs. Jakes in Promised Land. (Photo by Mary Sue Gellatly)

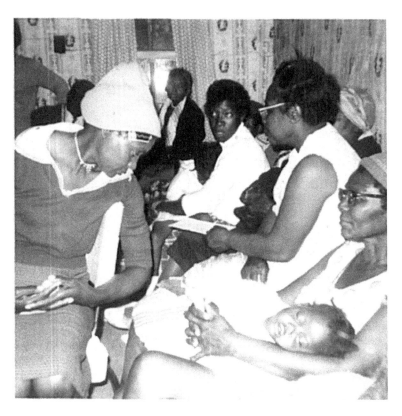

Women and children attend the freedom school at Reverend
Jakes's home in Promised Land.
(Photo by Mary Sue Gellatly)

A historical marker in Money, Mississippi, memorializes the life and legacy of fourteen-year-old Emmett Till, whose savage murder in 1955 was a catalyst for the civil rights movement. (Photo by Lee Anna Sherman)

Volume 2   HERE THE VOICE

HEADLINES: SHAW M.S.U STUDENTS IN

Aug.18: After several days of
days of non-violence work shops
three of Shaw M.S.U students went
to the public library here in our
town. The three students were
Eddie Short, James Johnson, and
Willie Wright, along with two
summer volunteers Grace Morton
and Mel Fahnestock. Theychecked
out recent novels and books on
sports and electronics. After 20
minutes James Johnson left the
library followed by four policeman. Ten minutes later the others
left with the two volunteers followed by more police, while Sheriff Capps and other groups of
police and a number of bystanders
watched with appalled and confu-
sed expressions.

FROM THE EDITOR'S DESK

To every Negro individual
all over this world, we can no
longer be fools, for it is time
to stop sleeping and wake up
and live. For we must live the
life we ought to live and not
what we want to live.

The Mississippi Student Union in Shaw ran an article in
their newsletter on August 18, 1964, recounting the public
library action taken by Eddie, James Johnson, and Willie
Wright, along with Freedom Summer volunteers Grace Morton and Mel Fahnestock. (Photo courtesy of Eddie Short)

Vicksburg: Early this morning, bottle hurled through window of barbershop owned by Mr. Eddie Thomas, Warren Co. FDP delegate

McComb: As white volunteer Mc transport potential Negro registra... he stopped at red light, one man qu... drove off and was followed by truck... narrowly missed going through window

Ganz drove back from Pike Co. courthouse in Magnolia to ... was followed by four men in unmarked pick-up truck. When ...ly got out of truck and began running at him. Ganz quickly... to McComb. Passenger in truck threw bottle which ... Ganz' car.

Natchez: Five-gallon can of gasoline, a bomb-like apparatus, found under Blue Moon bar here. Bar belongs to Jake Fisher, whose brother's bar was found bombed in Louisiana over the weekend.

Yazoo City: Two local Negro citizens today filed applications for cards at local library here without incident. Police talked with two "politely" and later contacted mother of one.

Shaw: Three Negro members of Shaw Mississippi Student Union entered town library today and success- fully registered for cards. When Eddie Short, James Johnson Jr., and Willie Wright left, they were followed by four police officers and watched by a number of bystanders.

?: Jackson: Three busloads of FDP delegates and alternates to National Convention, as well as FDP staff members, left from Jackson amidst hundreds of well-wishers late this evening.

(over)

A display at the National Civil Rights Museum in Memphis listed Eddie's Shaw public library integration action along with other examples of "incident reports" received at SNCC headquarters in 1964. (Photo courtesy of Eddie and Mary Sue Short)

Shaw's movie theater, shown here in 2016, has not been rebuilt since it burned down the same night Eddie and other black activists sat in the white section. (Photo by Lee Anna Sherman)

Dave "Honeyboy" Edwards, a Delta blues guitarist and singer born in Shaw in 1915, is honored with a marker on the Mississippi Blues Trail, which also recognizes such giants as B. B. King, Bo Diddley, Charley Patton, Elvis Presley, and Sam Cooke. (Photo by Lee Anna Sherman)

6

Groundings

The children of sharecroppers ... were introduced to
"plowin', plantin', and pickin'" as soon as they were
old enough to be useful in the fields.
—Bryan Stevenson, *Just Mercy*

Shaw, Mississippi, 1943 to 1964

One bitter night when Eddie was about ten, his daddy left
the shack, taking with him a burlap sack that held the
last of the family's garden harvest, the "Irish" potatoes, sweet
potatoes, and other root vegetables that Eddie had helped
his father plant and tend, hoeing and weeding and irrigating
with a bucket filled by hand at the outdoor pump through the
spring and summer and fall. The next day, a winter day with
nothing in the root bin for Janie Bea to cook, the temperature
dropped low. The wind leaked in through the newspaper and
brown paper bags pasted on the plank walls as insulation. She
fed chunks of wood into the old stove, but it gave off only the
barest warmth as it strained to keep up with the deepening
cold. The children huddled around the stove.

Then something happened that was rare in the Delta:
it started to snow. Janie Bea watched out the window for a
while as the white flakes drifted down, dusting the dormant

cotton fields and coating the cold, hard ground and drifting in through the chinks around the windows and doors. She told her children to bundle up in every stitch of clothing they owned and climb into their bed, where they lay side by side under the piecework quilt she had brought with her when she married Willie James Short sixteen years before. For a full day and a full night, the five Short children lay under the cotton quilt, the heat of each small body warming the child beside it. Janie Bea got into her own bed with her smallest baby at her breast. She fell asleep listening to her children's breathing in the silence of the snowfall.

The day after the snowstorm, Janie Bea looked out the window to see her brother James coming up the snowy road, his arms loaded down with bags and bundles. Eddie and his siblings ran out, barefoot in the snow, to help their uncle carry the food inside. It was far from the first time the Phillips brothers—"Uncle J. C." (James Cleveland), "Uncle Preacher" (Marion), and "Uncle Brother" (Ermin)—had brought emergency provisions to Janie Bea and her children. The three brothers, good churchgoing men, kept a watchful eye on their sister and her children. It was Uncle J. C. who would rescue Eddie and Mary Sue some ten years later when they got a flat tire on a dark night a few miles outside Shaw.

Uncles pitching in to help their nieces and nephews was commonplace in Mississippi's black communities, where extended family units were the norm. A woman's oldest brother was, except for her husband, the family member most responsible for her children and was given the same respect as a father. As for Willie's absences, he was not alone in juggling multiple families. In the era of Jim Crow, when black men were shut out of good jobs, many left their homes in search of work. In Shaw, male fieldworkers often supplemented their cotton wages during the winter season by heading to Florida to pick oranges and other citrus fruits. The lure of factory jobs in the industrial North drew able-bodied men by the thousands to Chicago and other cities ripe with opportunity, leaving behind a marriage gap in rural southern communities like Shaw. There were more black women wanting to marry and have children than there were marriageable black men.

Social scientists R. Robin Miller and Sandra Lee Browning explain that this imbalance of men to women led to an "alternative family form" in which a black woman settles for "a piece of a man" rather than being alone—what they call "sharing a man." This "adaptive strategy," they say in a 2000 article in the *Journal of Comparative Family Studies*, allows "the woman to experience the 'normalcy' of being part of a couple." They write: "Faced with a restricted marriage pool, black women can accept a 'piece of a man' instead of none at all.... They can settle for the intimacy and support (emotional and financial) that a part-time lover and partner can provide."

While not excusing his daddy's extramarital relationships, Eddie notes that such arrangements were "very common" in the community where he grew up. Eddie's younger sister Bernice cuts her daddy no such slack. She remembers him standing up in front of the Mt. Tabor Baptist Church, leading the choir in rousing hymns with lyrics like "Pick me up, Lord, pick me up." "I used to think, 'I wish the Lord would pick you up and slam you down,'" she says with a wry smile.

Today Bernice and her husband, Jake Shaw, live in the same modest home in Johnson's Addition where they raised their children, including Dameon, who went on to become mayor of Shaw in 2007. One of the first Head Start workers in Mississippi, she's still on the job fifty-plus years later with no firm plans to retire. She estimates that a thousand students have come through Shaw's Head Start program during her tenure. With pride, she notes: "Everybody knows Bernice Shaw."

Despite Bernice's jaundiced view of her daddy's ways, she remembers moments when he stepped up for his family endearingly, using his broad, mostly self-taught skill set on behalf of his children. "We had an old Singer sewing machine with a pedal," she recalls. "Daddy made us a few dresses." She still can picture the pink-and-white polka-dot frock he sewed for her, trimmed with ruffles, when she was eight years old. Willie James Short was a man of enormous contradictions.

BACK WHEN WILLIE COURTED Janie Beatrice Phillips, he won her hand in marriage with his wit and his charm and his seeming ability to do anything he put his mind to. He made her laugh in spite of herself, told her she was beautiful, made her believe his assurances of the secure life they would have together. He worked hard. His reputation as a fast picker was well known around Shaw. Once the crops were in, he hustled to make extra money any way he could. He took a mail-order class in radio repair and did a brisk business fixing white folks' Motorolas and Zeniths. He repaired other appliances for white people, too, and painted their houses, wallpapered their parlors, and mowed their lawns.

Black-and-white snapshots of Janie Bea show a fetching woman smiling at the camera, her large eyes dark and expressive. In one photo, she wears her Sunday finery, her crisp cotton dress accessorized with drop earrings, a string of beads, a fashionable hat, and a matching handbag. She looks happy, like she had on the days her husband came home with money in his pocket and a grin on his handsome face.

Eddie loved his daddy. During the times Willie provided for his family with energy and ingenuity, the times when he raised chickens and hogs and made them ready for Janie Bea's cookery, Eddie's heart swelled with pride for this man who led the family with such mettle and skill. Eddie remembers his daddy teaming up with a couple of local guys to slaughter hogs out behind the family's plantation shack. His recollection bespeaks the economies of scarcity: "Nothing was wasted. Mama used the pork for just about everything. She cooked the meat, boiled the fat, added pieces of pigskin to the cornbread batter. We called it 'cracklin' bread' because the meat made a crackling noise as we chewed it. We ate the heart, the head, the ears, nose, feet, intestines. Those we called chitlins. We cured the pork with salt in the cotton house out back to keep it from spoiling."

Those times, Eddie would come home after school and smell pork boiling on the stove. He would hear his mama's sweet voice singing hymns as she mixed up a batch of cornbread while keeping an eye on her children, all of them born in the shack with the help of a midwife.

But Willie's charm was not reserved for Janie Bea. His beautiful singing voice in church, where he led the choir and served as a deacon, drew people to him, especially women. Not long after their first child was born, Willie started going out at night, leaving Janie Bea alone in the sharecropper's shack, nursing her newborn until the baby fell asleep in the bed beside her. Her loneliness felt like a stone beneath her ribcage. And that's how it went, year after year.

The times when Willie was absent, Eddie would come home from school and find his mama sitting in the old wooden chair beside the woodstove, a baby folded in her arms, no aroma of okra and beans with neck bones, no sung hymns accompanying the sounds of supper simmering. On those days, Eddie knew there would be nothing to eat but leftover cornbread and maybe a little buttermilk. On those days, Eddie struggled to love his daddy. On the days when Janie Bea sat still and silent beside the stove holding a baby in her arms, nothing to cook, nothing to sing about, resentment toward his father churned in Eddie's gut.

And then one day Willie left for good. It was 1957. The *Brown v. Board of Education* decision of 1954 was still an open wound among white southerners. The ruling had reenergized the Klan. White Citizens' Councils had formed, first in Mississippi and then across the South, to stand guard against the threat to white supremacy, which depended on keeping black citizens down on the plantation.

Many of the plantations around Shaw and Bolivar County were shoestring operations. While the landowners' livelihoods appeared kingly to Eddie, they were marginal in the larger economy. With the exception of a few rich planters like Senator Eastland, who owned an expansive acreage in Sunflower County, the planters Eddie's family worked for had modest farms. Their families had the basics of middle-class America in those days—indoor plumbing, electric lights and appliances, nice cars and pickup trucks—but the lap of luxury it wasn't. Their narrow profit margins would quickly collapse if their black sharecroppers started demanding flush toilets, electric lights, and fair wages. To keep a lid on any such uprising, white citizens enlisted black spies, people Eddie called "Uncle Toms" or just "Toms." This term of derision originated in Harriet Beecher Stowe's 1852 anti-slavery novel, *Uncle Tom's Cabin*, and was used to refer to blacks who are willingly compliant or subservient to whites. In Shaw, Toms betrayed their friends and neighbors, reporting civil rights activities to the Citizens' Council for a few dollars or even a bucket of molasses. White telephone operators listened in on calls and passed along their eavesdropped intel. White postal workers knew who got what in each day's mail delivery, often informing on their black neighbors when something turned up that suggested an affinity for liberty and dignity.

So when Willie subscribed to *Jet* magazine, launched in 1951 with the tagline "The Weekly Negro News Magazine," word got around fast. Among the white residents of Shaw, *Jet* was regarded as dangerously subversive. Every week, Willie would go to the post office, pick up his magazine, and find a quiet corner where he could dig in. TVs were rare in the homes of black families, though most families had a radio where folks could tune in to WDIA in Memphis, the nation's first radio station to hire a black DJ, which played R&B with a sprinkling of news. The local newspaper, the *Bolivar Commercial*, might as well have been called the *White Bolivar Commercial*, with its front-to-back articles about prominent white residents and their accomplishments, white schoolchildren's sports triumphs, and the engagements and weddings of smiling white couples. If it weren't for the nonstop racist editorials, readers of the *Commercial* would never have guessed that Bolivar County had a black community at all, let alone a black majority.

For people like Willie, who had learned to read well during his five years of schooling, *Jet* opened a window into the wider world of black life in America. Besides promoting pride among blacks for their ethnic beauty, *Jet* covered the civil rights groundswell that had lurched dramatically onto the national stage in 1955 with Emmett Till's ghastly murder and the travesty of justice that let his killers go free. It covered the courageous act of resistance by Rosa Parks, who was arrested that same year for refusing to give up her bus seat to a white rider in Birmingham, Alabama, some two hundred miles east of Shaw. It covered the nonviolent black uprising being led by Dr. King and the Southern Christian Leadership Conference.

In the pages of *Jet*, Willie saw cracks forming in the southern white power structure. He wanted to be one of the battering rams. He believed in the civil rights movement. Could a southern black man earn a decent wage? Could he someday pass a white woman on the sidewalk without having to cross to the other side of the street? Might he be allowed to call a white child, even a toddler, by her or his first name, instead of addressing her as Miss Nancy or Mister Billy while maintaining a submissive demeanor? Might this black man be able to walk into a courthouse, register to vote without impediment, cast his ballot—maybe for a black candidate—and then perhaps run for city council or be elected mayor of his hometown or state representative for his district? He could barely imagine such revolutionary changes in a region where racism was so deeply entrenched.

Hidden beneath his affable smile, the smile with which he had wooed and won Janie Bea, he carried a simmering resentment of the rigged system that robbed him of not only his rights as a citizen but also his dignity as a man. Could a southern black man someday live free of a white man's boot on his neck? Willie wondered. The thought of living free of oppression kept him awake at night, trying to picture what that would be like. If it were even remotely possible, he would sign up, he decided. He took the dangerous step of joining the NAACP. It wasn't long before news of his NAACP membership leaked out, just as his subscription to *Jet* had activated the spy network.

From then on, Willie had a target on his back.

One day when Eddie was fourteen, a local member of the Citizens' Council took Willie aside downtown and threatened to kill him and murder his family if he didn't leave town immediately. Willie knew the threat was no joke. Beatings, hangings, and disappearances of blacks were legion in the Delta. Barely two years had passed since Emmett Till was murdered. The photos in *Jet* of Emmett's ravaged body haunted Willie. He didn't want to die. And although he hadn't always been a model husband or father, he loved his family and would not put them at risk.

With a rising sense of panic, Willie got word to Andrew Hawkins about the danger he was in. Hawkins in turn reached out to an acquaintance in Jackson by the name of Medgar Evers, who was becoming one of America's most prominent civil rights leaders. Evers, the first NAACP field secretary for Mississippi, once had lived in a town called Mound Bayou just up the road from Shaw. Mound Bayou had been founded by blacks for blacks and was governed solely by black Mississippians. Evers, like Willie, knew that the threat against the Short family was real and imminent. According to Short family lore, Evers advised Willie to come to Jackson immediately. In Jackson, Evers took charge of Willie's escape, taking him to a barbershop and getting him a haircut, driving him to the bus station and buying him a ticket, and then handing him a few dollars of pocket money to tide him over till he could find work in Chicago.

In his role as NAACP field secretary, Medgar Evers helped black Mississippians like Willie escape the clutches of the Klan. But he did not live to see his own fortieth birthday. Two attempts were made on his life—a Molotov cocktail and an attempted hit-and-run—in the weeks before his assassination by white supremacist Byron De La Beckwith on June 12, 1963. Beckwith was a member of the White Citizens' Council. When Evers was gunned down that day in his own driveway, he was holding an armload of T-shirts printed with the slogan "Jim Crow must go."

A few days after Willie fled Shaw, Mrs. Arlena, proprietor of a club and cafe across the street from the Shorts, ran to the house and pounded on the door. "Missus Janie Bea! Y'all open up now!" When Janie Bea slid the latch and looked out, Arlena said: "Hurry up, girl, come on now! Mister Willie be on the phone." Smoothing down her hair absently with her fingers, Janie Bea hurried across the dirt road to Arlena's Place, still wearing her apron, and picked up the receiver. "That you, Willie?" The voice of her husband dredged up a tangled mess of feelings: faded love and matrimonial loyalty knotted with bone-deep hurt and raw fury. There was a part of her that thought "good-riddance" that day when she saw his feet point away toward Jackson. Still, he was the father of her children, six of them still living at home. So she listened to what he had to say. He had made it to Chicago, he told her. He was looking for work. He would send for her and the children just as soon as he pulled together enough money for their bus fare. In the meantime, he said, he would send her any extra dollars he could scrape together.

Janie Bea had so often heard her husband make promises over their years together. He had kept many. But the broken ones littered her mind like shattered crockery. Buttoning up her doubts, she relayed Willie's words to their children. Eddie was pumped, excited about moving to Chicago, the adventure of being in a new place and living again as a family. He loved and admired his daddy, no matter his failings.

Months went by, then years. No money ever arrived from Chicago. After a while, Eddie stopped waiting for his daddy to send for them.

ON THE DAY EDDIE was born, September 24, 1943, World War II was raging across Europe and Southeast Asia. Eddie was two, a toddler barely out of diapers, when the war ended and the soldiers came home to the Delta. They found a place mostly untouched by the war. The United States and its allies had faced down the regime of Adolf Hitler, liberated thousands of Jews from Nazi death camps, and dropped two bombs (built secretly in New Mexico under the strangely friendly codenames Fat Man and Little Boy) that vaporized millions of Japanese civilians in a flash of light. The world had changed forever. But like the fairytale character Rumpelstiltskin, snoozing away as the world passed him by, rural Mississippi remained much the same.

Amzie Moore, a local black leader who became legendary in Bolivar County, served in a black regiment and was assigned during the war to lecture other African-American soldiers about how "after the war was over, things would be different, that men would have the chance to be free." Moore recounted this in James Forman's *The Making of Black Revolutionaries*. "Somehow or another," Moore added wryly, "some of us didn't believe it."

Another black soldier from Bolivar County, Preston Holmes—who later became postmaster of Cleveland, Mississippi—confirmed the wisdom of that skepticism with his homecoming story. In the oral history *War Comes to the Delta*, Holmes said, "I was hoping I was coming back to [a] world much better as it related to black people." When he got to the bus station in Hattiesburg on June 22, 1946, standing tall in his crisp uniform studded with medals and sergeant's stripes, he walked up to the counter to buy a ticket home. "The lady said to me, 'Nigger, get back to the end of the line.'" Then, while he was waiting for his bus, a black man walked up to him and said, "Soldier, I don't want to get in your business, but the white men in this town don't allow colored soldiers in this town after dark in uniform." So he got a cab.

For the Short family, World War II came and went with little change to the rhythms of their lives. Their days turned not on the doings of presidents and generals but on the seasons of the sun and the phases of the fields. The war did, however, have one outcome that impacted Mississippi's cotton industry and sharecropping families like the Shorts: it sped up mechanization on farms and plantations following rapid advances in technology during the nationwide war effort. Tractors and tractor-driven picking machines began taking the place of mule-drawn plows and human fieldworkers. By the 1960s, the labor of sharecroppers was becoming expendable except on modest farms like the ones surrounding Shaw. Knowing that sharecroppers had few options, farmers could squeeze their workers in a vise of dependency.

Before Freedom Summer, when Vietnam war protests, bus boycotts, sit-ins, civil rights marches, and race riots were rocking America, the little Delta town seemed stuck in a time capsule. Like much of the rural South, culturally and economically it was locked in an era not far removed from enslavement of blacks by whites. The Emancipation Proclamation that freed black people from forced servitude toward the end of the Civil War turned out to be a mostly empty act for millions of southern blacks. Their freedom was hemmed in on all sides by white landowners, white law enforcement, white bankers and businessmen, and white politicians who had rigged the system to keep black laborers trapped in a cycle of debt and poverty.

Sharecroppers like Eddie's family were the inheritors of one of the main stand-ins for slavery. The "share" part of sharecropping was meant to suggest a partnership between owner and worker. A 1923 tract on Bolivar County, *Imperial Bolivar*, by William F. Gray, an early predecessor to Clifton L. Langford as editor and publisher of the *Bolivar Commercial* newspaper, explained it this way: "Former master and former slave quickly adjusted themselves to the new conditions.

Contracts were drawn under which the planter furnished the land and everything necessary to make the crops; the negroes the labor." But it was a cruel illusion. Behind this rational-sounding system, boss and worker agreeing to a fair-minded contract to share in the bounty of the fertile floodplain, stood the raw reality. In fact, all financial benefits—along with all status, dignity, and power on the plantation and in the community—accrued to the owner.

Sharecroppers performed grinding labor for penurious pay during the seasons of planting, picking, and weeding. They experienced gnawing hunger when fields were fallow and the pay stopped. The planters let them buy food on credit, sums that would be subtracted from their pay when the accounts were tallied. The sharecropping system ensured the farmworkers' never-ending debt to the planter, who managed all the bookkeeping and made sure the workers would never balance the ledger. In *Slavery by Another Name*, journalist Douglas A. Blackmon put it this way: "White landowners in the South almost universally believed that management of their farms could be successful only if, in one way or another, 'their Negroes' could be tied to the land. Coercion and restraint remained the bedrock of success in the cotton economy—and the bedrock of all wealth generated from it."

"Tied to the land" by debt and poverty was the new bondage for families like Eddie's on the Mississippi Delta. Everybody's hands, no matter how small, were needed in the cotton fields if the Short family hoped to keep their stomachs full and their woodstove warm through the winter when there were no crops to harvest and, therefore, no money for cornmeal or salt pork or lard. So in the autumn of his fifth year, Eddie headed to the family patch alongside his daddy and mama (when she was well enough to work) and his older siblings, Jeansetta, who was eight, and Ernest, who was seven. As the years unfolded, each of the younger siblings—Bernice, James, Lee Bertha, Freddie, and Calvin—joined the family in the fields. The plants, their fluffy white fibers popping from prickly brown seedpods, were taller than Eddie as he followed his siblings up and down the rows in his tiny pair of patched overalls.

By the time Eddie was seven, he was big enough to not only pick cotton but also "chop" it. Wielding a hoe longer than he was tall, he attacked weeds and vines—morning glory, pigweed, cocklebur, johnsongrass—that threatened the crop. By age twelve, he could pick more than a hundred pounds of cotton in a ten-hour day, bent over the three-foot-tall plants and dragging a nine-foot-long canvas sack in heat that could reach 113 degrees Fahrenheit, not counting humidity.

One morning as the sun was rising and the family was headed to their patch, he bragged to his daddy that he would bag 125 pounds that day. Willie looked at this child who stood so tall in his small body, and said, "You pick 125 pounds today and I'll take you downtown and buy you a pair of Florsheim shoes." Eddie had never had a brand-new pair of shoes. He had never had any shoes at all until one day when he earned twenty-five cents stacking firewood for his teacher Mrs. Mason. She had looked at his earth-hardened feet, whose thick, callused soles could withstand stones and thorns and any other sharp obstacle in their path, taken him to the secondhand store, and bought him his first pair.

Nor had Eddie heard of Florsheim, a Chicago-based

brand worn by the well-to-do and later on, in the 1980s, by Michael Jackson when he moonwalked for millions of fans. A newspaper ad in 1922 boasted that "the Florsheim Shoe" offered "style of unusual distinction" and "character ... expressed in every detail." Eddie wasn't aware that Florsheims bore the "exclusive look desired by well-dressed men." He only knew that from the way his daddy smiled when he said the words "Florsheim shoes," they had to be something stupendous, something worth the extra effort of picking more cotton than ever before.

Even more motivating for Eddie than the shoes was the chance to excel, to prove his worth and earn his daddy's approval. So Eddie revved up his usual pace, his fingers flying over the cotton fibers while avoiding the razor-sharp pods, with the speed and precision he had gained from his years of experience. He exceeded his goal that day by several pounds. His daddy made good on his promise, taking Eddie downtown and paying five dollars for a shiny black pair of Florsheims.

Like any news in this tight community, word got out fast among Eddie's pals, who rushed over to see the fine leather shoes for themselves. When he wore the shoes to church that Sunday, he felt prouder than he ever had in his life thus far—proud of how he looked in the finely made shoes and even prouder that his daddy had bought them for him. "Eddie kept 'em *shined*," says his younger sister Bernice, who remembers those shoes more than fifty years later, so momentous were they in the family history. "He called it 'puttin' a spit shine' on 'em."

BUT THE MONEY EARNED picking and chopping cotton wasn't enough to feed, clothe, and warm the Shorts as the family grew to eight living children between 1940 and 1955. The plantation owners paid two-and-a-half cents per pound picked. A fast picker earned about three dollars for ten hours in the field. In their best year, the industrious Shorts, laboring from "sun to sun" spring, summer, and fall, earned a total of one thousand dollars, after the landowner took his 60-percent cut for land rental, fertilizer, seed, and equipment. During the winter, when the acres of cotton fields lay brown and fallow, the meager wages stopped.

Still, the bottomlands of the Mississippi Delta were rich with edible resources if you knew how to find and use them. The Delta is the triangle-shaped floodplain of two rivers—one huge, the Yazoo; and the other monstrous, the Mississippi, the "Big Muddy." Over endless millennia, the Mississippi had powered toward the Gulf of Mexico, curving and twisting, flooding again and again and yet again across the northwest corner of the state. When those muddy floodwaters drew back and subsided into the river channel, they left behind a wilderness of swamps and bayous that vibrated with life. In their plantation shack, the Shorts had only thin plank walls standing between them and the wild earth, so they were attuned to every sprouting, foraging, wallowing, finning, ripening, nesting, brooding, hatching, and whelping that happened within a day's walk of their front porch. This earth sensing was bequeathed to Eddie by his father and was a gift that stood him in good stead during the times his daddy acted less generously, disappearing for weeks or months at a time.

During the times of Daddy's absence, when Janie Bea, getting sicker and sicker with a lifelong heart murmur and dangerously high blood pressure, watched her children from her chair by the stove, Eddie put his survival skills to use. He would set out at dawn to hunt rabbits and raccoons and possums with his daddy's shotgun, the family's black-and-tan beagle, Fido, scouting out in front. If there were rabbits to be found, Fido would scent them and plunge into the briars, bringing back the prey locked in his jaws.

Eddie's younger brother Freddie remembers the day Eddie came home from rabbit hunting with the shotgun in one hand and an empty burlap sack in the other. Suddenly, a flock of blackbirds flushed from the field. Eddie took aim and fired. The rain of pellets brought down eighteen birds in that single shot—at least, that's the number that stuck in Freddie's mind when he told the story decades later. Eddie and Freddie gathered up the birds and carried them home, where Mama made dumplings flavored with the bits of meat she picked from the carcasses.

Sometimes Eddie went down to the bayou with his buddies and, wading into the slow waters, raked the muddy streambed with a stick to stir up the silt. Whiskered catfish, big-mouth buffalo fish, and other bottom feeders would swim to the surface for oxygen. Eddie would grab the slippery fish with his bare hands and chuck them into a bucket. One time, he grabbed what he thought was a fish. But when it broke the surface, he saw that he was gripping a three-foot-long snake around the neck. It was a water moccasin, also called a cottonmouth, a semi-aquatic snake dreaded in the Delta for its painful, sometimes fatal bite. In a panicky burst of pure adrenaline, he reflexively choked the poisonous snake to death.

Whatever he could catch or pick that was edible, Eddie brought home to his mama, who could turn anything into a savory stew or fry it up in a cast-iron pan with collards from the family's garden plot or wild greens (edible weeds) Eddie and his siblings picked from the roadside and carried home.

Freddie remembers days when the rain pummeled the earth and Eddie would lead his little brothers to a low spot near the railroad tracks, where the boys would scrape a shallow hollow in the dirt. As the rain hammered the ground, soaking the boys to the skin through their T-shirts and overalls, the hollow filled with water, creating a pond. The Short brothers would crouch there, watching, and crawfish would start to appear in the pond as if from nowhere. "I didn't know where those crawfish came from when it rained," Freddie said, "but it looked like they came from the sky."

Eddie's knowledge of crawfish behavior came not from encyclopedias or scientific articles, where he would have learned that the small crustaceans swimming into his makeshift pond had burrowed into the mud in late summer and waited in water-filled tunnels for the rains to return. Rather, his crawfish insights came from folkways passed down generation to generation among people who could not afford to overlook a food source. The boys would gather up the shellfish, like miniature lobsters opening and closing their outsized claws, and take them home to their mama. Janie Bea would drop the meaty tails into a pot of boiling water and then peel them, roll the sweet white meat in flour, and fry them in lard for supper.

BY THE TIME WILLIE left for good, the family had moved off the plantation and into Shaw's shantytown, the black neighborhood called Johnson's Addition. From their shack, it was a few blocks to Joe Canonici's Midway Grocery Store, the collection point for fieldworkers doing day labor on the plantations. They would climb into the back of a dusty pickup truck owned and driven by black residents employed by planters for fifty cents per worker.

Janie Bea's children's earnings were even more vital now that Willie was out of the picture. Though Eddie had cultivated a backyard garden, the turnip greens, okra, tomatoes, black-eyed peas, and butter beans weren't enough to keep the family going, More than ever, Janie Bea needed commodities, surplus foods distributed to poor families by the federal government. Her monthly allotment of milk, cheese, and peanut butter supplemented the bounty of Eddie's garden.

Janie Bea also tried her hand at direct sales. In an era when door-to-door sales were common and convenient, especially in isolated or rural communities, Janie Bea was among the millions of saleswomen and men plying the streets and neighborhoods of America with their cases and catalogs. Sellers of Fuller brushes, *Encyclopedia Britannica* sets, Hoover vacuum cleaners, and countless other products were knocking on doors and pitching their wares.

Janie Bea was pitching a line of dresses called Maisonette Frocks for the Indiana-based Ward Stilson Company, which had a nationwide sales force. "Mama would get a five-dollar deposit for sellin' a dress," Eddie's sister Bernice recalls. Janie Bea would put on her best clothes and, despite her weak heart, walk the dirt roads of Promised Land and Ice House

Quarter and Boatwright and Johnson's Addition with her Stilson catalog under her arm. She was much loved around town, admired for her sincere faith and a singing voice that could kindle the Holy Spirit in even the hardest heart. When she knocked on doors, she was welcomed in and offered a seat at the kitchen table, where she would sit beside the woman of the house and slowly turn the pages of the catalog, giving the customer ample time to view (and covet) the stylish dresses pictured there. As a further enticement, every dress was shown with a fabric swatch—a small square of actual dress fabric that customers could touch and imagine wearing.

Janie Bea's once-slender figure had gradually spread and swollen with childbirth and sickness. The poignancy of her plight—a poor, ailing, single black mother schlepping a catalog graced with drawings of bone-thin, tiny-waisted, white-skinned women who looked like they didn't have a care in the world—cannot be overstated. And yet, without a shred of irony or self-pity, she would flip the glitzy pages for her neighbors, pointing out the charms of dresses labeled with descriptors like "Frost Tweed Print," "Invitation to Loveliness," "Country Club Two-Piecer," and "Summer Sun and Fun." When she made a sale, her customer would receive her garment in the mail and Janie Bea would add a few dollars to her household budget.

In the black neighborhoods of Shaw, stylish dresses in lovely fabrics may have been on women's wish lists, but they were seldom in the budget. Still, women who taught at the black school and businesswomen who ran bars or hair salons had the means to buy Janie Bea's wares, wares that she herself could not afford. In the days when Willie was around, Janie

Bea had once or twice felt flush enough to buy a new blouse from a peddler on a payment plan of fifty cents a month. But the frocks in her Ward Stilson catalogs were out of reach for a sharecropper's wife.

Over time, Freddie's hurt at his daddy's disappearance festered into hatred. He had been five the day Willie hastily packed his few belongings and left home with a promise to send for the family soon. Eddie, on the other hand, long held out hope that his daddy would indeed send for them. He wanted to believe in the father he loved and admired. In truth, though, he was enough older than Freddie to know the score. As time went by, he fought down his bitterness for the sake of his mama and younger siblings. His mama's health was declining fast. Eddie stepped into the role of main breadwinner to supplement the family's federal food assistance. He was fourteen years old.

COAL TRAINS STEAMED THROUGH Shaw on tracks that ran so close to the shack the Shorts lived in that the porch rattled as the trains clattered past. Eddie and his brothers would grab a bucket and walk along the tracks, picking up chunks of coal that had dropped as the train jostled along. The coal supplemented the wood that burned in the family's woodstove, the main source of heat in the shack.

Another of Eddie's younger brothers, James, admired his big brother's ingenuity and persistence in finding work, especially after their daddy went away. "Eddie was a hard worker," James said looking back. "He always found some work to do, whether it was helping Mr. Addie Johnson look after his cows or harvesting pecans for Mrs. Washington."

When Eddie neared his teens, he added some new survival skills to his already hefty repertoire of hunting, gardening, plowing, gleaning, and doing odd jobs all over town. Seeing that there was money to be made downtown, he started spending free nights and weekends down at the Willie Roach Pool Hall or the 119 Club, perfecting his poker and pool games until he played like a pro. Then he hustled games for money.

At Willie Roach's, alongside the railroad track on the edge of downtown Shaw, people would sit watching from a wooden bench along the wall. A guy named Charlie Sharper ran the gambling table, where folks placed bets on pool games amidst the clack of billiard balls and the clink of glasses. Before long, Eddie and his friends were regulars, eating burgers, and, when he got older, drinking a few beers, playing cards, and shooting dice at a small table covered with green felt.

On a good night, when the balls were falling in Eddie's favor, he could make as much as twenty dollars. Just down the road, a Pabst Blue Ribbon neon sign blinked invitingly in the window of the 119 Club, a card joint owned by John L. Truitt. Passersby were beckoned from across the street by R&B tunes blaring from the Seeburg jukebox, those shiny, gawdy machines that played 45-rpm vinyl records automatically at the drop of a coin. They were everywhere in America in those days. Indeed, they revolutionized American nightlife.

"A roomful of people could now be entertained for a nickel," wrote Ink Mendelsohn in a 1989 story in the *Chicago Tribune*, "The Jukebox Still Rocks." "A coin-operated music machine was a perfect source of cheap entertainment," he wrote. He went on to report that "in the South, in poor agricultural areas, jazz and blues were played in shanty bars and cafes that came to be called juke joints. Historians agree that the word 'jukebox' first came into use among Southern black people and is derived from an African language."

Alex Crevar offers further details about the juke joints of the Deep South. "Traditionally seen as dens of the devil's music—jook is believed to originate from an African-derived Gullah word meaning disorderly—the surviving joints have become redefined as sanctuaries," revealed his 2013 article in the *New York Times* titled "Driving the Juke Joint Trail." "Within their ramshackle walls, a sense of community and a love of soul-searching rhythms reign supreme."

When Eddie joined forces with Mary Sue during their year in Mississippi, these ramshackle sanctuaries—"places of refuge and protection," as defined by *Webster's*—with their soul-searching rhythms did indeed offer a sense of community to the young activists as the heat rose in the little town of Shaw. It came to pass, as well, that the two activists found refuge and protection in one another.

Janie Bea wears her Sunday best for church in July 1967.
(Photo courtesy of Eddie Short)

In its heyday, Shaw boasted four or five cotton gins, including this one near the downtown section. (Photo by Lee Anna Sherman)

Italian immigrants Louise and Joseph Canonici owned a grocery store in Shaw where black customers and civil rights workers were treated respectfully. (Photo courtesy of Eddie and Mary Sue Short)

Twelve-year-old Eddie shows off his new Florsheim shoes, a reward for picking 125 pounds of cotton in one day. (Photo courtesy of Eddie Short)

Janie Bea poses for the camera at Arlena's Place, a club with a phone across the street from her house. (Photo courtesy of Eddie Short)

7

Awakenings

While the exclusion laws were rarely enforced in Oregon,
[their] tragic legacy was that they discouraged blacks from
coming at all.
—R. Gregory Nokes, *Breaking Chains*

Nashville, Tennessee, 1963, and Portland, Oregon, 1942 to 1964

One sweaty, sultry night in Nashville a year before Freedom Summer, six footsore college students piled wearily
into a car on the north end of town, the historically black
section of the city famous for country music, R&B, and rock 'n'
roll. Mary Sue was one of the six. She had finished her junior
year at Willamette University and was making her first foray
into civil rights work as a volunteer for a voter-registration
project sponsored by the National Student Christian Federation. After a long, hot day knocking on doors in black
neighborhoods, encouraging people to sign up to vote, she
and the other students were exhausted, ready to sleep so they
could hit the streets with their clipboards and fliers again
in the morning. They were headed back to their lodgings, a
house rented for the project by the federation.

It was late, well after dark. At the house, the project

leaders—a young white pastor named Wilson Yates and his wife, Gail—were starting to fret. Where were the six volunteers? They should have been back by now.

Nashville's civil rights movement was years ahead of many other southern towns. Student activists and civil rights lawyers had fought—and won—many of their challenges to Jim Crow by the time Mary Sue was there. In 1960, Nashville became the first major city to desegregate public facilities. As the top recording center in the United States outside of Los Angeles and New York in the early 1960s, it was known far and wide as Music City USA. With a booming commercial segment that was hip and cosmopolitan—not only hosting white artists like Johnny Cash, Elvis Presley, Patsy Kline, and Bob Dylan but also giving wide exposure to black musicians like B.B. King, Chuck Berry, and Ray Charles—Nashville was a city awash in new ideas, unlike the rural byways and hidden hamlets of Mississippi where time had stood still for a hundred years.

But even in Nashville, race relations were tense. As the students were heading homeward through the dark, silent streets, a police cruiser roared up alongside their car. The white officer at the wheel stared into the car, whose interior was lit just enough by a streetlamp to let him see the six faces inside. What he saw caused him to pick up his police radio. Three young men (two black and one white) and three young women (one black and two white) were riding together, sitting side by side on the slick vinyl seats. The next second, swirling lights, blood red, split the darkness around the car. A siren wailed.

The young civil rights workers looked at each other in confusion. "Just sit tight," the driver said as he eased the car over to the curb. Before they could start rummaging in their pockets and purses for their IDs, four or five more squad cars roared up the street and blocked the intersection, lights flashing and sirens screaming.

"Get out of the car!" commanded the policeman who had pulled them over. Mary Sue and the others climbed out and stood on the sidewalk, the young men dressed in pressed shirts and slacks, Mary Sue and her two female companions in summery dresses with nylon stockings and low-heeled shoes. Always frustrated by a shortage of off-the-shelf fashions for tall girls and stymied by the price tags, she had taken sewing lessons in high school and made a lot of her own outfits—including the dress she wore that night in Nashville—on her mother's old treadle machine and then on a modern portable tucked in the closet of the master bedroom. As she stood on that nighttime street, she felt the incongruity of the scene. Her knee-length, full-skirted dress with its modest cap sleeves and delicate yellow-and-orange floral print seemed wildly out of place in that frenzied scene of squad cars, lights and sirens, and surly cops with billy clubs and loaded guns.

As she was being taken to jail in the back of a police cruiser, Mary Sue began to understand, with the clarity only someone who has personal experience can have, that the fight she had joined was only partly about voting rights. The deeper fight, she grasped viscerally for the first time that night, was for the essential human dignity of black Americans.

The charge was disturbing the peace, even though the

site of the arrest had been perfectly peaceful until the squad cars splintered it with their sirens and lights. The three young women faced an additional charge: prostitution.

At the courthouse, a policeman stood her in front of a camera and snapped her mugshot, then placed her fingers on an inkpad and pressed them, one by one, on a fingerprint card. As she was booked into the jail, she never suspected how radically that experience would alter her life, that her own struggle on behalf of justice would not only land her in jail many more times but also ultimately steer her choices in the most profound ways.

The men were locked in a cell, while the women were ordered to sit on a wooden bench in the reception area. Mary Sue's floral-print dress gave a dissonant splash of color to the drab room. For the rest of the night, the three young women sat shoulder-to-shoulder, shifting uncomfortably on the hard bench, fighting sleepiness, waiting for morning and the legal counsel that was being arranged at that very moment by their project leaders, whom they had phoned when they were granted a call as required by law.

In the morning, when the deputy led the students into the courtroom, Mary Sue was relieved to see the promised lawyer, a distinguished black man in a smart blue suit billed as one of Nashville's top civil rights attorneys, standing beside the judge's bench. The charges were dropped within minutes.

Mary Sue's arrest—her first, but far from her last, as it turned out—was for her more annoying than alarming. For one thing, she knew the National Council of Churches and other human-rights organizations were keeping a watchful eye on civil rights volunteers from the North. It would be less than a year before the three civil rights workers were murdered in Mississippi during the first week of Freedom Summer, but the risks were already well known. For another, she was savvy to the subtext of the harassment. As she was being fingerprinted, Mary Sue translated the charge of disturbing the peace in her mind to "disturbing the white-ordained order of the South." Even before coming to Nashville, she had been aware that she might tangle with law enforcement. She was here not just to register voters but also to be a witness to white abusiveness toward black citizens. If necessary, she would take the abuse along with them—knowing, of course, that any discomfort she might endure was mostly symbolic. At the end of the project, she would go home to Oregon. Her black compatriots *were* home. They were fighting for themselves, their own families and towns, their region, which would change only when the nexus of law and protest stared down Jim Crow until it blinked.

As for the charge of prostitution, Mary Sue knew it was a cover for "people driving together while black and white." When she thought about her friends and family back home, she smiled to herself to imagine their reactions to the outlandish accusation. Her college roommate, Wendy Crane, described Mary Sue's outward appearance as "very natural"—no makeup, simple hairstyle (no teased-up, heavily lacquered bouffant or "bubble" hairdo as was popular at the time), practical fashions (pleated skirts and cardigan sweaters)—and her inner life as "genuine, ethical, and quietly strong."

The event was an epiphany. As she sat all night in the Nashville courthouse, the foul taste of racism grew more bitter in her mouth. This time, she had taken a spoonful of what southern blacks had endured for centuries. Hers, of course, was only a baby's spoonful of the fetid water blacks had been fed since the first slave ship landed in Virginia in the 1600s. She never fooled herself into thinking her onetime run-in with southern racism had given her more than a particle of shared understanding. Still, after that long night on the hard bench of Nashville's criminal justice system, she knew she couldn't just wrap herself in her Oregon cocoon once again, turning away from this stain on her nation.

When a quarter-million people gathered at the end of that summer for the March on Washington for Jobs and Freedom, Mary Sue was there to hear Dr. King deliver his "I Have a Dream" speech—arguably one of the most momentous speeches ever written, ever given, ever quoted, ever broadcast, ever prickling the skin and troubling the conscience of the human race. She had traveled to Washington, D.C., in a yellow school bus on August 28 with her fellow activists from Nashville, the students she had canvassed with—and been arrested with—on that hot summer night that solidified her will to fight for social justice. She had called her parents and made an earnest plea for funds to finance the trip. Money was always tight for the Gellatlys. But their daughter's voice conveyed an urgency to march with the thousands, to witness the historic moment on the Washington Mall. They wired the funds to Nashville.

When the bus pulled into the capital city, it was one of a sea of identical yellow school buses lining the streets. She made a mental note of her bus's exact location so she could find her way back. As she stepped into the flow of marchers streaming toward the mall, she caught the infectious energy of a quarter-million souls demanding their human and civil rights, the rights guaranteed in the nation's founding documents. The equality with which they were endowed by their creator depended on a level playing field where everyone had the same shot at prosperity. Pressed in the crowd, sensing the life force pulsing around her, almost hearing the heartbeats of her fellow marchers, Mary Sue once again gave herself to the struggle. She knew she would come back to the South soon.

At age twenty-three (two years older than Mary Sue), civil rights leader John Lewis was the youngest speaker on the mall that day. As chairman of SNCC, the young activist from Alabama soon would be gearing up for next year's Mississippi Freedom Project with other young black leaders like Bob Moses and Stokely Carmichael. That day while Mary Sue strained to hear the speakers from far back in the crowd, the Freedom Project plans were just beginning to take shape. She had no inkling of her soon-to-be link to Lewis. Nor did she know that her Nashville activism had been paved in part by Lewis, who helped lead integration actions in Music City USA. Yet, as Professor Garth E. Pauley of Calvin College argued in 2010, the legacy of Lewis's speech was the Mississippi Summer Project and "the voting rights campaigns it inspired." Indeed, a line Lewis penned and delivered on the mall that day, "One man, one vote," became a rallying cry for the Summer Project, Pauley notes.

None of this, however, registered clearly for Mary Sue on the mall. She was too far away from the microphones, too pressed in by the seething throng. Yet the college girl from Oregon would help carry Lewis's slogan into deepest

Mississippi when, as a SNCC volunteer, she helped organize Shaw's voter-registration action—an event that followed the car bombing by a week. Holding aloft hand-printed placards saying "One man, one vote" and "We shall overcome," Mary Sue and Shaw's young black activists would demonstrate against election corruption at the Bolivar County Courthouse. Lewis's demand in 1963, "We want our freedom, and we want it now," had, by the summer of 1964, taken hold in the heart of black Mississippians. Turning back was not an option.

When people look back at the March on Washington, they mostly remember the hallowed words of Dr. King. But the impassioned voice of John Lewis, although somewhat hampered by stammering and crimped by his early public-speaking jitters, must not be overlooked. As Professor Pauley writes: "Even though Lewis was forced by other speakers at the March to 'tone down' his rhetoric, he still delivered a powerful indictment of racial injustice and the politicians' failure to address the nation's chronic civil rights problems. Moreover, he called for a massive campaign of nonviolent direct action to bring down the system of racial segregation and discrimination in the South known as Jim Crow."

The call to action of John Lewis, who went on to become one of America's towering civil rights heroes, foreshadowed the summer to come.

BORN ON MARCH 30, 1942, Mary Susan Gellatly grew up on the hilly west side of Portland, a busy port town snugged up against acres of forestland to the west and fronting the Willamette and Columbia Rivers to the east and north. As a child, Suzie, as she was called then, would tie her sensible shoes and button her hooded raincoat for the half-mile walk to Capitol Hill Elementary School and, when she got older, the mile and a half to Wilson High.

From her family's modest two-bedroom home, the route rambled through the Capitol Hill neighborhood along mostly unimproved roads with no sidewalks. First she would turn onto Canby Street and walk past houses built on the site of an old orchard, subdivided years before. A few of the fruit trees in neighbors' yards were the gnarled remnants of the plantings that had once dominated the slope. At a certain spot where the road dipped low, Mary Sue would turn her face toward the east. From under the boughs of two ancient chestnut trees, she had a clear sightline to Mount Hood, Portland's iconic sentinel, constant yet constantly changing.

To the Chinook Indians, it was Wy'East, meaning simply "The Mountain." European explorers renamed just about every geographical landmark after famous white men. In this case, it was British admiral Lord Samuel Hood's name that was attached to the highest volcano in the Cascade Range, its snow-capped eleven-thousand-foot peak dominating the Rose City's eastern horizon. Mary Sue would observe the mountain's moods as they shifted with the weather and the seasons. In winter, the snowcap might reflect the pinks and lavenders of the sunrise one day and the next shine white against a sky of robin's-egg blue. More often than not, though, the grays of rainclouds draped its flanks and obscured its peak. This mood, too, was beautiful to Mary Susan. The mountain looked most like itself, she thought, when it was washed in clouds.

In June 1964, as she stared out the Greyhound bus's

window on the long highway to Ohio for her Mississippi Summer Project training, she measured this new landscape against her childhood horizons, against the mountains, against the trees so tall she had to tilt her head back to see the tops. Those vertical symbols of the Pacific Northwest were as familiar to her as arriving home from school with soggy shoes in a driving rain to find her mother in the kitchen and dinner under way—the sizzle of pork cutlets, the simmer of beef stew. They were as familiar as her father's collection of hand tools, stored with precision in a closet next to the water heater—saws and wood planers and pipe wrenches, a brace and wood bits, hammers and screwdrivers, all spotless with his fastidious maintenance.

After the bus had passed through the Cascades and over the Rockies, it rumbled downslope onto the plains toward the Great Lakes and the industrial heartland of America. She felt the bonds of home loosen. She sat up a little straighter in her seat and watched the endless plains roll by.

MARY SUE'S CHILDHOOD IN Oregon had been mostly happy. But by 1964 when she headed out for Freedom Summer, her family's equanimity had been rocked by loss. Her older brother, Richard, known as Dick, had been an Army chaplain's assistant stationed in South Korea. He was eighteen when he shipped out, his thick, wavy, light-brown hair combed straight back from his face. A sharp dresser who favored corduroy pants, white buck shoes, and Stradivari dress shirts bought with his earnings from an *Oregonian* newspaper route, he had charmed his classmates at Lincoln High School, where he was the drum major for the marching band. Dick was a gifted musician who had mastered instruments including the classical (piano), the sacred (pipe organ), and the oddball and offbeat (glockenspiel and vibraphone, the "vibes").

When Dick went overseas in 1957, the Korean War of the early 1950s was long over. American troops were there to keep the peace and help the country rebuild. Harold supported his son's enlistment, while Verna, a pacifist with Quaker leanings, objected to wars in general and, in particular, to Dick's becoming a soldier. She steeled herself to endure his two-year deployment.

Then one day in July 1958 came a knock on the door. Verna opened it. A man in a Western Union uniform stood on her porch. "Telegram, ma'am," the messenger said, handing her a small white envelope. Her arm must have felt leaden as she reached for it. Her fingers must have seemed clumsy, as if she were wearing stiff gloves as she fumbled with the seal. She strained to focus her eyes on the words typed on the paper inside. Dick had been stricken with polio, the telegram said. He was paralyzed from the neck down. Verna's knees gave way. She grabbed for the closest chair and sat down. More details would arrive tomorrow, the telegram said.

The next day's telegram was delivered midshift to Harold at the Shell plant where he worked, an oil refinery standing on the banks of the Willamette River amidst a cluster of oil storage tanks. He opened the envelope with his name showing in the cellophane window and took out the amber-colored paper. He stared at the message, comprehending and yet not comprehending. He spoke a few words to his supervisor and climbed into his gray 1952 Plymouth. As he drove the twenty-five-minute route home, the one he had been taking every day for twenty years, he felt as if a cold fog had rolled in off the river and seeped into his head. He didn't see the Willamette flowing slow and gray alongside Front Avenue on Portland's industrial north side. He didn't notice the phalanx of warehouses along Harbor Drive or the gradual incline of Barbur Boulevard as he traveled the last stretch to the small house he had built for his family with his own hands.

Verna, sixteen-year-old Mary Susan—who by then had adopted the shorter, less-formal name Mary Sue—and her fourteen-year-old brother, William, known as Bill, were at home that summer day, waiting for more news of Dick's condition. Bill was, like his sister, tall and thin, but his interests ran to gizmos and gadgets, to the inner workings of household appliances, to the mechanics of race cars and short-wave radios. They weren't close, these two younger siblings to Dick. But in that moment, the double helixes and genetic markers that bound them obscured their differences. They looked at each other when they heard the car crunch in the driveway. It was midafternoon, too early for Harold to be home. The back door opened, and Harold walked into the house. His eyes looked hollowed out, as if some part of his life force had leaked away. A white envelope was sticking out of his shirt pocket. Harold steered Verna into the couple's bedroom in hopes of breaking the news to his wife first. But Mary Sue and Bill followed on their heels. "Dick is gone," Harold told them. "He died yesterday."

Verna was the first to collapse face-down on the white chenille coverlet atop the double bed she shared with her husband. The other three fell beside her on the bed. The sobbing for their beloved Dick, whose life was taken by an invisible virus on a distant Asian peninsula, lasted for a long time that day.

Ironically, vaccines to combat the deadly disease were being developed and tested in the United States at the exact moment in 1955 and 1956 when Dick was finishing high school and joining the Army. By 1957, when Dick was playing the organ for members of the military attending church services in Korea, mass vaccinations of American kids were taking place in doctors' offices and clinics all over the country. Polio plummeted from a peak of 53,000 cases in 1952 to just over 160 in 1961. An army of volunteers for the March of Dimes were ringing doorbells across the United States, raising millions of dollars a few dimes at a time to wipe out polio, even as the virus was invading Dick's body at Camp Casey, thirty miles from Seoul. Dick had just missed the window for taking the life-saving vaccine.

That the family would never see Dick again was unthinkable.

As THE NEXT-OLDEST CHILD, Mary Sue felt a pull to step into the void Dick had left behind, as unfillable as that void might be. Like Dick, she had a gift for music. And she, like Dick, or maybe because of him, was drawn to the pipe organ. So when she enrolled as a music major at Willamette University later that year, she decided to specialize in church music.

Willamette University, like most colleges in the 1960s, was in a period of transition. "Willamette was a pretty conservative school, but even so it felt like we were on the edge of turbulence," recalled her college roommate and fellow music major, Wendy Crane. Along with other students, Wendy and Mary Sue were "kind of rebels," defying certain requirements left over from Willamette's Methodist roots in the 1800s. Skipping Tuesday chapel and boycotting convocation weren't exactly on a par with occupying the administration building or holding mass antiwar rallies as other campuses were beginning to do in the mid-sixties. Still, these small gestures of defiance reflected the broader restlessness among America's youth.

Freedom Summer stood at the nexus of protest in America, germinating inside a kernel of dissent that was about to burst and scatter its seeds of social unrest across the nation. The civil rights movement in the mid-sixties carried the same DNA that was spawning the antiwar movement, the women's movement, and the gay rights movement. Freedom was the theme binding these disparate movements together. There were two sides to the freedom coin: freedom *from* and freedom *to*. Freedom from oppression, from inequality, from militarism. Freedom to live in a just society, to receive equal treatment under the law, to resist dying in an illegal war, no matter who you are. This was the caldron of social conflict Mary Sue dove into that summer when she headed to Mississippi.

"Mary Sue had lots of strength in her convictions," Wendy said decades later. "She had a calm faith, a sense that life has meaning beyond just our own personal selves." When Mary Sue signed up for the Mississippi Summer Project, she told Wendy she "felt a call" to join the effort down south. Wendy's outward admiration for Mary Sue's decision was tempered with unspoken fear for her friend. "I didn't express my concerns out loud," she said many years later. "But I worried about her safety—oh my gosh! What could happen?"

Mississippi might as well have been a million miles from Willamette University, whose evergreen-boughed campus was an oasis of quiet scholarship and contemplation in Oregon's capital city of Salem. Mary Sue's studies in classical and church music were, in a way, an oasis within the oasis. As Oregon's lawmakers debated legislative issues in the capitol building just across the street from the north edge of the campus, Mary Sue spent much of her college life cloistered in the music building. There she practiced celestial masterpieces of composers such as Johann Sebastian Bach and Dietrich Buxtehude on a small pipe organ tucked away in the basement. She delved into courses on the thematic structure of classical composition, relishing the complexities of theory and the way it opened secret doorways in her understanding of music. She remembers one popular professor whose students teased him for whistling and trilling as he strolled across campus in a joyful public demonstration of the "baroque ornamentation" he taught in class.

It all seemed light-years from the civil rights movement that was roiling the South. There another college-age student, James Meredith, became the first black student to enroll in segregated Ole Miss (the University of Mississippi) in the fall of 1962, when Mary Sue was a sophomore at Willamette. Five hundred U.S. marshals stood watch on campus to protect him. White mobs rioted. Two people were killed. Nevertheless, Meredith persisted.

DATING WASN'T TOP-OF-MIND FOR Mary Sue during her school years. In high school, she had a couple of casual boyfriends and went to a few school dances, but she never got serious about anyone. The best part was wearing a beautiful dress and for one evening feeling pampered and admired. She remembers one homecoming dance in particular. Her six-foot-tall date, buff in a tux and crewcut, knocked at her door holding a white corsage. As her parents looked on, he pinned the flowers to her dress. She felt dazzling in the gown—pale aqua with a scoop neck and a full, knee-length skirt of chiffon over taffeta—handed down from her cousin Pat and altered by Mary Sue's mother to fit her slender figure. Her date's father drove the pair to the school gym, where they sipped punch and danced to hits by the white heartthrobs of the day, rockers like Ritchie Valens, Bobby Darin, the Drifters, Elvis, Roy Orbison.

Another time, she wore an "absolutely beautiful" watermelon-pink dress that she got to keep after modeling it on a TV ad for the Tall Shop, a clothing store for tall girls and women where she worked part-time in high school. She loved the dancing and the music and the swirl of tuxes and cummerbunds, flowing pastels and patent leather. But it wouldn't be until she met Eddie in Shaw that dancing led to real romance.

Mary Sue's school days were spent mainly in quiet conformity. Except for her height—she reached six feet tall in middle school, making her nine inches taller than the average girl her age—Mary Sue blended in with her classmates. She worked hard, took pride in earning good grades, went to the Methodist church where her dad directed the choir, and practiced piano on the family's old upright. By high school, she was giving piano lessons after school and on Saturdays.

She took a handful of modeling lessons at her mother's suggestion to improve her poise, self-assurance, and posture. She earned money picking strawberries and green beans in the summer, money she used to pay for music lessons and to buy fabric for the wardrobe she sewed on her mom's old Singer treadle machine.

Years later, she said, when new acquaintances learned of her civil rights activism in the Deep South, they assumed she must have been a rabble-rouser in her teens. They couldn't fathom that an introspective honors student who was tongue-tied around cute boys, diligent, and friends with girls who were like her—shy, serious, and studious—would charge off to Mississippi and poke the biggest hornet's nest of racism in the United States of America. "I went from zero to sixty in thirty seconds," Mary Sue says now.

As a teenager in Oregon, Mary Sue knew a little bit about Jim Crow from books and news reports. But like most Oregonians, she didn't know about the history of racism and segregation in her own state. She had never heard, for instance, that the Oregon Territory's provisional government passed a law excluding blacks from the territory in 1844. She didn't know that under this law, a black person already living in the territory would be severely whipped ("upon his or her bare back, not less than twenty nor more than thirty-nine stripes") if he or she failed to leave within two to three years. This "lash law" was quickly rescinded as being too harsh. But in its place, the government enacted a law that condemned black residents to, in the words of Oregon journalist R. Gregory Nokes, "a potential outcome not unlike slavery." Under this new provision, a black man or woman who failed to leave the Oregon Territory on time would be arrested, tried, and if found guilty, publicly hired out to the "lowest bidder" as a laborer for six months before being evicted from the territory. Nor did she know that a number of Oregon's early pioneers and farmers brought slaves with them in their covered wagons.

Racist laws passed in Oregon after the freeing of America's slaves by adoption of the U.S. Constitution's Thirteenth Amendment in 1865 remained on the books well into the mid-twentieth century. As Nokes asserted in his 2013 book, *Breaking Chains: Slavery on Trial in the Oregon Territory*, racism "remained deep-seated in Oregon" for a hundred years after slavery was abolished in the United States. The 1862 legislature, Nokes reported, imposed an annual five-dollar poll tax on black citizens, as well as citizens of Chinese, Hawaiian, and interracial heritage. Four years later, in 1866, the legislature passed a law forbidding marriage between white people and people of other ethnic and racial groups. This anti-miscegenation statute stayed on the books until 1951.

Oregon's state lawmakers withdrew the state's ratification of the Fourteen Amendment to the U.S. Constitution. Ratified in 1868, it required states to guarantee equal protection under the law to all American citizens, regardless of race. Oregon thumbed its nose at federal law, "reflect[ing] the stubborn refusal of white Oregonians to consider African Americans worthy of equal rights," in the words of Nokes. Astonishingly, it wasn't until 1973—nearly a decade after Mary Sue rode into danger for the sake of social and political justice—that the Oregon Legislature re-ratified the Fourteenth Amendment. As for the Fifteenth Amendment, granting voting rights to black citizens, Oregon's lawmakers waited nearly a century to ratify the amendment, which had been written into the U.S. Constitution in 1870.

In Portland, like most northern cities, black citizens were not subject to the overt, in-your-face segregation of the Jim Crow South—signs nailed to every restroom and drinking fountain designating "white" and "colored." Motels and restaurants in Portland were listed in *The Negro Motorist Green Book* as places where black travelers would be served and accommodated. But even if discrimination was not on display for all to see in Portland, it was encoded in the real estate practice called redlining. Within the red lines drawn around specific neighborhoods, black citizens could not rent or buy a house. Many Portland neighborhoods were "sundown" neighborhoods—all-white neighborhoods where segregation was maintained by discriminatory laws, intimidation, and violence.

When shipyards were hiring workers to build warships for World War II and black workers came north to take those jobs, they had few options for housing, being relegated to one small district in the northeast section of Portland called Albina. The hastily constructed city of Vanport, built precariously on the floodplain of the mighty Columbia River in the year of Mary Sue's birth, housed thousands of black workers and their families for a few years until the river breeched an earthen levy and washed away entire apartment buildings in an afternoon.

SHAW, MISSISSIPPI, AND PORTLAND, Oregon, share an important attribute of geography: each sits on an ancient floodplain, where high waters spill out of river channels and spread onto the land. The Mississippi River, twenty-three hundred miles long from its crystalline headwaters in Minnesota's glacial Lake Itasca (home to bigmouth bass and pike and bullhead trout) to the tropical waters of the Gulf of Mexico (where sea turtles, blue crab, and red snapper live and bottlenose dolphins cavort), carries the greatest volume of water of any river in the continental United States. The Columbia River (home to Chinook salmon and sturgeon and steelhead), running twelve hundred miles from Canada's Rocky Mountains through Washington and then along the Washington-Oregon border to the Pacific Ocean, is the fourth largest by volume. Together, these two mighty rivers pour nearly one million cubic feet of water into the oceans every second. In the Mississippi Delta, the Yazoo River adds its overflow to that of the mighty Mississippi. In Oregon, the Willamette River joins the Columbia at Portland, its waters gathered from forested tributaries across its own vast floodplain.

The volume of water, its speed and force and power, compounds during periods of heavy rain. Before European settlers started cutting trees, planting crops, and building permanent structures along the riverbanks, the swollen and churning currents would overflow their natural course and spill across the plains and valleys unencumbered, a natural cycle of ebb and flow that created, over millennia, the fertile soils where farmers and their families settled and thrived. These were the fertile soils from which Mississippi's cotton rose toward the sun, fat and soft, and pricked Eddie's fingers when he worked the long rows with his family, year after year. These were the fertile soils where Oregon's green beans hung heavy on their vines, where strawberries grew fat and stained

Mary Sue's fingers ruby red when, as a child, she picked them for half a cent per pound, summer after summer.

The blessings of a floodplain are also its curse. The super-rich soils that beckoned settlers to homestead in Mississippi and Oregon in centuries gone by were deposited by the same floodwaters that from time to time washed away towns, ruined crops, and drowned anyone who couldn't outrun the fast-moving waters. Decade after decade, officials labored to tame the mighty rivers and protect the citizens who lived beside them. But despite the building of levies and berms and dikes, a time always comes when human structures can't hold back the deluge of historic storms.

Disparity in suffering based on race and poverty is typical in floods, hurricanes, tsunamis, and other cataclysms of nature, as Caltech scientist Lucy Jones points out in *The Big Ones: How Natural Disasters Have Shaped Us.* "When flooding strikes, it doesn't strike an area or its residents equally," Jones notes. Two floods in the early twentieth century are emblematic of how racial bias in government planning and resource allocation brings extra calamity to black workers and their families. It was the spring of 1927 when a killer flood broke through a seemingly impervious system of levees to wash away hundreds of human lives in Mississippi. Two decades later in Oregon, in 1948, a flood of epic size raced through the low-lying town of Vanport on the perimeter of Portland, displacing thousands of families and killing at least fifteen people. In both floods, black citizens were far and away the greatest victims.

The devastation on the Delta was the stuff of epic storytelling when Eddie was growing up. He recalls hearing his grandparents tell stories about the Great Flood of 1927 while sitting on the porch of the plantation shack. His daddy's family was sharecropping in Leland not far from Shaw when the levees burst. Black workers had built Mississippi's levees, forced into servitude by their plantation bosses and supervised by white men with guns. During the deluges that periodically hammered the land, when biblical rains swelled the river dangerously and black sharecroppers were too few to keep the floodwaters back, "African American men were conscripted off the streets, often at gunpoint, to fill out crews," according to Jones.

So it was that in the spring of 1927, as the river raged higher and higher, hundreds of black men raced against the inevitable, filling sandbags and piling them on the levee. On April 21 near the Delta town of Greenville, just twenty-six miles from Shaw, they felt the quivering and the shifting of the earthen levees beneath their feet. Jones writes: "The levee was trembling as the water started to percolate through it. African Americans working on the levee realized it was failing and tried to leave, but they were forced back at gunpoint. When the failure finally came, many of them were swept away to their deaths."

The levee crumbled like a chunk of dry cornbread against the force of the rampaging river. Water poured across the Delta in great churning waves, following the laws of gravity and hydrology, leaving a million acres of the ancient floodplain under ten feet of water. People who could escape the water ran for high ground. Thousands of families, black and white alike, took refuge atop the levees that were still intact and waited for help. When the Red Cross at last showed up with rescue boats, only whites were allowed to board. "The African Americans were left behind—without clean water, without food, without protections from the continuing rain," said Jones.

In Portland, people still talk about the Vanport Flood of 1948. An exhibit at the Oregon Historical Society's downtown museum tells the story: "On Memorial Day in 1948, the Columbia River, swirling fifteen feet above normal, punched a hole in a railroad embankment that served as a dike, starting a flood that would leave eighteen-thousand people homeless and alter race relations in Portland forever."

The city of Vanport was built on a floodplain in 1942 to house the thousands of workers who came from all over the country to build battleships at Kaiser Shipyards. When Kaiser Shipyards ramped up for World War II, Vanport became Oregon's second-largest city. The African-American population in Oregon grew more than tenfold, from two thousand to twenty-five thousand.

On the afternoon of May 30, 1948, when Mary Sue was six years old, the Columbia River, "swollen by weeks of heavy rain," breached the dike that had been holding back its raging currents, according to an entry by Carl Abbott in the Oregon Historical Society's *Oregon Encyclopedia.* The swampy site absorbed enough of the fast-moving floodwaters in sloughs and low spots to give residents a slight head start, about thirty-five minutes to escape before the water rose into their apartment buildings. "The rising water tumbled automobiles and swirled Vanport's wooden apartment buildings off their foundations like toy boats," says Abbott. Fifteen people died, according to the official death count, but many in the black community suspected the count was much higher. Thousands of black citizens lost their homes in the floodwaters, but there was no place for them to relocate in Portland because the city's real estate "code of ethics" restricted African Americans to the tiny patch of the city called Albina by prohibiting homeowners and their agents from selling to black people.

ALTHOUGH OREGON'S RACIST LEGACY was mostly unknown to Mary Sue—as it was for most Oregonians, who tended to congratulate themselves on their tolerance—she did have some awareness, albeit sketchy, of apartheid in the South. Even the little she knew about the injustices of segregation and the indignities of racism made her blood boil.

So in 1964, during her senior year at Willamette University, when she heard the call for volunteers for the Mississippi Summer Project, she knew the call was hers to answer. She decided that very day to apply. When people asked her why she would risk her own safety for people she didn't know—why she would leave her safe, predictable life in the land of volcanoes and ancient forests, of wild rivers flush with salmon and rainbow trout, to fight racism in the swampy bottomlands of catfish and water moccasins, King Cotton and the Ku Klux Klan—she would explain that it was something she believed in, something she was driven to do by her conscience. But the answer she never voiced aloud was: "Why *wouldn't* I go?"

For her, it was a moral imperative. She wasn't deeply religious at the time, but she nevertheless took seriously the teachings of her Methodist upbringing. One passage from the Bible, Rom. 12:1, guided her decision to risk everything in Mississippi. The apostle Paul said, "Therefore, I urge you, brothers and sisters, in view of God's mercy, to offer your bodies as a living sacrifice, holy and pleasing to God—this is your true and proper worship."

ON MARCH 15, 1964—JUST three months before she would board the bus for Freedom Summer—Mary Sue performed her senior recital. Her parents, professors, and pals, including roommate Wendy Crane, filled the pews in the soaring sanctuary of the gothic First Methodist Church when she climbed the stairs to the organ loft. Taking a calming breath, she sat down at the massive Boston-made Aeolian-Skinner pipe organ. A rose window, its intricate panes of glass stained in shades of mauve and royal blue and amber, graced the chancel. The last murmurs of the audience gave way to silence, filling the historic church with expectation. The nervousness she felt knowing that her degree hinged on this performance dissolved as soon as her hands touched the keyboard.

Her program was challenging. She played three pieces by German-Danish Baroque composer Dietrich Buxtehude (Ein feste Burg ist unser Gott, "A Mighty Fortress Is Our God"; Ach Herr, mich armen Sünder, "Oh Lord, Poor Sinner That I Am"; and a fugue). Next was *Prelude and Fugue in G* composed by J. S. Bach, followed by Charles-Marie Widor's *Sixth Symphony*. She finished with three pieces by twentieth-century French composer Jehan Alain (Variations sur un theme de Clement Jannequin; Le Jardin suspend, "The Hanging Garden"; and "Litanies").

Three months later, as she headed out for her training in Ohio, the timeless compositions by European musicians across five centuries resonated in her consciousness. She carried them, too, during her year in Mississippi—classical and sacred music from another time and place. The music in her personal playbook soon entwined with Negro spirituals and gospel hymns and freedom songs derived from the field hollers and black churches of the South, songs of liberation. Her alto voice merged with the voices of activists black and white, at demonstrations and mass meetings, even echoing from jail cell to jail cell when she and other activists sang freedom songs in police custody. Singers could be jailed, but songs could not.

Eventually, it all blended together for Mary Sue with R&B riffs blaring from jukeboxes in Shaw's black clubs, where she and her fellow activists decompressed on Saturday nights. As she sipped her vodka and grapefruit juice, tapping her foot to Sam Cooke in a club where hers was the only white face, the outlines of her Oregon alma mater softened in her mind, turning faint and fuzzy like a wash over a watercolor. Only the struggle retained sharp focus for her now.

Harold and Verna Gellatly in their Portland home, 1960.
(Photo courtesy of Mary Sue Short)

Gellatly siblings Bill, Mary Sue, and Dick, Christmas 1948. (Photo courtesy of Mary Sue Short)

8

Leanings

We're women and men together,
We shall not be moved.
Just like a tree that's planted by the water,
We shall not be moved.
—Pete Seeger's version of a traditional Negro spiritual

Shaw, Mississippi, August 1964 through March 1965

It was late August 1964. Freedom Summer was over. Hundreds of student volunteers had packed up and headed back to their homes and campuses in the North and the West. But a few had stayed. Mary Sue was one of the twelve or thirteen volunteers who took staff positions with SNCC and embarked on new assignments in towns where the freedom struggle was still very much alive.

So one blistering hot morning, her blue-gray satchel in hand, Mary Sue stepped aboard a Greyhound in Hattiesburg bound for the Delta, notorious for its monumental intransigence on issues of race. As the bus rolled north on Highway 55, she pressed her face close to the window and watched the Piney Woods give way to the endless flatness of the Delta, the Mississippi and Yazoo floodplain stretching flat and wide to the far horizon. This girl who had grown up in the shadow of volcanos—the peaks of Mount Hood and Mount St. Helens and, farther to the east, Mount Jefferson, all visible from her Portland neighborhood when the air was clear—was accustomed to living in a world of verticals. As the bus hummed along, getting closer to her new posting, she was astonished by the unbroken horizontal plane that was the Mississippi Delta. But as it turned out, the contrast in geography was the least significant of the contrasts between Mary Sue's tall-timbered homeland and the flat-fielded cotton mecca that was her destination.

She arrived in Shaw at a seminal moment. Despite Eddie's dogged efforts to integrate the diner, the library, Liar's Park, and the theater, now a pile of debris, Shaw had remained somnolent during the first weeks of Freedom Summer. Rising against a hundred years of oppression, it seemed, would need a bigger spark than just an influx of white college students. In his 2010 book, *Freedom Summer: The Savage Season That Made Mississippi Burn and Made America a Democracy*, journalist Bruce Watson describes the frustration of volunteers assigned to work in Shaw.

"Shaw's project was a backwater," Watson writes bluntly. "With no local movement to build on, mass meetings drew just a few adults.... All summer, the rotting shacks of Shaw had seemed to drown in despair."

Then in a heartbeat, everything changed. "Suddenly," Watson says, "Shaw awoke."

It was a single comment that catalyzed the movement, according to Watson. The comment came from the mouth of

Bolivar County sheriff Charlie Capps as he was interviewed by the *New York Times*.

"I know it may sound foolish," the sheriff opined, "but 95 percent of our blacks are happy." When the quote ran in the *Times* on July 19, 1964, it swirled through Shaw like a dust devil. Capps—who presided over Bolivar County's chapter of the White Citizens' Council and who was, not insignificantly, himself a planter with two thousand acres of farmland in Bolivar County—fancied himself a moderating force, a voice of reason, in the unfolding racial debate. Turns out he was wrong. His comment to the *Times*—so blithe, so cocksure, so patronizing—enraged the black community for miles around Shaw.

The pushback was swift. Volunteers at the Freedom Center pinned the article to the bulletin board for everyone to see. At the mass meeting that week, the statement was read aloud to groans and jeers of protest.

The brouhaha made national news, again filling significant column inches in the *New York Times*. In a follow-up story on August 9 titled "'Happy' Negroes Dispute Sheriff," the *Times* reported on the reaction Capps's comments provoked. "A copy of the story was posted by Northern civil rights workers at a Freedom Center in one of the Negro districts in the town of Shaw," the *Times* story noted. "It thus came to the attention of many Negroes who visit the center daily and who attend meetings sponsored by Negro and white civil rights workers several times weekly."

Twenty-plus black residents of Bolivar County sent rebuttals to the *Times* in what the paper called "an unusual

Negro reaction in this cotton-growing county." The *Times* ran some of the comments, with spelling and grammar errors intact: "The Negroes that says they are doing fine they are lying because they are scared of losing their little two cents jobs." "Only a fool would be happy in Mississippi down here chopping cotton for 30 cents an hour, just think, ten long hours only $3 a day."

Specifically addressing a vile comment from *Bolivar Commercial* editor Clifton Langford that ran in the original "happy blacks" article, several Shaw residents pushed back with ironic wisdom. Langford had told the *Times*, "We don't want classrooms mixing in our children with some colored child who thinks only of sleeping with some girl or throwing craps." One black woman sent her response as follows: "You have already mongrelized the white race and the black one, too. The only thing that you haven't done is claim your children."

Sheriff Capps's assertion—the myth of contented black people perpetuated by whites whose livelihoods were built on the backs of black workers—gave the movement in Shaw a potent new shot in the arm. Eddie's reaction to Capps's quote was visceral. It wasn't just that Capps had spouted a view convenient for the existing power structure. More insulting was that he had presumed to speak for the black community. Eddie was enraged.

Turning anger to action was, and always had been, Eddie's great strength.

After disembarking from the bus at the Truck Stop, Mary Sue stood beside the highway and looked around. The memory of that arrival is fuzzy in her mind, but somehow she found her way to the home of her host family, Andrew and Mae Lou Hawkins, where she would live for the next few months, and then to the Freedom Center to meet the local volunteers. She met Eddie a few days later.

The plantations that sprawled for miles around Shaw were off-limits to so-called agitators like Eddie and so-called invaders like Mary Sue. They and their fellow civil rights workers felt the danger acutely and took precautions whenever they approached a sharecropper's shack with voting-rights information. Danger notwithstanding, their mission required reaching out to plantation workers, who were among the most impoverished and oppressed citizens of Bolivar and Sunflower Counties.

One of the biggest, richest plantations in the Delta belonged to U.S. Senator John Stennis, who, along with fellow Delta senator James Eastland, was, in the words of *Washington Post* writer Robert G. Kaiser, an "old-time Southern segregationist." Stennis had voted no on every civil rights bill that had ever made its way to the floor of Congress, including an anti-poll tax bill in 1948 and an anti-literacy test bill in 1962. In 1956, he and Eastland had both signed the "Southern Manifesto," vowing to block or delay passage of any and all civil rights legislation.

Countless bills never saw the light of day. Eastland, as chair of the Judiciary Committee, deep-sixed legislation before it ever got out of committee. Eastland owned a six-thousand-acre plantation in Doddsville, Sunflower County, just five miles down Highway 49 from Ruleville. He liked to brag that he had "special pockets" in his pants where he secreted bills he didn't like.

When Eastland retired from the Senate in 1978, Kaiser described him in the *Post* as a "living caricature of the southern senator: white hair, stooped shuffle, ever-present big cigar." He would "rise regularly in the Senate to rant against 'mongrolization' of the races."

These senators represented the racist-to-the-marrow leaders of the white resistance in Mississippi. But secret pockets could not forever contain the forces of freedom. By 1964 and 1965, countervailing winds were pushing against the likes of Stennis and Eastland.

As a fighter within those countervailing forces, Eddie was taking an enormous risk by joining the Freedom Summer effort. His associations with Andrew Hawkins and Fannie Lou Hamer were in themselves big red flags to local white supremacists and their spies. Sometimes at night, when the fields stretched dark and empty across the land, Hawkins would take the wheel of SNCC's donated car, a gold-and-white 1954 Studebaker, and drive to the neighboring town of Ruleville, where he would swing by Fannie Lou Hamer's house. Together, the duo would head down the dark highway toward the sleeping plantations.

These stealth excursions, the activists knew, were fraught with danger. Civil rights workers, black or white, who encouraged local sharecroppers to seize their voting rights were not just frowned upon by the white planters; in their minds, it was a sedition against the white race and an assault on the southern way of life. Black activists canvassing at night were especially vulnerable, given Mississippians' history of wanton violence against black citizens and the utter lack of consequences for such crimes. White folks could, quite simply, get away with beating or killing their black neighbors. A dark night, a cold river, a band of thugs with a pickup truck—that's all it took to make a person disappear in the Delta. These raw facts, these unembellished truths of being black in Mississippi, were a spectral presence in the car as the activists traversed the rough dirt roads on the outermost edges of vast cotton acreages to call on sharecroppers' shacks.

On nights when moonlight shone on the fields, Andrew turned off the headlights to better avoid detection by the planters. After making sure their car hadn't been seen, the activists would get out and rap softly on the sharecroppers' doors. In low voices, almost whispers, they greeted the men and women within. In the shadowy corners at the back of the shack, clusters of children often would peer shyly and curiously at the visitors. Visitors were rare. The remoteness of the sharecroppers' cotton patches precluded most social calls. If the tenants agreed to let the activists in, they would set about persuading the tenants to claim their constitutional rights. It was a hard sell. But the activists kept at it, month after month.

BEGINNING IN THE MID-1800s, Bolivar County was carved out of "as grand a primeval forest of virgin oaks, cypress, hackberry, gum ash, and hickory as ever graced a level, fertile land," wrote William F. Gray in his 1923 tract, *Imperial Bolivar*. Gray described a wilderness teeming with wildlife, a "jungle equal to any African jungle," a "land of ridges, flats and sloughs, bayous, lakes and rivers, with millions of acres covered with cane [bamboo] from ten to twenty feet high under the giant forest trees."

It was the fertile soil of this "jungle" that beckoned to the white pioneers, the "empire builders," as Gray called them in his tract. That, and the remoteness of the region, which would give them free rein to hold slaves even as the North was condemning the buying, selling, and owning of human beings. These unexploited lands, he noted, were "in the heart of the South and free from abolition influences that had begun to affect the border slave states." Black labor, Gray pointed out, made King Cotton possible in the Delta: "Between the period of 1850 and 1860 the great black axe-men of the plantations … mowed down the forests like wheat before the sickle."

Gray waxed poetic as he described the transformation of a primeval forest—once home to millions of wild pigeons, ducks, geese, cranes, swans, and countless other species—into a cottony goldmine for white landowners. "The forests began to fade, and clearings and fertile fields sprang up in the wilderness. It was wonderful!… With the echoes of the axe and the saw dying away, there came the braying of the mules, the lusty singing of the ploughman, the welcoming hum of cotton gins, the clear early morning tintinnabulations of plantation bells, and the animated bustle of agricultural activity," he enthused. "Then Bolivar County began swiftly moving towards her imperial destiny."

Despite the great hacking down of the primeval forests and wetlands on the Mississippi River Delta, human settlement remained sparse. In 1900, Shaw was among a handful of "small centers of inhabitation along the main line of the Y.&M.V. Railroad," Gray reported.

By the 1960s, the fertile land of the Mississippi Delta had been worked by blacks for the enrichment of their white overlords, mostly Irish and Italian immigrants, for a hundred years. Eddie and his family, descendants of slaves, were the twentieth century's living legacy of the Delta's history of subjugation. In the 1960s, Shaw was still a place where white families exploited their black neighbors and treated them with contempt. It was a place where white men could abuse black children and women with the same impunity as their slaveowner ancestors. Eddie's younger brother Freddie recalls, "There was one that we called 'the babysitter.' He would come through the neighborhood and pick up little black girls. And he would say he's taking them to babysit for him. Nobody would ever say anything about it because of fear. But we knew who he was."

It was a place where white schools had neatly trimmed ballfields and crisp new textbooks, while the ill-equipped black school ran on hand-me-down books and split sessions scheduled around the chopping and picking of cotton. White kids got long, lazy summer breaks. Black kids sweated out the summer months in school so they would be available to planters for chopping in the spring and picking in the fall. Freddie remembers heading home after wickedly hot days in the classroom while the children of white planters were kicking back on summer break:

In August we'd always be in school in the blistering hot sun.... And they'd be out for summer vacation. And when we would come by on a truck, they would just stand out and just yell, niggers, niggers, niggers as far as they could see us.... We learned to ignore it, of course. So, we know the apple don't fall far from the tree. They didn't just learn that, you know, by birth. They had to hear it somewhere.

The *Bolivar Commercial* seemed to take pleasure in twisting the knife of discrimination in its pages, full of golden prose about the lovely white girls and athletic white boys whose every act was newsworthy. On September 3, 1964, just a few days after Mary Sue arrived in Shaw, editor Clifton Langford published an ode to lazy summer days, knowing of course that the county's black children were in school all summer so they could be released to pick cotton in the fall. He wrote:

> To many a freckle-faced youngster September is a foreboding sound. For it is this month that complete freedom dies for millions of boys and girls, and the schoolroom once again demands its place in their lives. To the youngster who roamed the hills with an adventurous spirit during June, July and August, this confinement often comes hard. To the freckle-faced lad who spent his time swimming in that nearby stream or lake, or hiking through the woods, or just lying on the bank of some stream waiting for a fish to bite, looking up into a summer's sky, school is the worst of all mankind's inventions.

In the guise of a paean to innocent childhood summers, Langford was making a mockery of the black children of Bolivar County. These children attended school in the summer so planters could exploit them in the fall. These children rarely learned to swim and often drowned in that "nearby stream or lake." If these children went fishing, it was so their families could eat. Freckles are, of course, evidence of sunshine on skin with little melanin.

ONE AFTERNOON IN THE fall of 1964, Eddie and Mary Sue, along with Shaw's hardcore band of young activists, were feeling emboldened. Civic awareness among fieldworkers was rising. Defiance was, for some, taking the place of fear. The activists decided to drive their 1954 Studebaker to several nearby plantations to canvass in broad daylight. It was a brazen act. "We knew it was dangerous," Eddie recalls. "The white plantation owners didn't want us talking to the sharecroppers. Besides, the dirt roads were private property. Technically, we were trespassing."

That morning, a hard rain had slickened the roads. Buckshot mud, as deep as a man's shin, coated the narrow lane that tracked the outskirts of the plantation of a man named Larkin Turpin. The old car's tires, worn to bald, couldn't gain traction in the ooze. It was like driving in slush. When Eddie stepped on the brake, the car's front end stopped but the rear end kept going, sliding off the one-lane road into the ditch. Eddie revved the engine. The wheels spun furiously. Before Eddie could gather his thoughts, a pickup truck appeared in front of them, seemingly out of nowhere. At the wheel was the plantation owner, Mr. Larkin Turpin. His face was a portrait of rage when he saw the carload of activists, all of them black except Mary Sue.

By now, Mary Sue had been in Mississippi long enough to look instinctively at the gun racks of the pickup trucks she encountered. For Eddie, scanning for shotguns in pickup trucks was a survival skill along the lines of keeping your bare hands away from hot woodstoves. So the fact registered in their minds immediately: there was no shotgun in Turpin's rack. The planter's cussing and snarling, therefore, carried little threat in the moment. Turning his truck around precariously in the mud, the planter yelled out the window, "You better not be here when I get back!"

Eddie was certain the planter would return with his gun. As soon as Turpin's truck was out of sight, the activists scrambled out of the Studebaker to lighten the load. Mary Sue slid into the driver's seat and took the wheel. As she stepped lightly on the gas, Eddie, his adrenaline pumping crazily in his veins, reached under the bumper and lifted the rear of the car out of the ditch. As a man of God, who was baptized in the bogue at age eleven, Eddie felt a divine hand in his superhuman strength that day. Speeding away as fast as the mud allowed, they all held their breath, Mary Sue keeping one eye on the rearview mirror till they were clear of Turpin's land.

ANOTHER OF SHAW'S VOLUNTEERS, a Californian still in his teens named Bob Scoville, wasn't as fortunate in evading detection by the white planters. One day while out canvassing on the outskirts of Shaw, he ventured onto a cotton plantation. A sheriff's deputy showed up and arrested him for trespassing. In the back of the cop cruiser, the young man rode to Cleveland, where he was locked in the Bolivar County jail. Scoville looked around the cell. A half-dozen white men in sweaty T-shirts and grimy jeans were smoking cigarettes and staring at him from narrow wall-mounted bunks. His mind was racing with images from the previous week, when a volunteer from Harvard University, Morton Thomas, had been thrown into the same jail, probably the same cell, where his fellow inmates—probably the very inmates now staring at him—had "beat the crap" out of him. Scoville had seen Thomas's swollen face and blackened eyes a couple days after the beating.

With that picture stark in his mind, he suddenly felt the hot breath of a man on his neck as the man leaned close and unfolded a bandana. A jagged piece of a broken mirror glinted in the dirty fabric. The man spoke. "We didn't have this when your friend was here," he said. On the outside, the only people who knew that Scoville had been jailed were a group of religious activists, whom Scoville identifies as "priests," that happened to be walking by the courthouse when they saw the young white prisoner in custody. Unbeknownst to Scoville, the priests had called the FBI. Within a couple of hours, a jailer showed up with a ring of keys and, unlocking the cell, escorted Scoville down the narrow steel corridor. He wasted no time driving back to Shaw.

Scoville was a college friend of Fred Winn's, one of the first Freedom Summer arrivals in Shaw back in June. Raised in Marin County, an affluent bastion of liberalism, Scoville was still in high school when he heard acclaimed black author James Baldwin speak. Thereafter, he kept an eye on politics and civil rights. He was nineteen years old, attending Sonoma State College and living in Sausalito, when he heard about the murders of the three civil rights workers. Appalled and energized to join the cause, he joined the struggle in Mississippi when Bill Light, a mutual friend of Winn's and Scoville's, came to California to raise funds and stayed with Scoville in Sausalito. "Can I go back with you?" Scoville asked.

In Mississippi, Scoville became a driver for one of the black leaders, Laurence Guyot, at Freedom Summer headquarters in Jackson. In late August, when the Mississippi Summer Project was winding down and volunteers were heading home, Scoville was assigned to work in Shaw. There he stayed through the winter, sleeping on a cot among the donated books in the Freedom Center, reading books about black history and the civil rights movement in his off hours.

In the spring of 1965, some of Shaw's black activists asked Scoville to drive them to Selma, Alabama, where Reverend Martin Luther King Jr. was leading some of the seminal events of the civil rights movement, the three marches across the Edmund Pettus Bridge from Selma to Montgomery. The "old, old man" of Dennis Flannigan's "like being in heaven's choir" recollection, seventy-five-year-old Miller Lark, was among the black activists who rode with Scoville that day in March 1965. "Miller Lark probably had more influence on me than anyone else in my life," Scoville said many decades later. "He was a great man, a wise man, a courageous man."

Lark, Scoville, and the others saw Dr. King and heard him speak in Selma. But when Stokely Carmichael got wind of the trip, he was not pleased, according to Scoville. "Carmichael was the coordinator for District 2, which included Shaw, so he was basically our supervisor at the time," he said. "He was very prominent." The two young men had words. Carmichael argued that Selma was too dangerous for a man of Lark's age. The risks were too high. Scoville responded that as a white volunteer, his job was to support the local people in what they wanted to do, and they had wanted to witness history.

Another driving mission was launched, this one to raise sorely needed funds to keep activism alive in Mississippi. So Scoville and Eddie, who by this time were good friends, headed to a Quaker community in upstate New York and other sympathetic communities in the Northeast, where they spoke to audiences in churches and auditoriums about the plight of Mississippi's black citizens and the dire need for money to sustain voting-rights initiatives in Shaw and other Mississippi towns.

Despite the project's money woes, "the project in Shaw was very good, very strong," Scoville recalls. He attributes much of that strength to Mary Sue and Eddie. Mary Sue, who he described as disciplined, even "straitlaced," had a "calming influence" on the other activists. "She was very mature, very focused. She held things together." Eddie's biggest strength was his deep and abiding roots in the community. "Everyone knew him, and everyone trusted him," Scoville said.

A FEW DAYS AFTER the stuck-in-the-mud episode on the Turpin plantation, Mary Sue and another volunteer were tasked with moving a three-generation sharecropping family from one plantation to another. The move had to be done at night, out of sight of the landlord. The Thomas family—a couple named Jack and Mary, eight young children, and Mary's mother, Mrs. McCrea—were in perpetual debt to the planter on whose land they lived and worked. As sharecroppers, they were under the thumb of the landlord, who kept all the records of weeds chopped, cotton picked, and hours worked, subtracting the cost of tools, fertilizer, and seed. During the fallow times when there was no work on the land, the planter would sell them supplies on credit, which they would, in theory, be able to pay back from their future wages.

In a voice dripping with irony, Mary Sue calls this system "creative accounting." Even with the whole family working sun to sun, there was never enough money to pay off the landlord for the prior year's expenses, let alone break even. And sharecroppers could forget about putting money aside to escape the bondage of King Cotton. The Thomas family's only option on this dark February night was to disappear, to take the offer of a clean slate from a neighboring planter who needed workers. They would then start the cycle yet again.

Sitting at the wheel of the Studebaker, Mary Sue left the Hawkins home around ten o'clock, creeping along the unlit road that hugged the far edge of the plantation. Her fellow volunteer followed in a pickup borrowed from a sympathetic black townsman. It was as dark as tar when they rolled up to the wood-plank shack. Mary and Jack were waiting inside, standing beside a cold woodstove holding their few belongings, their faces tight with worry. The children, toddlers to teens, had been taken earlier in the day to the homes of extended family members. If something went wrong, if the planter got wind of the escape and showed up with a posse and a gun, the kids, at least, would be safe.

A small wooden crate sat on the table. As Mary Sue picked it up to load it into the car, she made a quick visual inventory: half a bag of cornmeal, a small sack of flour, a tin of baking powder, a little salt. She looked around the shack but saw nothing else that was edible. The meagerness of that crate's contents has stuck in Mary Sue's memory for fifty years. "I was heartsick seeing that there was so little to feed so many," she recalled.

In a couple of minutes, they had loaded the food and the family's handful of possessions into the two vehicles. Through the darkness they traveled along the silent roads, their breathing shallow, their muscles taut, their senses tuned to the possibility of pursuit, till they arrived at the new plantation where the Mary and Jack hoped to hang on for another year.

For Mary Sue, the word *freedom* had taken on a meaning she hadn't sought, a personal meaning that welled up in her as she stood her ground against the white resistance in Mississippi. The inner strength she had shown, always, growing up on the westside slope of Portland took on a new dimension here among the cottonfields of Bolivar County. It's not that she had worried a lot about being accepted in a world where she was taller and quieter and more industrious than most of her peers. She found all the camaraderie she wanted in her circle of smart girlfriends and all the validation she needed in her large extended family, even accepting as a compliment the remarks of her well-meaning auntie who would always greet her with, "Oh, my, how wonderfully tall you've grown!" If she didn't feel the full embrace of her agemates in Oregon, she responded by picking more beans and swimming more laps and studying harder and practicing on the family's old upright piano. But in truth, she had chafed ever so slightly under the scrutiny of others.

When she signed up for the Mississippi Summer Project, her conscious reason was to join the fight for racial justice.

And she did that, fought with all her heart for the dignity and equality of Mississippi's black citizens. But as often happens, life wrote an unexpected subtext in the margins of her story of courage and activism: in helping to free the oppressed people of the Jim Crow South, Mary Sue freed herself. The college girl from Oregon became, in Mississippi, the undaunted woman who would not be cowed by officialdom, who could find her own way into a courthouse under siege, who would look defiantly at a pissed-off cop while, just a few feet away, local black activists were openly, boldly, freely demanding their rights.

Back in Shaw at day's end, she was free to dance to the R&B licks of black artists, to be the only white person in a black nightclub. It seemed an interstellar distance from her family's front porch in Portland where, a few years earlier, her first date had stood in his tux and polished shoes as she opened the door in her blue chiffon dress. If now and then Portland chanced to cross her mind, she would smile to herself, wondering what the folks back home would think if they saw her now, swinging across the dance floor in the arms of Eddie Short. In those moments, her spirit was unfettered.

IN NOVEMBER 1964, A week before the nation's presidential election, the Mississippi Freedom Democratic Party conducted a four-day mock election to give unregistered black voters a chance to have their say. On the ballot, distributed from barbershops, churches, cafes, and automobiles combing the backwoods, were Lyndon Johnson and Barry Goldwater, as well as four black congressional candidates who had been disqualified by the State Election Commission. Some 45,230

Negroes in Mississippi voted, 45,218 of them for Johnson and 12 for Goldwater.

On January 4, 1965, eleven Shaw activists drove to Washington, D.C., where hundreds of people were gathering for the so-named Congressional Challenge. It was the first day of the Eighty-ninth Congress. New members were about to be sworn in. But activists from all over Mississippi, unwilling to let go of the results of the mock election, still championed the seating of the winning Freedom Democratic Party candidates, rather than accepting the results of an all-white election that had disenfranchised most black citizens. "The House was asked to set aside the regular results of the elections, to refuse to seat the white congressmen and to seat the Freedom Democrats," Mary Sue recalls. "They were asked to call for new elections in which all adult citizens would be able to vote, regardless of race."

Mary Sue met with several congresspeople and government officials, challenging them to champion the cause of equal representation for the citizens of Mississippi and other Deep South states. Stokely Carmichael was there during a silent vigil in the pedestrian tunnels between the Capitol and congressional offices. Later, he wrote about the moment in his memoir, *Ready for Revolution:*

> As congressmen and their aides made their way through these tunnels, they turned a corner and found themselves passing between two lines of silent, working black men and women from Mississippi. The people, spaced about ten feet apart, stood still as statues, dignified, erect, utterly silent.... I looked into

the legislators' faces as they passed. Most could not take their eyes off those careworn, tired black faces. Some offered a timid greeting, a smile, or tentative wave. Others flushed and looked down. All seemed startled. Some clearly nervous, even afraid. All seemed deeply affected in some way.... That grave, mute presence became the most effective and eloquent of testimonies. To those passing Congressmen, the issue of Southern political injustice could no longer remain an abstract statistic, distant and dismissible.

The challenge was defeated on a roll call vote. But civil rights lawyers had been busy taking depositions and compiling evidence of the voting-rights violations that had long been the norm in Mississippi. They submitted to Congress three thousand pages of testimony describing systematic harassment, intimidation, violence, and reprisals against black citizens trying to vote. When the Voting Rights Act was signed into law a half year later, President Johnson's pen could be said to trace a direct line to these dramatic actions.

THE WINTER OF 1965 was long and treacherous. Workdays at the Freedom Center began early in the morning and lasted well into the evening. At night, Eddie would walk Mary Sue home to the Hawkins house along the muddy road, their shoes collecting buckshot mud.

"I'd have four inches of mud on my shoes," Mary Sue recalls. When her flats became so encrusted that they were all but ruined, Eddie loaned her his dress shoes (men's size 8) to wear to an all-staff SNCC meeting she needed to attend in Atlanta. The shoes fit perfectly. Wearing Eddie's shoes felt like wearing armor against danger. It also felt like taking her friend along with her. When she looked at her feet, warm and dry and well shod, she felt comforted by Eddie's presence—a presence that by then seemed as natural as breathing.

Outwardly, they lived those chilly winter days as if the next day would dawn like any other, the sun rising above the cottonfields, their mission pushing forward unhindered. But inwardly, anxiety percolated minute by minute just under the surface of their courage. As SNCC volunteer Penny Patch, a student from Swarthmore College, wrote in a collection of essays titled *Deep in Our Hearts: Nine White Women in the Freedom Movement*: "We were living in wartime conditions. We were always afraid."

Wartime conditions form bonds among combatants that grow faster and deeper than bonds in peacetime. It's the "band of brothers" that soldiers experience. They have each other's back. They will take a bullet to save a buddy. It was like that in Shaw for Mary Sue and Eddie. Mary Sue describes a "heightened awareness" of the people around her, her brothers and sisters in the movement. With every nerve prickling with attention, every sense on high alert, the activists noted that life became supercharged. Time became compressed; each day held an eternity of emotion, an eon of experience. Race, education, birthplace—these traits dissolved into irrelevance for Mary Sue and Eddie. Justice, equality, dignity—these ideas drove out everything superficial that typically serves to divide the human family. The universal ideals of human rights took up all the oxygen in Shaw as the two young people, side by side, leaned their shoulders into their mission.

Inevitably, it seems, their relationship evolved from comradeship to mutual admiration to deep friendship and, finally, to romantic partnership. They were caught off guard, these foot soldiers in the civil rights trenches of Mississippi's darkest backwaters. Saturday nights, after a nerve-rattling week of twelve-hour days on the frontlines of social justice, Eddie, Mary Sue, and their little band of freedom fighters would lock up the Freedom Center and walk the few blocks to a makeshift nightclub in Johnson's Addition named after the once-famous Chicago nightspot Club DeLisa. Unlike its namesake, Shaw's version had not a scintilla of glitz. It was tacked on to the home of Mr. and Mrs. T. S. Bartley, who, like so many black residents of Shaw, were entrepreneurial spirits who created their own opportunities for income in a town where jobs beyond the cottonfields were almost nonexistent.

No matter how dark the unlit road or how much mud they waded through, the young activists could relax for a few hours in the warm glow of the club. They would order a "set-up"—glasses, ice, and mixers. Liquor laws banned clubs from selling mixed drinks back then, so customers brought their own bottles and mixed their own cocktails. For Eddie and Mary Sue, it was Canadian Club and grapefruit juice. Eddie would drop a nickel in the Seeburg jukebox while Velma Bartley grilled hamburgers. Eddie—whose dancing and singing skills had been legendary in Shaw ever since his eighth-grade triumph performing "Stagger Lee" at the Mound Bayou talent show—had a natural stage presence. At Club DeLisa, he would grab Mary Sue's hand and pull her onto the dance floor. They made an unusual pair, this compact black man with the smooth moves of a born entertainer and the tall white girl, ungainly in her long limbs, smiling through her awkwardness. Eddie brought out in her the playfulness she usually kept hidden behind her serious façade. As Eddie remembers, they danced the jitterbug, the funky four corners, the slop, and the funky chicken to the licks of great R&B artists like Marvin Gaye, Aretha Franklin, and Sam Cooke. Cooke's hit song "A Change Is Gonna Come," described on the BBC's *Soul Music* program by *New Yorker* magazine writer David Cantwell as "a brooding but bright civil-rights anthem," was all over the radio airwaves in 1964 and 1965. The last stanza captures the mood of struggle and hope in Shaw in those days:

> *There have been times that I thought*
> > *I couldn't last for long*
> *But now I think I'm able to carry on*
> *It's been a long, a long time coming*
> *But I know a change is gonna come,*
> > *oh yes it will.*

The song could have been the anthem, too, for the converging lives of Eddie and Mary Sue. One night, many months into their shared mission in Shaw, Eddie walked her home as was his custom. At the door of the Hawkins house, he said goodnight as usual. But then, in the quick beat of a youthful heart, everything changed. He sensed something he could not have imagined not so very long ago: her eyes lingering on his just a moment longer than usual. There was something new in that longer look, an affection in her expression that went beyond the friendship they had formed.

In the next instant he rejected, reflexively, a fleeting impulse to answer her gaze with a kiss. If such a kiss were witnessed by a white gang member or one of their paid informants, Eddie would be a target for murder.

The next day, when he and Mary Sue were working in the Freedom Center, he got up from his chair and, glancing around to ensure their privacy, he walked over to where she was sitting. She looked up. He leaned over and pressed his lips to hers. She was surprised. Yet she felt quite natural receiving this kiss from this man who, by then, was her best friend and her protector. It felt right, maybe inevitable, that this stalwart man from sharecropper roots in the deepest South would become her sweetheart.

After that night, they moved forward together not only in the cause of justice but also in the embrace of romance. The love they shared then wasn't a wild, passionate, I-can't-live-without-you love, they explained years later. Rather, it was a fond coming together of two kindred spirits in a time of fear and uncertainty. They needed each other in that moment, and in that moment, they held fast to one another.

ONE EVENING, EDDIE AND Mary Sue decided to drive twenty miles north on Highway 61 to Winstonville, a Delta hamlet only a tenth the size of Shaw, to meet with some fellow activists. During the heyday of the Delta Blues, Winstonville was a hotspot for traveling musicians. Today, a Mississippi Blues Trail historic marker alongside the highway is a reminder of Winstonville's Harlem Inn, once known as "the showplace of the South." The marker tells visitors: "The inn was once the Delta's most important venue for touring national blues performers. B.B. King, Little Milton, Bobby 'Blue' Bland, Howlin' Wolf, Tyrone Davis, and T-Bone Walker were among the many stars who appeared, and Ike Turner and his Kings of Rhythm from Clarksdale gave some of the earliest performances here." The Harlem Inn was long gone by the time Eddie and Mary Sue set out that night in 1965, having burned down in 1949. But Winstonville had not faded away completely. Civil rights activism had brought a new spark to the community.

The night was dark as they headed out. They hadn't driven more than a few miles north on Highway 61 when they felt the sickening *kthunk, kthunk, kthunk* of the right front tire going flat. Eddie pulled onto the shoulder and looked at Mary Sue. The risk they were taking driving together at night was suddenly amplified a thousandfold. There was no spare tire in the trunk of the gray 1949 Plymouth that had been donated to Shaw's project after the firebombing of the Chevy. And so, with the darkness deepening around the disabled car, they sat side by side on the torn vinyl seat and weighed their options. Eddie could go for help. But leaving Mary Sue alone by the road was dangerous, and Eddie's walking alone was an equally bad idea. They agreed that they had better odds of surviving the night if they stuck together. They knew they were just a mile or two from a gas station and diner owned by prominent black activist Amzie Moore, a giant of a man whom Bruce Watson describes as "standing over six feet tall, with a thick neck and bald head." Moore's home in Cleveland was a well-known gathering place for civil rights leaders, always hopping with activity and conviviality. Eddie and Mary Sue decided they would try to make it to

Moore's gas station, the closest safe haven, on foot.

They set out at a brisk pace. Crickets droned in the surrounding fields, and mosquitoes lit on their necks and ankles as they walked. Pretty soon, they passed a whites-only liquor store and exchanged glances, sharing the unspoken hope that no one in the store would spot them. But once they were beyond the glow of the neon signs advertising Crown Royal and Smirnoff's, a vehicle pulled out of the parking lot in a crunch of gravel. The headlights were pointed toward them. The vehicle slowed to a crawl alongside them, matching their gait. The two kept walking, looking straight ahead. The driver's side window rolled down. "Well now," the man at the wheel remarked to his companion, who was leaning forward to get a good look at Mary Sue and Eddie, "would ya look at that nigger walkin' along the road with that white woman!" Then he stepped on the gas and pealed out. The taillights of the blue pickup truck were like two red eyes in the deepening darkness.

Mary Sue and Eddie watched the taillights grow dimmer as the truck disappeared into the distance.

Mary Sue and Eddie knew this wouldn't be the end of the incident. The men would, no doubt, be back with a posse. Eddie's mind ticked through their options. Running was not among them. His daddy's long-ago warning still made Eddie's skin crawl. "Don't you never run," Willie had taught his sons. "Don't give 'em no excuse to shoot you." They were sitting ducks out there on the dark highway. They had no choice but to keep walking and hope they made it to the gas station in time. They picked up their pace, walking as fast as they could without breaking into a flat-out sprint.

Another set of headlights lit up the roadway before they heard the vehicle coming up behind them. But before panic could set in, the car passed without stopping and the night closed around them again. In their minds, they could see the glow of the gas station. They could almost smell the burgers sizzling on the cafe's grill, just about hear the voices of customers chatting and laughing with Daisy, the waitress, while the sounds of R&B played on the radio. In their minds, everything would be fine just as soon as Amzie Moore's haven of safety wrapped them in its warmth.

Before they could reach that oasis, though, the headlights of another vehicle cut through the darkness heading toward them. Blinded by the lights, they heard the car slow down. They stared into the beams as they braced for the harassers. But as the car drew up beside them, they recognized the two-toned blue 1960 Chevy sedan. The window rolled down, and they saw Uncle J. C. Phillips looking at them. This man, this brother of Janie Bea, with his massive biceps built over a lifetime of hard work and his "heavy-to-the-right" hairstyle, this stand-up guy known for his raucous storytelling and his infectious laugh, had no hint of humor in his face at that moment. They climbed in beside him and, as they rode back to Shaw, listened penitently to his gentle scolding about the unwise risk they had taken.

The eyes and ears of the tiny, tight-knit community had once again come into play. Someone had tipped off Eddie's family about his plight. The one black officer on the Shaw Police Department, a man whom folks whispered was "white controlled," had pounded on Janie Bea's door. Eddie's little brothers, James, Freddie, and Calvin, and his little sisters

Bernice and Lee Bertha, lay in their beds listening as the cop told Janie Bea the scuttlebutt, through the town's lightning-fast, word-of-mouth network: some white men in a truck had seen Eddie and Mary Sue walking down Highway 61 and were plotting to kill him.

Freddie, who was twelve at the time, remembers it as "one of the most horrifying nights" of his childhood. After that night, Eddie recalled, "Mama had nightmares that someone killed me."

Shaw's black officer came to the door often during Eddie's activist years, Freddie says. "One evening, my mother was sitting on the porch, and he came up and said that the police had taken Ed to jail. And that he had shackles on his feet and handcuffs. And my mother just fell out right there on the porch, screaming and crying," Freddie recalls with tension in his voice fifty years later. "The one thing my mother always prayed for was that her children would outlive her, because she didn't think she could stand it if she lost another child."

Eddie says he was never shackled during his several arrests. But the policeman's wild claims exemplified the superheated atmosphere enveloping Shaw. That Janie Bea would believe the hyperbole shows a town on the edge of terror.

Dennis Flannigan (center, holding up ballots) and his brother, Richard "Dick" Flannigan (to Dennis's left), join other volunteers in counting ballots cast in the Mississippi Freedom Democratic Party's mock election in November 1964. (Photo by Mary Sue Gellatly)

Shaw residents Dave Hayden and Daisy Greenwood vote in the mock election. (Photo by Mary Sue Gellatly)

On January 4, 1965, delegations from across Mississippi, including Bolivar County, gathered in Washington, D.C., to protest the seating of Mississippi's unconstitutionally elected representatives. (Photo by Mary Sue Gellatly)

Wearing his trademark black felt fedora, Eddie joined other Shaw activists for the Congressional Challenge in Washington, D.C., on January 4, 1965. (Photo by Mary Sue Gellatly)

Then known as the Pan-Am, Amzie Moore's gas station and cafe on Highway 61 was the safe zone Eddie and Mary Sue headed for when their car's tire went flat in 1965. (Photo by Lee Anna Sherman)

Now called Moore's Lounge, the building is home to the Flying Eagles Motorcycle Club. (Photo by Lee Anna Sherman)

Amzie Moore's home in Cleveland, Bolivar County, was a gathering place for civil rights leaders. (Photo by Lee Anna Sherman)

Bolivar County's Amzie Moore was a hero of the civil rights movement in Mississippi. (Photo by Lee Anna Sherman)

9

Standings

If volunteers ... and other "outside agitators" displayed
bravery in journeying to Mississippi to challenge discrimination, what about the men and women from the Deep
South who risked their jobs and homes, lives and loved
ones to join these idealistic crusaders?
—Steve Estes, in *The Civil Rights Movement*
in American Memory

Cleveland, Mississippi, February 1965

The word *freedom* was the emblem of the Mississippi
Summer Project—a broad, all-encompassing word
whose meaning extends beyond the nuts and bolts of voting,
even beyond the temporal concepts of civil rights and democracy. Freedom, as defined by *Webster's*, is "the state of being
free from the control or power of another." Synonyms are
words like *independence, liberty, self-determination*. Opposites
include *captivity, enchainment, subjugation*.

In the minds of Shaw's young activists, freedom meant
nothing less than the unboundedness of being, the limitless-
ness of a human life. As such, it was nonnegotiable. That's
why organizers called their songs freedom songs and their

schools freedom schools and their local headquarters freedom centers or freedom houses. That's also how freedom days got their name. Throughout Freedom Summer, individual city and county projects took carloads of black citizens to the nearest courthouse to register to vote. While the registrants lined up at the registrar's office, a force of sign-carrying, song-singing activists demonstrated outside.

For projects like Shaw's, which was extended for an extra year, Freedom Day lived on. On February 11, 1965, activists would caravan black citizens to the Bolivar County Courthouse in Cleveland, Mississippi, where they would attempt to register to vote. In Shaw, Eddie, Mary Sue, and their comrades in civil justice were making plans to ferry as many people as possible to the courthouse in Cleveland for voter registration and a protest march.

It was less than a week after the firebombing of their donated car and just five days after Shaw's black activists had caravanned to Cleveland to give depositions against corrupt elections officials. But if the car bombing had been meant to scare the activists, make them slink home in fear and abandon their cause, the terrorists were surely disappointed. The harder the white establishment leaned on the freedom fighters, the stronger was the pushback.

DENNIS FLANNIGAN HAD RETURNED to Shaw after being treated for impetigo in his hometown of Tacoma after picking up the infectious skin disease on his first stint in the Delta. When the impetigo cleared up, he got right back to work for social justice, making a trip to New York to raise funds for the project. Among the donations he scored was the green 1956 Chevy station wagon that was subsequently firebombed at the Freedom Center. During the twelve-hundred-mile journey from Staten Island to Shaw, which he shared with two other volunteers, the car sucked up nine quarts of oil, all the while belching noxious fumes from its tailpipe. Still, it gave wheels to the cause for a while.

Dennis had joined the Mississippi Summer Project after being expelled from the University of Puget Sound in 1963 for writing and publishing an underground newspaper called *The Brail*—a snarky mockery of the university's official paper, *The Trail*. Describing his publication as a raw and unplugged parody ("*The Onion* of its day"), Dennis, a conscientious objector, reports using "strong verbs" to vent his outrage against the Vietnam War. The entire press run of *The Brail*, one thousand copies, sold out in three hours. It also caused paroxysms of anger among the university administrators. And so Dennis was "pitched out" of the university.

He soon found another outlet for his outrage: the civil rights movement. Like Mary Sue, Dennis had grown up in a lily-white enclave in the lily-white Pacific Northwest. Washington state, like Oregon, was a place settled by immigrants from northern Europe and the United Kingdom, immigrants like his Norwegian and Irish grandparents. And like Mary Sue's hometown of Portland, Tacoma was a redlined city, where black families were excluded from most neighborhoods through real estate covenants.

Dennis shared another inheritance with Mary Sue: he was endowed with a compassionate heart, in his case reinforced by the do-unto-others teachings of the Catholic church, in which he was raised. He knew bigotry when he saw it, and it chafed at his soul, even as a child.

Something as simple as a sandwich could, for such a person, be the switch for a lightbulb moment. Dennis's lightbulb switched on one warm summer day when he was thirteen. Looking to earn a few bucks, he was mowing the lawn at a fourplex apartment owned by his older brother, James, in the Hilltop, a neighborhood of mixed ethnicity and one of the few places where Tacoma's black residents could find housing. Renters living in the plain gray building of turn-of-the-last-century vintage were mostly military families and young blue-collar workers. Around lunchtime, the door of one of the apartments opened and a young black woman, most likely the wife of an enlisted man, called out to Dennis. "Hello, child," she said, her voice pleasant, her expression kind. "You been workin' hard in the sun. I could make you a tuna sandwich if you like."

Dennis, who even in the most familiar settings was shy and awkward, felt the blood rush to his face as he fumbled for an answer. "Um, no thank you, I'm not hungry," he mumbled, looking away and turning back to his lawnmower. "Not hungry," he knew, was a lie. For one thing, he was always hungry that year as his arms and legs and feet outgrew his clothes faster than his mother could replace them. Besides, his mind while he mowed had been fixated on the double-dip chocolate cone he planned to buy at the ice cream parlor across the avenue just as soon as the grass was cut.

"She was simply offering a semi-hardworking boy a sandwich," he recalled decades later. "Why did I turn it down?

I turned it down because she was a Negro, because I didn't know any black citizens on a personal basis back then and I felt ill at ease."

As he headed toward home that evening, his conscience stung with confusion, regret, shame. He couldn't stop thinking about the kindness of the woman, a kindness he had spurned for reasons he didn't fully understand but knew were wrong. "I'm not on firm ground here," he thought or, rather, felt in the pit of his stomach, recalling the smiling face of the kind woman. The incident grabbed hold of his consciousness and never let go.

If an uneaten sandwich can steer a life, then the spurned tuna in Tacoma surely threw a curve in the life of Dennis Flannigan. After his mid-sixties stint in Mississippi, which was in itself a kind of penance, he took his first real job back home as director of the Hilltop Housing and Relocation Office in 1969. His administrative assistant was a young black woman from the neighborhood, Claudette Patterson Nash, whose parents owned the ice cream parlor where he had eaten many double-dip cones in his youth. Claudette and her family, at one time well-known gospel singers in the black community, remain close to Dennis as he nears his eightieth birthday.

Dennis's letters to friends and supporters in Tacoma during Freedom Summer were later published under the heading "Letters from Mississippi" in the University of Puget Sound newspaper, *The Trail*, which he had parodied with *The Brail*. Many years later, after Flannigan's distinguished career as a civil rights activist and four-term representative in the Washington State Legislature, the university rectified the long-ago violation of Dennis's free-speech rights by granting him an honorary doctorate. As Jessica Robinson reported on National Public Radio in 2012: "The school kicked him out for his activism in the 1960s. Now it's honoring him in part for his career in the legislature."

As FREEDOM DAY DREW near, momentum mounted in Shaw. The Freedom Center hummed with hubbub, adolescents and adults coming and going, cranking out fliers on the mimeograph machine and hand-lettering slogans like "One man, one vote" and "We shall overcome" on pieces of cardboard to make placards for the march. Anyone who was able and available walked through the black neighborhoods—Johnson's Addition and Promised Land and Boatwright and Ice House Quarter—knocking on doors and handing out fliers. Others drove out into the countryside to talk with black sharecroppers. The message was simple: Claim your rights. Secure your freedom.

A mass meeting in Shaw was planned for the evening of February 10, the night before Freedom Day. Aaron, Buddy Boy, Eddie, and Mary Sue locked up the Freedom Center and walked the three short blocks to the Church of God in Christ. They were optimistic but a little uncertain about what to expect after all their careful preparations. Would people come in numbers? Or would they dribble in, just two or three brave souls, while others avoided the risk of standing up?

Then people began to arrive. There were babies in arms. There were elders stooped with age. There were teenagers bursting with spirit. There were the church mothers, those steadfast, formidable pillars of every black church. In other, wealthier, communities, church mothers wore flamboyant hats, their vivid colors redolent on their proud heads. In Shaw, however, church mothers rarely could afford fancy headgear. Still, they raised their voices clear to the rafters with the rhythms of their faith, freedom songs derived from the hymns and gospel songs and traditional Negro spirituals that were as much a part of them as the fertile floodplain and the life-giving river and the eternal bonds of family. Now, in the era of civil rights, new renditions of those familiar songs were on the lips of activists across Mississippi as they gathered and marched and reached for their rights.

By seven o'clock, the church was packed. People crowded close together in the pews, their anticipation audible in the buzz of conversation. When the church was full to overflowing, a stanza of full-throated notes broke loose from one of the church mothers, who was sitting in her regular seat in the right front pew. The notes seemed to flow not so much from the soul of the old woman as from some hidden spring, the headwaters of a metaphysical river, an ancient, abiding river whose currents carry the history of a people.

As if someone had flipped a switch, the buzz became a chorus. The wooden church felt like the inside of a tightly stitched drum, the sound's vibrations amplified, sounds the activists felt to their bones. If, on that winter's night, anyone had walked past the little wooden church, they would have heard a joyful noise rocking and pulsing from within the rough walls. On this night before the march on the courthouse, they would have heard the lyrics from an old African-American spiritual adapted for the civil rights movement:

Ain't gonna let nobody turn me 'round, turn me 'round,
 turn me 'round!
Ain't gonna let nobody turn me 'round,
Keep on a walkin', keep on a talkin',
Marchin' up to Freedom Land!

Ain't gonna let segregation turn me 'round ...
Ain't gonna let no jailhouse turn me 'round ...
Ain't gonna let no sheriff turn me 'round ...

A church deacon rose to his feet and asked the people to bow their heads in prayer. Then Andrew Hawkins stood up and turned toward the crowd. He looked upon the faces of the men and women of Shaw. In a voice that resonated, clear and calm, in the humble church, steady with conviction, he reminded his friends and followers why voting was the keystone to equality, why their strength resided in standing together, how real power arose from collective action.

When he finished, the people stood, one by one, and testified to their resolve:

"I already went to the courthouse four times to register, and I'm goin' back tomorrow. I'll keep on goin' till they let me register!"

"If you goin' to trust God on some things, you gotta trust Him all the way. He goin' to protect us."

"I'm doin' this for my grandchildren. I won't let 'em have to live the way I had to."

"I'll quit out the field to do what's right."

"If they jail me, I'll keep on tryin'. Nothin' gonna stop me."

"If they kill me, at least my children'll know why they got to vote and why we all got to fight for justice."

The next morning, Eddie, Mary Sue, and the other young activists watched anxiously from the Freedom Center as people began to arrive. As they watched, people came in twos and threes, by foot, by car, by truck, people who by now, on this winter day in 1965, had faced down their fears. The freedom movement in Shaw had come out of the shadows.

By late morning, seventy-five people were gathered outside the center in clusters, talking among themselves, nervous but ready to go, ready to claim their rights. Cars and pickups were idling, ready to carry the activists to the courthouse. The people piled in, six or seven to a vehicle, and they rolled north on Highway 61.

Official Cleveland was ready. On the front steps of the yellow-brick courthouse, whose Gothic columns soared upward as if to point at the iron-barred windows of the jail above, deputies stood, swinging their billy clubs. Their handguns glinted in their holsters. FBI agents in white shirts and felt fedoras snapped photos of the picket line so white employers would know which employees to fire or harass. It was a déjà vu reprise of the first Freedom Day back in July 1964.

No one was surprised that the plan had leaked out. Everybody in Shaw knew there were spies among the activists—"snitches" or "Uncle Toms"—who were passing information to the White Citizens' Council and the Klan in exchange for cash or goods, even something as small as a bucket of molasses. But the spy network was expanding, growing beyond the hometown snitches who were willing to sell out their neighbors, even beyond the local white supremacists and Klansmen who had long terrorized the black residents of Shaw. Now, like spiders weaving a sticky web to ensnare their prey, the state of Mississippi, in concert with the FBI, unspooled into the little town of Shaw a series of confidential informants and special agents to gather information on the activists. It wasn't until years later that Eddie and Mary Sue learned the full extent of the spy web among them.

Running the FBI was J. Edgar Hoover, the bureau's founding director, who ruled it and its predecessor, the Bureau of Investigation, like a personal fiefdom for forty-eight years until his death of a heart attack in 1972. Hoover kept detailed records on, among others, politicians, movie stars, and civil rights leaders, using the clandestine information to threaten and manipulate people he perceived as enemies. "Hoover built his FBI files into an intimidating weapon, not just for fighting crime but also for bullying government officials and critics and destroying careers," wrote Kenneth D. Ackerman in his book *The Young J. Edgar Hoover: Hoover and the Red Scare, 1919–1920*. In a *Washington Post* opinion piece on November 9, 2011, Ackerman reported, "By 1960, the FBI had open, 'subversive' files on some 432,000 Americans."

Mary Sue was one of those nearly half-million Americans whose names were in Hoover's files.

A STATUE STANDING ON the courthouse grounds seemed to mock the activists' efforts on that so-called Freedom

Day. Atop the tall column stands a Confederate soldier at attention. Engraved on the yellow stone are the words: "To the memory of our Confederate dead, 1861–1865." Below that inscription are two crossed swords, a Confederate flag, and another inscription reading, "Dead upon the field of glory, hero fit for song and story." The bitter message—the lingering mournfulness of white southerners over their defeat in the Civil War—was not lost on anyone, black or white.

The deputies allowed only two people at a time into the courthouse to complete the long registration process. The activists wore their best clothes—boys and men in jackets and ties and dress slacks; girls and women in plaid skirts and cardigan sweaters and headscarves against the chill. While the would-be voters went in, the other activists formed a single-file line along the front of the courthouse. Carrying their hand-printed signs, they marched and sang freedom songs. White men drove pickups around the block, their shotguns propped in their gun racks with the usual menace. Across the street stood more white men, yelling racial slurs at the marchers.

At one point, Mary Sue, who was documenting the event on her Kodak Instamatic, ran out of film. As she walked toward a nearby drugstore to buy another roll, white men tailed her in their trucks, shouting, "Nigger lover!" When she got back to the courthouse with her film, she decided to go inside to see what was happening with the registration process. She strode up the steps to the main entrance and reached out to pull open the door. One of the sheriff's deputies on duty stepped in front of her, blocking her way.

"Now just hold on there, Miss," he said, his expression smug, his tone officious. "Just folks wantin' to register to vote in Bolivar County can come in."

Her anger rose up quickly, her face flushing with indignation, her mind racing with the injustice—the illegality—of this man's action, blocking a member of the public from entering a public building. She took a deep breath and considered her options. She would not be intimidated by a bully cop. Walking back down the steps, she casually rounded the corner of the building. When she was out of the cop's view, she headed for a small, unguarded side door she had noticed earlier. Glancing back over her shoulder, she stepped up to the door and pulled on the handle. It opened. She slipped in. Ha!" she thought. "I got in after all."

She hurried down the hall to the election office, where two black citizens from Shaw were trying to digest lengthy sections of the Mississippi constitution and then interpret them to the satisfaction of the elections clerk. These so-called literacy tests were required by the state constitution's "literacy clause," codified in the 1890 Mississippi state constitution explicitly to block the post–Civil War voting rights of freed slaves. As stated in that document: "Every qualified elector shall be able to read any section of the constitution of this state; or he shall be able to understand the same when read to him; or give a reasonable interpretation thereof."

In addition to interpreting passages from the constitution, prospective voters were required to present a receipt for a two-dollar "poll tax" in order to cast a ballot. Two dollars in 1965 is equivalent to fifty-five dollars today. To a sharecropper making three dollars for ten hours in the fields, this was an impossible financial burden—as, of course, it was meant to be.

After Mary Sue had observed the registration process to her satisfaction, she made a point of making her exit through the main door where the deputy was still on duty. As she strode past, she cast him a sidelong glance. His mouth fell open as he watched this audacious young woman who had dared to defy him. The college girl from Portland, Oregon, had bested the cop from Cleveland, Mississippi, and with the eyes of the North on him and his city, there wasn't a thing he could do about it. "He was furious," Mary Sue said later, a small smile suggesting the triumph she had felt back then.

By midafternoon, heavy rain began to fall, soaking the activists' carefully pressed clothes. But if they were not deterred by cops or bullies in armed pickup trucks, they weren't about to be fazed by a cloudburst. In a rare expression of civility, if not exactly compassion, the officials allowed the would-be voters to stand inside the building, out of the downpour. The picketers kept marching outside.

Not one black citizen who tried to register that Freedom Day in Cleveland passed the literacy test. On the other hand, no one was hurt or killed or locked up that day. In that sense, the action was a victory of sorts. With each action— each meeting, each march, each petition, each protest—the guaranteed rights of black citizens appeared nearer at hand. Day by day, black citizens in Mississippi were wresting full citizenship from the stranglehold of bigotry.

By then, signs that the voting-rights tide was turning could be seen in Washington, D.C. Civil rights leaders had been leaning hard on Congress and President Johnson to pass a sweeping national bill that would give teeth to enforcement of voting laws across the nation. The poll tax had been outlawed by the Twenty-Fourth Amendment to the U.S. Constitution on January 23, 1964. But Mississippi and several other Deep South states remained defiant. When Freedom Summer rolled around five months after the amendment took effect, elections officials were still charging poll taxes.

Then an epic event in American history cranked up the pressure on lawmakers. On March 7, 1965, TV viewers across the nation tuned in to the evening news to witness a sickening eruption of racial hatred. In Alabama, as voting-rights protesters led by Dr. King marched peacefully toward the Edmund Pettis Bridge between Selma and Montgomery, state troopers in riot gear took a war footing against the mostly black crowd. Swinging nightsticks and cracking whips against the demonstrators, they unleashed a spasm of brutality and cruelty that stunned America and pried loose much of the resistance in Washington, D.C.

A week later, on March 15, President Johnson made a statement to Congress that included these words: "We cannot, we must not, refuse to protect the right of every American to vote in every election that they may desire to participate in. And we ought not and we cannot and we must not wait another eight months before we get a bill. We already waited a hundred years and more, and the time for waiting is gone." The Voting Rights Act, signed into law at last on August 6, 1965, would ban states from turning away voters because of race or color and provided protection for people trying to vote. It would also provide federal examiners to register voters and require federal approval for local areas to change their voting laws or procedures. It would direct the federal government to challenge the unlawful use of poll taxes in state and local elections.

Shaw's volunteers and local activists make signs for the
Freedom Day voter-registration drive in February 1965.
(Photo by Mary Sue Gellatly)

Shaw's activists, many of them still in high school, march at
the courthouse in Cleveland, Mississippi, while adults try to
register inside. (Photo by Mary Sue Gellatly)

With deputy sheriffs and FBI agents looking on, activists march for voting rights in Bolivar County. (Photo by Mary Sue Gellatly)

Law enforcement was out in full force for Bolivar County's first Freedom Day demonstration in the summer of 1964. (Photo by Wallace Roberts)

On May 8, 1967, Bolivar County sheriff Charlie Capps (on the far left) and F. H. Nance, a member of the Mississippi Levy Control Board (on the right), met with FBI director J. Edgar Hoover (center) during their visit to FBI headquarters in Washington, D.C. (Photo courtesy of Bolivar County Library)

10

Imperatives

Picket lines
School boycotts
They try to say it's a communist plot
All I want is equality
For my sister my brother my people and me
—Nina Simone, "Mississippi Goddam"

Shaw, Mississippi, April 1965

On April 1, 1965, under an unforgiving sun, fifty activists—students, parents, townspeople, civil rights workers and volunteers—gathered at the Freedom Center, the launching point for civil rights demonstrations in Shaw. This time, the focus was schools.

Marching was not their first strategy. A month or so earlier, Shaw's black parents and students had drawn up a petition outlining their demands for better educational services for Shaw's black children and sent it off to the white superintendent and the all-white school board, as well as to the principal of McEvans School, Fred Altheimer, who was black. The petitioners requested a public hearing on these matters to be held on or before May 7.

Shaw's black citizens were done accepting crumbs for their sons and daughters. The petition was bold and direct. There was no "If you please, sir," no "If it wouldn't be too inconvenient." In fact, the petitioners didn't ask. They demanded. Their rights to equal education, they said, were being withheld. The administrators ignored the petition. The snub triggered the demonstration, organized by the Shaw chapter of the Mississippi Student Union.

Together, the people turned their faces toward McEvans High School, which everyone pronounced "Mack Evans," as if it were two words. Together, they walked, their feet kicking up puffs of dust on the dirt road, their voices rising in song. Mary Sue's alto and Eddie's tenor blended into the harmonious chorus of freedom songs like "Woke Up This Morning," a revamp of the old gospel song "I woke up this morning with my mind stayed on Jesus." The civil rights version went, in part, like this:

Woke up this mornin' with my mind stayed on freedom
Woke up this mornin' with my mind stayed on freedom
Woke up this mornin' with my mind stayed on freedom
Hallelu, hallelu, hallelujah

Walkin' and talkin' with my mind
My mind stayed on freedom
Singin and prayin' with my mind
My mind stayed on freedom
Hallelu, hallelu, hallelujah

Another freedom song that rang out that day in Shaw was based on a song written by Lester Cobb:

Ain't scared of your jails 'cause I want my freedom,
I want my freedom, I want my freedom,
Ain't scared of your jails 'cause I want my freedom,
I want my freedom now.

Ain't scared of no police dogs 'cause I want my freedom,
I want my freedom, I want my freedom,
Ain't scared of no police dogs 'cause I want my freedom
I want my freedom now.

ELEVEN YEARS HAD PASSED since the U.S. Supreme Court decided *Brown v. Board of Education*, mandating the integration of public schools. Just as Mississippi violated federal voting laws, so it flouted the ruling on schools. Shaw's schools were still segregated, still grossly unequal in per-pupil spending, teacher training, and classroom equipment, including textbooks. The white school board controlled the curriculum and limited what black children learned, particularly about black history and their own legacy as a people. "We only learned about three important black people—Eli Whitney, George Washington Carver, and Booker T. Washington," Eddie says. "We had no idea that we had anything to be proud of as a people."

While Mississippi's white educators and lawmakers squandered eleven years thumbing their noses at *Brown*, whole cohorts of students in Shaw grew up. Kids who were first-graders when the *Brown* decision came down were about to graduate from segregated McEvans School. Kids who were in cradles in 1954 were stuck in the inferior school, lagging far behind their white agemates in basic skills. For these children, a substandard education, broken by periods of chopping weeds in the spring and picking cotton in the fall, diminished their earning power and shortchanged their potential.

"We are citizens of Shaw and taxpayers, and our money helps support the schools," the petitioners asserted. They called for the hiring of qualified teachers at McEvans School. They demanded a complete library and a home economics class. They insisted on a full nine-month academic year and an end to the split session. They wanted civics lessons. "We believe," they asserted, "that the teachers have a right to teach freedom to our children and shouldn't be punished or fired because they try."

Finally, the black parents and students of Shaw demanded that their local officials follow the federal mandate established by *Brown*. Waiting, delaying, hemming, and hawing were no longer acceptable to these black citizens of the Mississippi Delta, who were by then feeling the power of their collective strength. If the established power structure in Washington, D.C., was, as it seemed, impotent to force change in the South, it would spring from the grassroots, from the people on the ground who were subject to Jim Crow every day.

Integration at all grade levels beginning in September 1965 was the nonnegotiable demand of the Shaw petitioners as they marched to the school grounds, singing together.

SPIRITS WERE HIGH AS the marchers trod the dirt road toward McEvans School. But the mood soon turned ominous. As the crowd rounded the corner of the two-story red brick school building onto the playground where they would hold their rally, several police cars rolled up. The marchers kept walking until all were assembled on the playground, where they stopped. The cat had been let out of the bag, it appeared, because standing there on the playground was Sheriff Charlie Capps. His all-white posse of deputies arrived in a crunch of dust and gravel and took up positions near the entrance. Pulling up just behind them were several Shaw police officers in their squad cars, red lights twirling.

"Y'all need to disperse," Capps called out. "Y'all need to go on home."

Instead of dispersing, the marchers broke out loudly in song.

"Y'all are under arrest!" Capps yelled at the marchers. Turning to his deputies, who by then were standing outside their cruisers eyeing the marchers with their hands on their holsters, he ordered, "Take 'em to jail!"

The cops loaded as many marchers as they could into their squad cars, hauled them to Cleveland, then came back for more. At the courthouse, all fifty were booked for disturbing the peace and refusing to obey an officer.

After they were booked, the activists were herded up a flight of stairs to the jail and led down a long, narrow concrete cell block where they were locked in cells segregated by race, gender, and age. The black girls were put into the only "juvenile cell" for underage prisoners. The black boys and men, Eddie included, were packed into one adult cell, about twenty-by-twelve-feet square. Thirteen black women were locked in a space designed for six. Mary Sue shared a cell with three white women who had been jailed for unrelated offenses, including car theft.

Thin, lumpy mattresses on steel platforms riveted to the walls served as bunks. There weren't enough platforms to go around, so the jailers hauled in extra mattresses and tossed them on the floor. Even then, not everyone could stretch out. The prisoners rested sitting up, leaning against the hard concrete walls or against one another as late afternoon sunlight leaked in through a tiny barred window.

The activists knew Mississippi jails were dangerous places—that people had been beaten, raped, and killed in cells just like the ones confining them now. Fannie Lou Hamer's brutal beating in the Winona, Mississippi, jail, which had left her with permanent injuries, was legendary in the Delta. Mary Sue, as one of Shaw's paid activists, wanted to ease the worry and tension of her comrades, especially the youngest among them. So she sang. As her cellmates sat up straight and looked at her in surprise, her voice carried up and down the cell block. Before the first verse ended, there came an echo. The girls and women had picked up the song midstanza. They clapped and rocked to the rhythms. The volume rose. As the words of liberation rang from cell to cell, the sopranos and altos soon were overlaid by tenors and baritones as the men and boys chimed in. The notes bounced off the jailhouse walls, resounding around the concrete corners and down the dim corridors.

The irony of freedom songs, anthems of black liberation, filling the cells of a Mississippi jail may have been lost on the jailers. But it wasn't lost on the freedom fighters of Shaw.

The songs died out. A few hours passed. The captive activists were dozing uncomfortably in the heat. Suddenly, Mary Sue awoke to her name being called. She looked up, sleepy eyed, from her flimsy mattress. "Mary Sue Gellatly," the guard was saying as he unlocked the cage door with a big key and slid it open with the screech of metal on metal. "Come on now," he ordered. "You're wanted downstairs."

"What's this about?" she asked, suddenly wide awake. But the guard said nothing. Smoothing the wrinkles out of her cotton skirt, she followed him along the cell block and down the metal stairs to the main floor of the courthouse. The jailer stopped outside an office door stenciled with the words "Bolivar County Sheriff." Opening the door, the guard nodded toward Mary Sue, indicating that she should enter. "Here she is, Sheriff."

Sitting behind a big oaken desk was Charlie Capps, the man who had ordered her arrest on the schoolgrounds just hours earlier. Described by journalist Bruce Watson as "a thin, dapper plantation owner," Capps was dressed in a dark blue suit, a white shirt, and a tie. He looked "very much like a businessman," Mary Sue recalls. She was aware that despite his reputation as one of the state's few moderate sheriffs and his prestigious role as president of the Mississippi Sheriff Association, he was also president of the White Citizen's Council in Bolivar County. She stood in front of Sheriff Capps's desk, holding her chin high and her shoulders back. She looked him in the eye and waited for him to speak.

The sheriff cleared his throat as he stared up at the young woman from Oregon. In a tone Mary Sue described later as that of a "smooth talker," Capps informed her that he had received a phone call from Bishop Raymond Grant, the Methodist bishop for the state of Oregon, where Mary Sue had been active in her neighborhood church. Bishop Grant had made it clear to the sheriff that he and other prominent Oregonians were keeping a close eye on what was happening to Mary Sue in Mississippi. He had issued a veiled warning: nothing bad had better happen to the young Oregon activist while she was confined in Capps's jail.

Capps's indignation was undisguised. The bishop's inference was that Mississippi was less than civilized, the sheriff groused, frowning at Mary Sue. Capps was just getting warmed up. He demanded to know why a nice white girl like Mary Sue was meddling in Mississippi's affairs. Everything would have been just fine, he asserted, if outsiders like her had stayed out of his state. Mary Sue stood still and silent as Capps ranted and rambled for another ten minutes. "He treated me like a misguided girl," she recalls.

Finally, Capps waved his hand at the guard, indicating that he was done with this miscreant from the alien state of Oregon. Walking back to her cell, she felt her repressed anger rising, as it had so many times during her months in the South. The call from Bishop Grant was a reminder of why she and hundreds of other white students from the North had been recruited to Mississippi. The "outsiders" so reviled by the editor of the *Bolivar Commercial* and Sheriff Capps, "invaders" like Mary Sue Gellatly, aimed an unprecedented spotlight on the recalcitrant state. When word of her arrest reached Bishop Grant, her own safety was assured, as was the safety of her black comrades. Acutely aware that northern leaders like Bishop Grant were looking over Mississippi's shoulder, Klansmen and other white supremacists were forced to rein in the worst of their racist behaviors, at least for a while.

While the activists languished in their cells, news of their arrest rocketed through Bolivar County's neighbor-to-neighbor network. Some of the area's black growers, including Mack Carter, put up their property as collateral for bail. Money flowed in, too, from supporters in the North. Civil rights lawyers jumped into action. By evening, all the activists were set free. But they weren't off the hook. A trial date was set. Later in the month, their attorneys moved the case to the federal district court, seeking a fairer trial venue. Eventually, the case was dismissed.

SHAW'S ACTIVISTS, FULLY AWARE of their First Amendment rights of free expression, never asked permission to march, figuring that the mayor would turn down their requests anyway. It was no coincidence that four days after the school demonstration, Shaw's all-white council of aldermen passed this law:

> An ordinance to regulate and prevent the blocking of traffic on the streets of the Town of Shaw, Mississippi and setting for the purposes for which said streets and sidewalks are maintained by the Town and making it unlawful for any person or persons, with certain exceptions, to parade or march or to sit, kneel, or recline, or otherwise obstruct said streets and sidewalks, or to engage in public speaking, group shouting, or group singing or to assemble in organized

groups carrying signs, on the sidewalks or streets of said Town, or to interfere with the normal use of sidewalks and streets, without written permission from the mayor and providing that this ordinance be effective as provided by law.

Less than two months later, the activists chalked up one small victory when this anti-picketing law—whose validity had been challenged in district court by lawyers with the Lawyers Constitutional Defense Committee (LCDC) of the American Civil Liberties Union (ACLU)—was found to be unconstitutional. On June 1, 1965, U.S. District Court judge Claude Clayton—who had presided over a number of civil rights trials, including the trial of the law officers who had beaten Fannie Lou Hamer in the jail in Winona, Mississippi, and trials regarding the desegregation of the school systems in Sunflower and Bolivar Counties—issued a temporary injunction voiding the ordinance on the grounds that it was an unconstitutional abridgement of free speech.

THE DRAMA AROUND SHAW'S black schools, it turned out, was far from over. One night just days after the activists' march and arrest, McEvans School was vandalized. The damage was extensive. On June 18, twenty-nine black youths were arrested and charged with the vandalism. Mary Sue is adamant that whoever wrecked the school, their actions weren't connected to or condoned by the organizers or leaders of Shaw's civil rights movement. But when questioned by authorities, several of the arrested youths reportedly fingered some of Shaw's leading civil rights leaders and activists—Andrew Hawkins,

George Shelton, Robert "Bob" Weil, and Mary Sue. They reportedly claimed that the four had urged them to trash the school. The other students, however, refused to falsely accuse their leaders. Two of the youths later told attorneys that the police had painfully shocked them with electric cattle prods—the precursors to stun guns—to force their statements.

As outlandish as this might sound to American sensibilities, there were plenty of examples of cops using cattle prods on human protesters during this era. Cattle prods "became symbolic of Southern resistance to the civil rights movement in the 1960s," noted a 1981 *New York Times* article entitled "Alabama Prisoners Are Accusing Police of Using 60's Cattle Prods."

Based on the coerced confessions, Mary Sue and the three other leaders were arrested and jailed on June 26. Once again, prominent people from the North were notified of her incarceration. This time instead of a bishop, it was a ten-term congresswoman who had attended Mary Sue's alma mater, Willamette University, who rattled the cage of racism in Bolivar County.

Edith Green, a Democrat who championed women's rights, called the Bolivar County jail to demand information on Mary Sue's safety. When Green was stonewalled by the jailers, the congresswoman contacted the FBI. The FBI, in turn, contacted Sheriff Capps and told him that "a Congresswoman named Green from the state of Oregon" had unsuccessfully tried to get "telephonic contact" with Mary Sue while she was in jail. According to an FBI memo dated June 26, Capps's excuse for not putting Green through was a shortage of personnel. "The only man on duty is the jailer, and therefore, [Capps] has set a policy of not allowing any incoming phone calls to prisoners as a security measure when only one man is on duty. He has insufficient personnel to handle such situations." Capps informed the FBI that Mary Sue had been released on a five-hundred-dollar bond. He also let the FBI know that "Mary Sue Gellatly apparently has some connection with the National Council of Churches, in Portland, Oregon," as he had had "inquiry from the head of that organization about her on several occasions," and furthermore had "a teletype from a William B. Kate, Executive Secretary, Greater Portland, Oregon, Council of Churches, sent sometime back seeking information as to her welfare."

Meanwhile, the U.S. Department of Justice sprang into action. John Doar, deputy assistant attorney general for civil rights, ordered the Jackson FBI to investigate the charges against Mary Sue, the circumstances of her arrest, and the amount of bail paid for her release. Doar was a seasoned civil rights advocate, having walked through a white mob with black student James Meredith in 1963 when Meredith had integrated the University of Mississippi. In fact, Mary Sue had seen Doar in person and heard him speak when he made an appearance at her Freedom Summer training in Ohio.

On July 6, 1965—just a few days after Congresswoman Green contacted the FBI—a confidential source recounted to FBI director Hoover in a four-page memo a series of arrests, charges, jailings, bail payments, and other details regarding Mary Sue. Subsequently, according to several FBI memos, Sheriff Capps assured the feds that everything in his jurisdiction was just fine and no interviews would be necessary. After all, he implied, Mary Sue was nothing but trouble, as anyone could see by reading her lengthy rap sheet. The FBI apparently took his word for it. In any case, the agents did not interview Mary Sue.

Capps may have won this round. But he was by then painfully aware that Mary Sue's home-state network was keeping a close eye on him and his activities.

HELP FROM THE NORTH propped up the Shaw project more than once. Sometimes, it came in unexpected ways. On April 16, 1965—two weeks after the school march—Mary Sue was teaching a class of preschoolers at the Freedom Center when she noticed outside the window a caravan of three cars rolling slowly down the dirt road, all driven by white males. Whenever caravans of white males passed through the black neighborhood of Johnson's Addition, the activists made records, as they had been trained to do. Mary Sue hurriedly jotted down their Mississippi license plate numbers. In case anything happened, she would have evidence of possible perpetrators.

That afternoon, she was still on high alert when she noticed another car slowing down outside the center. As she again grabbed her pencil and notepad to take down the license number, she realized that the plate was not from Mississippi but Wisconsin, "America's Dairyland." She was mystified. License plates from Wisconsin or any other state outside the Deep South were rarely seen in Shaw.

Before she could puzzle out this new development, she saw a middle-aged white couple, dressed casually in cotton and khaki, climb out of the front seat and open the back doors, from which two young children, a boy and a girl, stepped out. The woman took the little girl's hand and the four, looking around tentatively, climbed the Freedom Center's old wooden steps. The man knocked on the door. Although the foursome seemed nonthreatening in every respect, Mary Sue still harbored some nervousness from the morning's suspicious car caravan. So it was with a bit of anxiety that she opened the door.

The warm smiles that greeted her dispelled her worries. The unexpected visitors, she learned, were Ivan Kaste, a journalist for the *Waukesha Freeman* newspaper, his wife, Nissley, a social worker also trained in journalism, and their two kids, twelve-year-old Fred and ten-year-old Betsy. The Kastes belonged to the Waukesha chapter of the Women's International League for Peace and Freedom (WILPF), founded in the early 1900s by social reformer and suffragette Jane Addams. The Waukesha league had adopted Shaw—chosen because of the rhyming of their towns' names—and had been sending books, clothing, and other donations for the past year. The Kastes explained that they were on a spring break trip to the South and had stopped in Shaw to see the project firsthand while dropping off donations of money and supplies.

The Kaste family had arrived in Shaw's postage-stamp-sized downtown earlier that afternoon. Uncertain how to find the SNCC office, Ivan had hailed a white policeman standing outside the "cop shop," as Eddie and Mary Sue called the police station. "Excuse me, officer," he said. "We need some directions." Walking up to the car, the cop leaned down and smiled pleasantly at the white travelers. "Sure, Mister. Where do y'all want to go?"

When Ivan said, "We're looking for the Freedom Center," the officer's smile vanished faster than a startled badger dives into its burrow. He stood bolt upright and stepped back from the car. His demeanor hardened like three feet of Delta mud in a drought. In the mind of the cop, this friendly white family seeking directions had morphed into dangerous subversives, troublemakers, agitators—outsiders who were unwelcome in his segregated town. Speaking through a clenched jaw, he reluctantly pointed the Kastes toward the Freedom Center. Later on, Betsy told her parents how scared she had been, sitting in the backseat during the exchange. The officer's tone, seeping out from attitudes she couldn't begin to understand at the time, felt threatening to the ten-year-old child.

Mary Sue showed them around the three-room Freedom Center, pointing out the bookshelves stocked with three thousand volumes, many of them donated by WILPF. Then she got behind the wheel of the old donated car and drove the Kastes around town and out along the country roads hemming in the cottonfields, introducing them to some of the local activists. Flossie Minley of the generous heart cooked lunch for them at her tiny restaurant.

Back at the Freedom Center, as the Kastes bade farewell to Mary Sue, a squad car crept out from behind some shrubbery. Mary Sue learned later that the cop tailed the Kastes until they were well out of town.

In a follow-up article in the *Waukesha Freeman*, the largest newspaper in Wisconsin's Waukesha County, Ivan Kaste described his impressions as he and his family journeyed through Mississippi along Highway 61: "We passed many dilapidated shacks housing Negro families. With their slanting roofs, crowded front porches and unpainted siding, these homes might well have been standing from Civil War days.... About eighty-five miles south of the Tennessee border, we left Route 61 temporarily and drove into Shaw, a village of about 2,000. The road into Shaw runs parallel to a sluggish stream called a bayou." Describing Mary Sue as "an attractive girl in her mid-twenties," he wrote that "in a different setting, she could easily pass for a junior league socialite."

When Mary Sue next received a package from the Kastes and found the "Southern Travels" article tucked inside, she laughed out loud at the irony of this depiction. Despite her respectable—some would say conservative—appearance, Mary Sue would have found little in common with many of the prominent women who have graced the ranks of the Junior League over the years. These women have included social and political luminaries such as former first ladies Nancy Reagan and Barbara Bush, child actress-turned-politician Shirley Temple Black, U.S. Supreme Court justice Sandra Day O'Connor, and Mary Pillsbury Lord, granddaughter of the Pillsbury Company's founding titan.

Ivan went on to write a series of articles about the Mississippi Summer Project for the *Waukesha Freeman*. As letters to the editor from members of other WILPF chapters poured into the *Freeman*, donations to the Shaw project continued to grow over the next three years.

The Kastes' affiliation with the league, however, elicited more than books and pencils and hand-me-downs for Shaw's project. It also brought the spotlight of suspicion. In June

1965, two months after the Kastes dropped in on Mary Sue at the Freedom Center, headlines in Mississippi newspapers trumpeted WILPF's alleged ties to communist ideologies and smeared Mary Sue with guilt by association. As reported by the *Jackson Daily News* on June 28, Mary Sue had "solicited out-of-state funds" from the league "to buy food for starving Negroes in and around Shaw."

Asserting that the league "has a long record of subversive activities," the article quoted a Mississippi state official named Erle Johnston Jr., commissioner director of the Mississippi State Sovereignty Commission. He had unearthed congressional testimony from 1938 about the league's alleged ties to communist and socialist groups. The testimony, besides being a quarter-century old, came from the archives of the House Committee on Un-American Activities, notorious in the 1950s for dragging countless Americans in front of its klieg lights and cameras to accuse them of subverting the American system with their left-wing ideologies.

IN THE SHORT TERM, nothing much changed in Shaw's black schools as a result of the march on McEvans. Still, the petition and jailings brought attention to the gross inequities suffered by black children year after year. It was only one action, barely noticeable by itself. But it added power to the collective activism that was rocking the South, much of it documented by broadcast and newspaper reporters. During the civil rights struggle of those pivotal years in the mid-sixties, even Bolivar County made national headlines from time to time, most notably Sheriff Capps's statement in the

New York Times about Mississippi's "happy blacks." In the limelight or not, Shaw's freedom fighters carried on. Progress was gradual, but come it would, even to Shaw.

One drop plus one drop plus one drop more, sooner or later an ocean makes.

Attorney John Doar with the U.S. Department of Justice
warns Freedom Summer volunteers about the risks they will
face. (Photo from www.crmvet.org)

The Bolivar County jail was housed on the upper floor of the courthouse. (Photo by Lee Anna Sherman)

Mary Sue and Eddie were each jailed multiple times in this cell block at the Bolivar County Courthouse in Cleveland, Mississippi. (Photo by Lee Anna Sherman)

Cells where Mary Sue, Eddie, and other activists were lodged offered little space and less comfort. (Photo by Lee Anna Sherman)

11

Stoppages

Why buy the white man steak
when you can't hardly eat neckbones?
—Mississippi Freedom Labor Union organizing flier

Shaw, Mississippi, April through August 1965

Spring was greening the fields and footpaths of the Mississippi Delta. In the slow-moving waterways, the bayous and bogues of Bolivar County—the Porter, the Silver, the Snake, the Knox, the Hasty—gopher frogs and mud snakes and buffalo fish were stirring. Squadrons of dragonflies patrolled the swamps in the gathering heat, their translucent wings catching and holding the light. Under the surface of the earth, long-slumbering cicadas waited for the heat of the summer to warm the soil and wake them in their hidden places of repose.

In Shaw, tensions were heating up along with the thermometer. It was going on a year since a battalion of idealistic college students and young lawyers from the North had arrived as workers and witnesses to Mississippi's civil rights struggle. Nine months had passed since Sheriff Capps had informed the *New York Times* that Bolivar County's blacks were happy as clams. Shaw's white residents were increasingly on edge. The fabric of southern life was being turned inside out. The future of towns like Shaw, which not long ago had seemed permanently carved into the concrete edifice of race and class, was looking more and more like a blank slate. No one could predict what would be written there next.

The kettle of unrest that had been simmering in Bolivar County for more than two years was about to boil over.

At the Freedom Center, an idea had been percolating for several months. A union of farmworkers—like the unions of autoworkers and truckdrivers and dockworkers in the North—would empower the local labor force to demand fair wages and working conditions. By banding together, the families whose joint labor kept King Cotton thriving in the Delta could bargain collectively against the planters. In March, nearly a hundred people, most of them local black activists, had canvassed the black neighborhoods of Shaw and the plantation shacks to begin seeding the idea of unionizing. The idea was taking hold.

One afternoon in early April, shortly after the school demonstration, Aaron German, Andrew Hawkins, George "Buddy Boy" Shelton, eighteen-year-old Charles Bond (who was "family-connected kin" to Eddie), and Mary Sue huddled at the Freedom Center and began to flesh out the idea, outlining the details of a plan. A mass meeting was set for April 9. The activists would present their proposal to the community. Word spread fast. When the day arrived, expectations among Shaw's black citizens were at full throttle.

The mood at the meeting was electric. George, Andrew, Aaron, and Charles stood before the crowd, while Mary Sue, as usual, kept a low profile in the back. This was—always had been—a local fight. They talked about the strength of solidarity, about the power of collective action. They talked about the impact of a work stoppage on the planters' profits. Aware that FBI informants likely were in the crowd that night, they even dared to utter the word "strike"—a refusal to work unless their demands were met.

That night, the Mississippi Freedom Labor Union—the MFLU—was officially born. The elected leaders were young men still in their teens. Eighteen-year-old George Shelton was chosen president. Aaron German, age nineteen, was named vice president. The people who were gathered in the church decided, together, that they would demand an hourly wage of a dollar and twenty-five cents, the federal minimum wage at the time. That meant a worker now taking home three dollars after ten hours in the field (thirty cents an hour) would earn twelve dollars and fifty cents for the same shift. No one, not even the most optimistic among them, expected the planters to accede to any raise in wages at all, let alone a fourfold increase. They agreed to strike if their demands weren't met.

A strike seemed inevitable.

Early the next morning, the activists gathered at the Freedom Center in high spirits. Mary Sue got on the WATS line and called in the news to headquarters in Jackson: a union had been formed. Like a wildfire crackling down a tinder-dry hillside, the news spread across Mississippi and into other southern states. The phone in the Freedom Center started ringing, the callers clamoring for information on how to form a union branch in their community.

Shaw's activists shifted into high gear, cranking out organizing fliers on the mimeo machine to rally the workers—fliers with words like these:

> Why make your child work for low wages when you all of your life have been working for nothing? Why buy the white man steak when you can't hardly eat neckbones? As cheap as chicken is, you can't eat it but once a week on Sunday. Wake up and think. We as Negroes should want to be equal and get high wages. For over two hundred years we have been working for nothing. Please join the union, because if you are not in a union, you just aren't anywhere.

When the union organizers took their wage demands to the planters, they were met with ridicule. The workers declared a strike. More than one hundred people, the pickers and choppers of the Bolivar County cotton industry, stayed away from the fields. Work on the plantations ground to a halt.

Fannie Lou Hamer jumped into the union cause within a week of its formation in Shaw. For her, the union signaled a paradigm shift in civil rights actions. Yes, the union was organized "to address the age-old lack of economic opportunity experienced by black Deltans," as author Chana Kai Lee writes in her book, *For Freedom's Sake.* Yes, it was formed "to fight against the immediate problem of exploitation of day laborers." But in Hamer's mind, unionizing was a radical act of self-determination for black laborers. And it was personal—as personal as a finger prick from a thorny cotton boll.

Hamer became the union's "adopted leader and figurehead," according to Lee. "Their plight was one Hamer shared." Elaborating, Lee says:

> She was the rank and file's role model; she was a former sharecropper and political activist. In a symbolic sense, Hamer was the personification of a kind of historical force that created conditions for the existence of the Mississippi Freedom Labor Union. Her life, work, and suffering constituted a necessary precedent to the MFLU; her publicly lived experience in the civil rights movement inspired a parallel movement among farmers and other exploited laborers.... Hamer's courageous tale was told and retold throughout the Delta between 1962 and 1964, creating a lush environment of boldness and daring for the growth of independent alternative organizations such as unions and cooperatives. In many ways Hamer had helped establish an inspirational and institutional foundation for the MFLU.

Meanwhile, the U.S. Department of Agriculture was set to meet in Greenville, a Delta town on the banks of the Mississippi River twenty-five miles from Shaw, to discuss farm policy. Black workers and families—workers who would directly gain or lose from any policy decisions made at the meeting—were not on the participant list. As one union organizer said, "The conference dealt with the fate of thousands of Negroes and none of us were invited to participate."

The first day of the meeting, Fannie Lou Hamer and six others walked in, and the second day, even more civil rights workers found their way into the premises, while sixty others picketed outside the building. Mrs. Hamer read the labor union forms aloud, and Andrew Hawkins stood up to ask a question.

With this success, small as it was, the union continued to grow. The union leaders held a workshop to further unite the union branches, and more than one hundred people attended, coming in not only from all over Bolivar County but also from neighboring counties such as Panola, Washington, Humphreys, Sharkey, and Issaquena. This group decided to set up a state office in Shaw, to be headquartered in the Freedom Center. They also discussed the possibility of setting up northern support groups for the union by writing to their relatives in the North and asking them to organize. Plans to help people who had walked off the fields or gotten thrown off plantations started taking shape.

As soon as the local activists started talking about forming a union, the city police and county sheriff stepped up arrests, and the White Citizens' Council doubled down on their spying and scare tactics. But white intimidation as a reliable go-to tool was getting rusty. Instead of meekly retreating to the cotton fields, hoes in hand, workers were joining forces to stand up for justice. They were wielding their greatest power: withholding labor. Their action—forming a union and striking for higher wages and better working conditions—was not only unprecedented in Shaw; it had been unimaginable before the SNCC initiative.

BUT THE UNION COULDN'T hold on for long. The strike had been called so quickly after the union formed that no safety net for striking workers had been put in place. Reports circulated that donated food from the North had been waylaid by corrupt elements. Freedom gardens went into cultivation quickly, but it would be months before they yielded fresh produce to feed the strikers and their families.

One such garden was at the farm of the Robert Watts family in Choctaw, a tiny community among the endless farm fields of Bolivar County. Their daughter Bernice had grown up in a "little red house" on the family's sixty-seven acres, where they raised cotton at first and then corn. "There was corn all around the house," Bernice recalls. "It was like a wilderness." Bernice was in high school when the MFLU formed. Her family, among a handful of black landowners in the area, made a patch of land available to the strikers.

"During the strike, we had a freedom garden on our property, about an acre," recalls Bernice, who still lives on the property. "Also, there was one in Ruleville." The Watts family's courage to stand with the strikers put them on the radar of white terrorists. When asked if she was afraid, Bernice answers without hesitation, "Oh, yeah, mmm-hmm." No one got hurt, she says, but "they did burn a cross out at our mailbox."

With plans to grow beans, greens, and "things you could eat immediately without cooking," Eddie, Mary Sue, and their fellow activists rode out to Choctaw to clear the weeds and vines from the new garden patch. Once the brush was cleared, Mr. Watts tilled the soil to make it ready. When Mary Sue woke up the morning after clearing the garden patch, her legs and arms were breaking out in an itchy, bumpy rash. At the drugstore in downtown Shaw, the pharmacist looked at her reddened skin and clicked his tongue. He told her she had poison ivy and sold her a tube of calamine lotion.

Meanwhile, out on the plantations, growers weren't about to sit by and watch their fields go untended and their profits sag. The new union threatened the keystone of white power in the Delta, King Cotton, the economic base of Bolivar County. When black sharecroppers' kids went hungry, as they so often did, the planters were unmoved. Not so when hardship menaced their own "freckle-faced" kids. They sensed that their comfy way of life was slipping out of their hands one stalk of cotton at a time.

Rather than meet their workers' demands or even negotiate, the growers sent their black drivers to round up scabs, workers from nearby towns and counties who were willing to break the strike. They offered extra pay to the drivers whose job it was to deliver workers to the fields in their pickup trucks in hopes that those men would urge people to break the strike and come back to the fields.

On June 1, 1965, Mary Sue, who by then was living with a host family by the name of Ferguson, and Eddie both got up with the sun. They positioned themselves in front of Joe Canonici's grocery store, one of Shaw's daily pickup sites for fieldworkers. As the workers started arriving for the six o'clock pickup, the activists urged them to join the strike. Mr. Howard Sias, a longtime driver, rumbled up in his rickety truck, and several workers, including Eddie's younger siblings James, Freddie, and Lee Bertha, climbed in. The three younger Shorts, who were school-aged, still lived with their mama in the shack by the railroad tracks. She needed the income their fieldwork brought to the household. So even though their big brother was on strike with the union, they were obliged to keep working.

Just as Mr. Sias was about to steer toward the fields, Mary Sue and Eddie jumped into the bed of the truck with the workers. Tensions were thick as Eddie and Mary Sue urged the workers to join the strike. Mr. Sias, who could see what was happening in his rearview mirror, was furious. He warned them that he had instructions from the Boss Man to carry activists and recalcitrant workers straight to jail in Cleveland.

Sixteen-year-old James grabbed twelve-year-old Freddie and they jumped off the truck, heading to a nearby store to make a phone call to SNCC headquarters to report the incident. Seeing his daily pay shrinking before his eyes—drivers were paid by the planters fifty cents per worker delivered to the fields—Mr. Sias suddenly gunned the truck and sped away with six people still in the back, Eddie, Mary Sue, and fifteen-year-old Lee Bertha among them. He raced to the county courthouse, where all six were arrested and charged with "malicious trespass."

When Eddie's mama, Janie Bea, learned that her daughter was in jail, she was furious at Mr. Sias. How could this lifelong acquaintance take Lee Bertha, who was only fifteen years old, to jail? He had driven right past the family's house with his truckload of hostage workers. Why hadn't he dropped the girl off at home? Janie Bea declared that her children would never ride in Mr. Sias's truck again.

Her decision was consequential, as it turned out. Only a week later, on the last day of chopping season, Mr. Sias was driving a load of nonstriking workers to the cottonfields, all of them packed into the bed of the truck. As he drove down Highway 61, a speeding semitruck slammed into the old pickup from behind. Four workers were killed and several others badly injured. Because of their mama's refusal to let them ride with Mr. Sias, James, Freddie, and Lee Bertha were not on the truck that morning. When they heard the news, despite their sorrow for their bereaved neighbors, the Short family felt the hand of God in their near miss.

A COUPLE WEEKS LATER, Eddie was away on a fund-raising trip to a church in Connecticut and Mary Sue was on duty alone at the Freedom Center. She was smoothing calamine lotion onto her painful, puffy calves when the front door burst open and banged into the wall with a crash. Startled, she watched a ruddy-faced man wearing a Bolivar County deputy's uniform storm in. "Are you Mary Sue Gellatly?" the deputy demanded. When she said yes, he snarled, "Well, then, you're under arrest." When she asked to know why, he repeated his statement and ordered her to come with him. She tucked her poison-ivy medicine into her purse and climbed into the backseat of the squad car.

She was getting used to the drill at the courthouse—the mug shots and fingerprinting—because this was her fifth arrest. When the officer took away her purse to lock it up with the other prisoners' personal belongings, she protested that she needed the lotion for her poison ivy. He looked at her with a smirk, as if it gave him pleasure to deny her. He then led her to the cell block on the second floor of the old courthouse, put her in a cell, and slammed the barred door shut, locking it behind him.

For five days, Mary Sue sat on the lumpy mattress in the cell awaiting trial for an unknown charge as her legs swelled and developed big, oozing sores. The pain and itching were almost unbearable. Meals were skimpy and came only twice a day (she remembers eating a lot of baloney sandwiches behind bars)—meals for which she would be charged on her release.

On the fourth day of her imprisonment, she was looking outside through the steel bars of her cell's tiny window, wondering when she would be freed.

Then she saw Eddie striding across the gravel parking lot. Just below her second-story cell, he stopped and looked up. She waved furiously through the bars. His face broke into a huge grin when he caught sight of her. Despite the itchy poison ivy and the anxiety and uncertainty of her plight, Mary Sue felt a warm tingle of joy as she looked at this man, so steadfast, so reassuring in his unwavering commitment to her and to the civil rights movement. She realized with a pang how much she had missed him while he was away. Bewildered by what she was feeling, she was unsettled by the sensation of warmth that was washing over her. She brushed it off as just a reaction to the loneliness of being locked up.

Finally, on the fifth day, she heard footsteps coming down the long, narrow cell block. A deputy, jangling a big ring of keys, stopped outside her cell. Unlocking the grated door, he told Mary Sue she was free to go and handed back her purse with the calamine lotion inside. The charge against her, "malicious mischief," stemmed from her Constitutionally protected civil rights activities in Shaw. But the trumped-up charge was a flimsy cover for her true offense. As the project director for Shaw's civil rights movement, Mary Sue was a threat to the status quo. With the eyes of the nation watching Mississippi's resistance to change, local law enforcement wouldn't dare harm the white college girl from Oregon, at least not with anything worse than harassment and intimidation. Throwing her in jail, making her sit on a hard bench and sleep on a thin, lumpy mattress for five days as her poison ivy sores blistered and oozed, was a transparent attempt to scare the tall, thin, opinionated girl from the Pacific Northwest. If she would only slink away on a Greyhound bus headed north, the officials figured, all the tension and unrest in Shaw would surely settle down.

But the civil rights movement in Mississippi showed no signs of slowing down. Despite nonstop editorials in the *Bolivar Commercial* decrying "invaders from the North" who, like Mary Sue, were fomenting unrest across Mississippi, the protests persisted. Even in the face of ugly threats aimed at black activists—the same brand of warning that spurred Willie James Short's move to Chicago nearly a decade earlier—intrepid local activists like Eddie kept knocking on doors, drumming up new voters, and urging folks to join the movement, get active, stand up to the Boss Man. Homegrown heroes like Fannie Lou Hamer gave the lie to the white establishment's mythology about contented black citizens who had been perfectly happy with their lot in life until "agitators" showed up from the North.

"We claimed the word 'agitator,'" Mary Sue says, looking back on those days. "We pointed out that in a washing machine, the agitator was what got the dirt out."

Black Mississippians, "sick and tired of being sick and tired" in the immortal words of Mrs. Hamer, stepped up in ever-greater numbers to claim their rights. Their bravery was infectious.

The white authorities, however, had brought out their cruelest strategy thus far. In today's parlance, it might be called the nuclear option. The state welfare department began withholding welfare checks and food allotments from striking families who depended on the federal commodities program to supplement their penurious wages. Times became desperate for many striking families. Faced with hunger, some went back to the fields.

Still, the strike went on.

BIG LABOR UNIONS IN the North—the AFL-CIO, the United Auto Workers, the Teamsters—heard about Mississippi's union and sent funds to supplement local fund-raising efforts. SNCC helped too, although its resources were spread paper-thin among local movements. On June 29, 1965, retaliation by local bankers was detailed in a WATS report from Cleveland to headquarters in Jackson. "The first National Bank in Cleveland has cancelled the MFLU accounts and refused to reopen them," the report stated. "The manager, Mr. Collier, said the reason was because they didn't agree with the policies of the union. This bank is a member of the Federal Reserve."

On July 15, the collective voice of Shaw's fieldworkers was heard in the nation's capital. At the invitation of the House Committee on Labor and Public Welfare, whose members included Oregon congresswoman Edith Green, Andrew Hawkins and Aaron German testified to the fact that federal cotton subsidies "go only to landowners and never to sharecroppers." *The Movement*, the monthly newspaper published by SNCC and distributed to various groups sponsoring projects in Mississippi, reported that Hawkins also called out Senator Eastland for unfair and unethical practices on his Bolivar County plantation. Eastland's workers, Hawkins testified, "received such low wages they were forced to operate illegal liquor stills to supplement their income." Hawkins also charged Eastland with using prison labor on his farm.

In August, George Shelton, president of the union, sent an open letter to readers of *The Movement*:

Dear Friends,

I am a member of the Miss. Freedom Labor Union and we need help badly, such as money and food. There are 100 people on strike here and need help. … They are striking for $1.25 an hour.

Your truly, George Shelton

Friends of SNCC and other groups in the North sent food, clothing, and money. In other areas, such as Greenville, the Delta Ministry provided help to strikers who had been evicted from their plantation shacks. A tent city rose up in Greenville, an event that was covered extensively by the press.

One afternoon, on the way to Memphis on union business, Aaron German, Buddy Boy, Eddie, and a couple of other activists wrecked their car in northern Bolivar County. Sheriff's deputies took them into custody. They were met at the courthouse by Sheriff Capps.

"You boys, this fine will cost you thirty-seven dollars, and if you ain't got that, we gonna have to take you upstairs [to the jail]," the sheriff reportedly said. Buddy Boy, who as union president had just received a donation from a union in the North, reached into his pocket and pulled out a one-hundred-dollar bill. The sheriff was furious.

"Nigger," he said, "if I'd known you had that much money, I woulda charged y'all a hundred!" The group didn't wait around. They hailed a cab and, for a twenty-dollar fare, got safely back to Shaw.

At its peak, the union had 1,325 members across Mississippi, with 350 people on strike in various counties. Other states were following Mississippi's lead, with Tennessee, Louisiana, and Arkansas forming their own freedom labor unions. Organizing and joining a labor union in the South were acts of great courage. The risks were huge. On the day William Springfield, a black tractor driver in Fayette County, Tennessee, was elected chairman of that state's union, he was fired from his job.

In Shaw, there was no conflict between the union and the larger civil rights movement—as there was in some localities—because the union activists and the civil rights activists were one and the same. They simply layered union work on top of their voter-registration work, freedom schools, canvassing, and mass meetings. "People in Shaw recognized that civil rights and economic opportunities were intrinsically connected," Mary Sue says.

THE MFLU RAISED NEW hackles in the southern white establishment. Even liberal and moderate commentators became alarmed when the fieldworkers laid down their hoes. Agitating for voting rights was one thing. But demanding fair pay—and withholding labor to get it—was a bridge too far. By supporting the fieldworkers' strike, civil rights leaders in the Delta had, in the words of *Chicago Daily News* staff writer Nicholas von Hoffman in July 1965, abandoned reason and nonviolence in favor of "revolutionary turmoil" and "hard-nose, stop-at-nothing, ultra-revolutionary" tactics.

Although Mary Sue's voting-rights work in Shaw had drawn the ire of Sheriff Charlie Capps, it was her leadership in the fieldworkers' union that cranked up surveillance to full bore. When news of the union's formation leaked out of Shaw, Mary Sue's name began popping up in scurrilous newspaper stories. For instance, a story under the headline, "Delta CR Worker Linked to Reds: State Agency Brands Shaw Woman," ran in the *Jackson Daily News* on June 28, 1965.

It's notable that Mary Sue had been canvassing, picketing, teaching, and organizing in and around Shaw throughout the fall of 1964 and the winter of 1965 without being arrested. But the minute the fieldworkers unionized, the target on Mary Sue's back glowed neon. Between April 1 and June 18, 1965, she was arrested five times, accused of sham charges (disturbing a session of public school, malicious mischief, malicious trespass, destruction of public property, and contributing to the delinquency of a minor)—charges she describes as "harassment arrests," intended to intimidate.

The two massive protest movements of the era—Vietnam and civil rights—to FBI director J. Edgar Hoover presented "the greatest threats to the stability of the American government since the Civil War," according to Pulitzer

Prize-winning writer Tim Weiner in a 2012 NPR interview with *Fresh Air* host Terry Gross. In Hoover's mind, "These people were enemies of the state." Hoover "repeatedly refused to involve the bureau in … protecting black civil rights workers in the South, insisting that these were matters for local police," attests Kenneth D. Ackerman in his November 9, 2011, opinion piece in the *Washington Post*.

Two of the FBI's divisions were tasked with investigating "civil unrest" and "racial matters." In every corner of every county and town where citizens, black and white, were organizing for social justice and civil rights, Hoover saw communist plots. The *Bolivar Commercial*, in a column on August 6, 1964, backed Senator Eastland's rantings about "Reds" (communists loyal to the red flag of the Soviet Union). The column cited as the "most reliable source of all" Mr. Hoover himself. "In February of this year [1964], testifying before a Congressional committee in Washington, Mr. Hoover stated that 'communist influence does exist in the Negro movement.'" The column went on to cite Hoover's commie-under-every-bed mindset, quoting the FBI director's belief that "America's twenty million Negroes and all others engaged in this struggle are a major target" for communist infiltrators.

Besides being under surveillance by the White Citizens' Council and the FBI (she is named in at least a dozen FBI reports filed under the headings "civil unrest" and "racial matters"), Mary Sue was also in the crosshairs of the Mississippi Sovereignty Commission, the state spy agency formed in response to *Brown v. Board*. The Sovereignty Commission was disbanded and its records sealed in 1977, and it wasn't until 1998 that the records were opened to the public after civil rights advocates fought in court to unseal the secret files. As *New York Times* reporter Kevin Sack wrote in an article titled "Mississippi Reveals Dark Secrets of a Racist Time" on March 18 of that year: "After a 21-year court fight, the state of Mississippi today unsealed more than 124,000 pages of secret files from a state agency that used spy tactics, intimidation, false imprisonment, jury tampering and other illegal methods to thwart the activities of civil rights workers during the 1950s, 60s, and early 70s. Like an eerie journey into a shadowy past, the files of the agency, the Mississippi Sovereignty Commission, provided a profoundly unsettling reminder of the state's determination to maintain Jim Crow segregation."

Today, reading through a website called Sovereignty Commission Online, an archival collection maintained by the Mississippi Department of Archives and History, you might get the idea Mary Sue Gellatly was among Mississippi's most-wanted outlaws. A series of teletype memos sent to FBI director Hoover in Washington, D.C., from confidential informants in the field chronicled her activities, including a sudden spurt of arrests in Bolivar County closely coinciding with the union's genesis at Shaw's Freedom Center.

That's because she was perceived, along with her fellow SNCC activist Robert Weil from Indiana, to be a ringleader of the new union. An investigator for the Sovereignty Commission reported in a memo on June 18, 1965, that the "Delta labor trouble" was "brought about through professional agitators" sponsored by civil rights groups. The investigator, Tom Scarbrough, went on to say: "It is believed by all authorities that the entire trouble which has been going on in the field of agitation in and around Shaw has been brought about by this bunch of immoral degenerates and beatniks whose main purpose is to destroy the racial harmony in these communities."

On June 25, the following message, marked URGENT, was sent from SAC (Special Agent in Charge), Jackson, to the director of the FBI via "Bureau Instant Telephone Call" about Mary Sue Gellatly (original capitalization, typos, and grammatical errors included):

SUBMECT PRESENTLY CONFINED BOLIVAR COUNTY JAIL, CLEVELAND, MISSISSIPPI, SERVING SIXTY DAYS, AFTER BEING FOUND GUILTY IN COUNTY COURT FOR MALICIOUS TRESPASS ON JUNE TWENTYFOUR LAST. SUBJECT WAS FOUND GUILTY ALONG WITH THIRTEEN OTHERS OF MISSISSIPPI FREEDOM LABOR UNION, FOR INSTANT CHARGE WHICH IS BASED ON THAT SHE AND OTHERS JUMPED ON A NEGRO LABOR HAULERS TRUCK AND REFUSED TO GET OFF IN ORDER TO KEEP HIM FROM RETURNING TO THE COTTON FIELDS. SUBJECT WAS ARRESTED BY THE TOWN MARSHAL OF SHAW, MISSISSIPPI, WHO IS ALSO A DEPUTY SHERIFF OF BOLIVAR COUNTY.

SUBJECT ALSO HAS A TRIAL DATE SET FOR JULY THIRTEEN NEXT FOR CONSPIRACY AND CONTRIBUTING TO THE DELINQUENCY OF A MINOR. BOND WAS SET AT SEVEN HUNDRED DOLLARS FOR EACH CHARGE. BASIS OF CHARGE WAS IN REGARD TO THE DESTRUCTION OF A NEGRO SCHOOL IN SHAW, MISSISSIPPI, BY TWENTY-

NINE NEGRO YOUTH, WHO IMPLICATED SUBJECT AND
THREE OTHER CIVIL RIGHTS WORKERS.

One report ("Mississippi Freedom Labor Union") to the
FBI director dated June 3, 1965, captures the granularity
of the surveillance against the Mississippi Freedom Labor
Union. It began: "CHARLES HORWITZ, 507 ½ N. Farish Street,
Jackson, Miss., advised a special agent of the FBI on 5/24/65
that the MFLU was formed in May 1965, to assist the plantation workers in the Delta area of Miss. The MFLU was
formed by civil rights organizations, according to Horwitz."
The report went on to highlight the intense media coverage
sparked by the union:

> An article appeared in the Jackson, Miss., 'The Clarion
> Leger' [sic] dated Tuesday, 6/1/65 entitled "Farm
> Hands Strike on Delta Plantation." The article was
> datelined Leland, Miss., by the UPI (United Press
> International) and set forth that about 80 Negro
> farmworkers complaining of long hours and low pay
> walked off their jobs at a cotton plantation in the
> Mississippi Delta in an unusual civil rights strike. The
> walk-out stemmed from meetings of the newly formed
> MFLU. The workers were asking for a minimum of
> $1.25 per hour.

The union was making headlines in the southern hub
city of Atlanta, Georgia, and even as far away as Chicago.
A headline dated July 16, 1965, in the *Southern Courier*, a
weekly out of Atlanta, captured the near hysteria stirred up

by a handful of striking farmworkers: "Revolution in the Delta: Farm Hands Go on Strike." Reporter Philip Ardery, describing the union's genesis, wrote the following:

> These workers have been poor and in debt for a long time. Why did it take till 1965 for them to decide to strike? The answer is the freedom movement, which spread through the Delta and across much of the rest of Mississippi as a result of last summer's civil rights project. The idea of a strike was born at a freedom school meeting in Shaw, Miss., last November, when a 75-year-old man, Miller Lark, stood up and suggested they go on strike instead of chopping cotton for only $3 per day.... Although the people of Shaw decided to go on strike, for a while 19-year-old George Shelton was about the only organizer. Now he is the chairman of the 325 union members in Shaw, and Shaw is the headquarters for the whole union. Every month representatives of the local MFLU unions [sic] in the Delta come to workshops at Shaw and discuss their problems and make further plans.

Accompanying the story is a photo of young George Shelton, who told the reporter that when he called on plantation owners to negotiate wages and working conditions, "They won't even talk to me."

A few days later, the *Chicago Daily News* ran the headline: "A Bitter Cotton-Chopping Strike: The Delta Negroes' Poverty Fight." Reporter Nicholas von Hoffman wrote: "The Delta is a violent land. Its whites, outnumbered 3 to 1, have always feared a Negro uprising, and now under the impact of pressure for change, the Ku Klux Klan has taken on strength here it has not had for 40 years."

By 1966, a file had been opened on the Mississippi Freedom Labor Union by Special Agent Birl Wilson of the FBI.

WHEN MARY SUE WAS arrested on June 18, 1965, one of her lawyers was Bruce Rogow. Just a year out of law school, Rogow had gone to work for the Lawyers Constitutional Defense Committee (LCDC) in Jackson. When Shaw's activists launched the Mississippi Freedom Labor Union, the LCDC became the official legal representative for the union.

Some twenty years later, the South Florida *Sun-Sentinel* newspaper profiled Rogow under the headline, "Bruce Rogow Rocks the Boat." Of the lawyer's time in Mississippi, reporter Buddy Nevins wrote:

> His job was to provide legal assistance to the flood of civil rights workers trying to break the back of segregation in the South. Rogow soon realized that there was real danger in his new job. Civil rights workers James Chaney, Andrew Goodman, Michael Schwerner ... had been murdered in Mississippi six months before he arrived, and civil rights lawyers had been warned to be on their guard. With his Northern accent and black friends, Rogow was an easy target. "Whenever somebody was overdue, we assumed the worst," he recalls. "We knew that what had happened to Schwerner, Chaney and Goodman could easily happen to any of us."

Usually, Rogow defended civil rights workers who, like Mary Sue and Eddie, were being harassed on minor charges. Sometimes, however, the charges were more serious. "Rogow recalls one incident when a sheriff's deputy had a heart attack after becoming enraged over a button worn by a civil rights worker that depicted black and white hands clasped together," the article said. "The deputy died and the worker who had worn the button was charged with manslaughter." Rogow defended the man, who was acquitted.

When the Voting Rights Act passed in 1965, Rogow decided to leave Mississippi. "I was too young to be scared, but I was burned out," he told Nevins. Bruce Rogow went on to a distinguished career practicing law in Florida and arguing a number of cases before the U.S. Supreme Court.

HAROLD GELLATLY HAD SUPPORTED his daughter's decision to go south for Freedom Summer and to stay on in Shaw as program director through much of 1965. But his support came from his love for her, not from a commitment to social justice. Harold was and always had been a dyed-in-the-wool conservative. Still, during his long-distance monitoring of events in Mississippi, new attitudes seeped into his thinking. By the summer of 1965, he had refined his law-and-order views, embracing a more nuanced understanding of criminal and social justice.

He wrote a letter on June 7, 1965, to his sister Margaret and her husband, Oris Dearborn, who lived in the remote ranching town of Ontario, Oregon, which read in part:

I have undergone a complete re-think on the matter
of arrests, jail, etc. in relation to MSue and the other
Civil Rights workers. Before this activity of hers, or
I should say, before she became active in this work, I
had the same attitude toward those who were arrested
as I had when Dad was sheriff [of Benton County,
Oregon, from 1908 to 1920]. In other words, I still
thought that the law and the law enforcement officers
were right and those who had been arrested were
wrong. That is just not the case in Mississippi and the
other southern states.... However, since MSue went
to Tenn. in 1963, I began informing myself about the
South, its people and practices etc. There can be no
justice without just laws and I mean just that. When
a law is passed with anything but an attitude for it to
apply to any and all people alike, and the enforcement
of it is on exactly the same basis, then that law is an
unjust law and if people who are hurt by it take it into
their own hands to point up the injustice of it, then
I can't hold them in disrespect as I was want [sic] to
do before I got involved in this situation.

Indeed, Harold's change of heart most certainly owed
something to his own confrontation with racial intimidation,
a confrontation in the front of his own hand-built house in
his quiet Portland neighborhood. Some six months before
he penned his letter to his sister, the *Oregonian*—the state's
largest daily newspaper—had run an article about Mary
Sue's civil rights activism in Mississippi. Her photo was
front-and-center in the half-page story, which was based on

an interview she gave to a reporter when she went home in November to raise funds for SNCC. She didn't mince words. "Mississippi is a police state 'of fear and injustice,'" she was quoted as saying. "The white community just puts a complete clamp on Negro life, so you cannot get out from underneath it without taking extreme risks, meaning your life."

Just a day or two after the *Oregonian* story ran, Harold got up early and stepped outside, as he always did, to pick up the newspaper, delivered every day by a paperboy on a bicycle. As he stooped to pick up the paper, something curious, something out-of-the-ordinary caught his eye. He stood up to see what it was. At the bottom of the gravel driveway, standing under an ancient cedar tree among the sword ferns and the ground cover, was a wooden cross. Tendrils of smoke twisted around the cross, which was charred and smoldering in the morning air.

Harold got the intended message in a beat of his racing heart. The symbol of racial hatred, so ubiquitous in the South, was aimed at him, his wife, Verna, and their surviving son, Bill, because of Mary Sue's activism, highlighted just days before in the *Oregonian*. Was it a warning? Was it truly sinister? Or was it just a mindless spasm of hatred and cowardice?

In that moment, the distance between Oregon and Mississippi, which had seemed vast just yesterday, shrank to insignificance. The boundaries of state or region could not—clearly did not—limit the scourge of racism in America. A chill passed through Harold's body as he thought of his daughter living in the heart of it all.

Verna was in the house, unaware of the smoldering cross in her front yard. Harold doused the smoking timbers with the garden hose and dragged the heavy cross into the backyard, out of sight of his wife and his neighbors. Then he took the timbers apart and left them behind the woodpile to be chopped up later for firewood. He didn't tell his wife or daughter about the incident until after Mary Sue had returned from Mississippi. Bill didn't learn about it until fifty years later.

WHILE SOME AREAS DID see a pay increase of twenty cents per hour, the MFLU effort mostly fizzled out. As winter began, survival became the main issue. Some cotton workers moved north, hoping to get better-paying jobs. Some stayed on strike and lived in tents, especially in the Greenville area. Life had been hard before, but it was even harder now. At the same time, plantation owners increased their use of machines to pick cotton, reducing the need for human labor. After that, growers planted more soybeans and corn, cutting the number of acres planted in cotton. With the dwindling of cotton came the shrinkage of the labor force. Plantation field hands and sharecroppers were a dying breed.

Despite the union's eventual demise, its impact was greater than its outward failure would suggest, in Mary Sue's judgment. Although the union didn't directly accomplish what it had set out to do, it was a powerful force in Mississippi's civil rights movement, she argued in the unpublished memoir she coauthored with Eddie in 2016, entitled *Fireproof Freedom*. Because of the esprit de corps it fostered and the publicity it generated, she said, the union helped inspire southern black citizens to break away from oppressive cultural and economic norms and create their own destinies. This solidarity helped energize and shore up activism in other critical areas of social justice—voter registration, Operation Head Start preschool programs, the election of black officials in southern states, and school desegregation.

Shaw's activists formed the Mississippi Freedom Labor
Union, which quickly led to a strike against cotton planters.
(Photo by Mary Sue Gellatly)

GEORGE SHELTON, SHAW ORGANIZER

George Shelton was elected to lead the Mississippi Freedom
Labor Union in 1965. (Photo by the Atlanta *Southern
Courier*)

One of Eddie's arrests included this charge for "obstructing a public road" when he was urging fieldworkers to honor the strike in 1965. (Photo by Lee Anna Sherman)

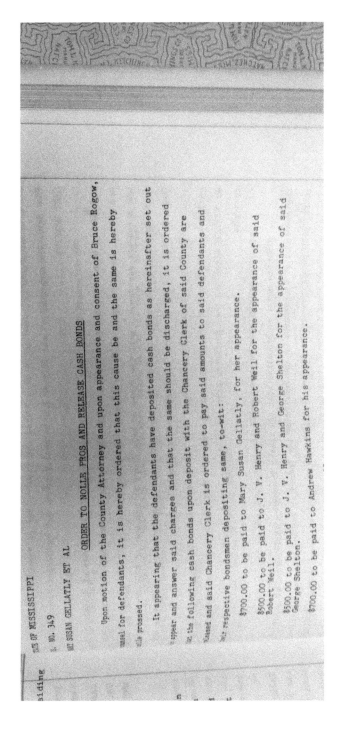

Civil rights attorney Bruce Rogow represented Mary Sue and other defendants charged with "malicious mischief." (Photo by Lee Anna Sherman)

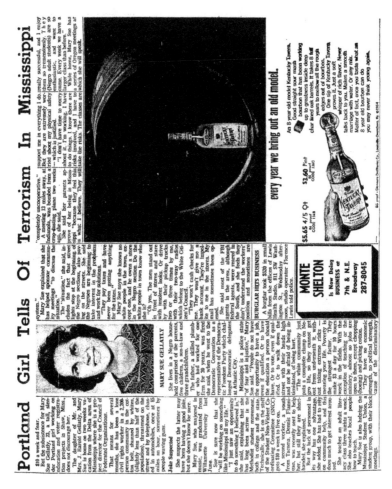

Portland's daily newspaper, the *Oregonian*, ran a story about Mary Sue's civil rights work on November 13, 1964.

12

Departures

My first glimpse of the flat, black stretches of Chicago
depressed and dismayed me, mocked all my fantasies.
—Richard Wright, *Black Boy*

Shaw and Chicago, late summer through fall 1965

Freedom Summer had, for Mary Sue and Eddie, stretched
into "freedom year," a year that straddled 1964 and 1965,
summer to summer. It was a year so much bigger than any
year ever plotted on a calendar, a year when things that would
have seemed fantastical, unthinkable, just months earlier
became concrete realities. Things like Eddie's sitting down
to order a burger and an Orange Crush at Shaw's segregated
Truck Stop and the waitress, after stalling and pursing her
ruby-painted lips in resistance, finally, grudgingly, setting the
food before him. Things like the abduction of three Freedom
Summer activists on the first weekend of Mary Sue's Freedom
Summer training. Things like the whole nation following
CBS's coverage of the disappearance and murders on TV.
Things like Mary Sue going to Mississippi anyway, in full
knowledge that no one could guarantee her safe return.

Like a tremor rising from the earth, it was a year that shifted everything, a year that tilted the old order, rocked the Delta so hard that nothing would ever be the same.

As EARTH COMPLETED ITS yearly rotation around the sun, bringing yet another summer to Mississippi, Mary Sue sensed that her work in Shaw was nearly done. It was time for her to leave the project in the capable hands of Shaw's black leadership. In August, she turned toward home.

On the morning of her departure, damp heat drenched the Delta as Eddie and Mary Sue locked up Shaw's Freedom Center for the last time as coworkers. As, side by side, they descended the old wooden steps, Eddie's mind waged war with his heart. Crowding his brain were the vast chasms between his world and Mary Sue's, the million-plus reasons their lives could not entwine. Still, his heart pounded out in protest. Countless times, it seemed, he had walked beside this determined young woman, drawing strength from her resolve. He tried to fashion something to say, but the words stuck in his throat like peanut butter. He wanted to call out, "Wait! Don't go." But his voice had deserted him.

He managed a smile, but it felt false. "Bye, Eddie," she said as she turned to go, her blue-gray vinyl satchel slung over her shoulder.

She strode down the unpaved road to the Truck Stop on Highway 61, where she stepped up to the counter and bought a ticket for her two-thousand-mile journey back to Oregon. As she stood on the shoulder of the highway, waiting in the heat and the dust, she was envisioning her homecoming among the hills and evergreens of Oregon. In that moment of departure, she felt at ease. She had cherished her time in Shaw and the righteous work she had accomplished with her sweetheart, Eddie Short. But pragmatic as always, Mary Sue was now looking forward. When she tried to imagine what the future held for her, the picture was still unfocused. She would worry about that when she got home.

The bus rumbled up in a flurry of dust. Sliding her battered satchel into the luggage compartment, she walked to the open door where the driver looked down from his perch, his hand resting on the door lever in an attitude of impatience. Mary Sue stepped aboard. As the bus pulled back out onto the road, she looked out the window at the cotton fields filling the horizons.

Eddie, meanwhile, imagined the bus carrying Mary Sue down Highway 61 until it disappeared into the simmering heat. In that moment, only one thing saved him from overwhelming sadness: a small scrap of paper secreted in his back pocket, a scrap of paper that he reached for then in his bereavement, his fingers touching its raggedy corners as if, like a talisman, it held some magic, as if it could ward off the ache that seemed about to engulf him. He had secured this scrap of paper just a few days earlier back in the Freedom Center. While Mary Sue was busy with some end-of-project details, Eddie had shuffled through the desk and found a list of contact information for SNCC's Mississippi volunteers. Making sure she wasn't looking, he had jotted down the seven digits of her parents' home phone number in Oregon. Folding it neatly, nonchalantly, he had tucked it into his pocket.

BY LATE SUMMER OF 1965, Eddie was widely known around town as a freedom fighter. His highly visible year of activism had included at least three arrests on trumped-up charges: obstructing a public road on May 26, 1965, destruction of public property on June 3, 1965, and, back in 1964, parading without a permit. Eddie was blackballed in Bolivar County. To the planters, managers, and business owners of the Mississippi Delta, Eddie and his fellow hometown champions of civil rights—guys like George "Buddy Boy" Shelton, Aaron German, James "Jimmy" Johnson Jr., and Willie Wright; girls and young women like Ruby Richard, the Hawkins sisters, and twin sisters Jeanette and Annette Miller, whose mothers were active in the local movement—were dangerous subversives. No one would hire these native sons and daughters of Shaw, young men and women as endemic to the Delta as the fields fat with cotton, the bayous lazy with catfish, the cypresses chirring with cicadas.

When the sharecroppers and fieldworkers had gone out on strike the previous spring, the planters had sensed that the days of exploiting black laborers, of paying wages so penurious that families like the Shorts were trapped in virtual bondage, were fast slipping away. Growers began turning to automation and away from cotton, planting new crops, soy especially, that could be picked by machines instead of human hands. White business owners fled rather than integrate, shuttering their shops, even burning them down. The old white men never returned to Liar's Park where once the *clack-clack* of dominoes had sounded across the bayou.

The old order was, if not yet dead, wheezing out its last putrid breath. Shaw's black citizens had risen against indignity and injustice, had rejected their generations-old oppression, had summoned their own liberation with courage and collective action. They had secured rights that had eluded them for centuries. But securing the vote, they discovered, was a pyrrhic victory without the ability to earn a paycheck. Eddie and thousands of other black Mississippians were cast out of the economic engine of the South when they dared to claim full citizenship. Even though he had started working when he was barely out of diapers, Eddie couldn't piece together enough odd jobs in Shaw to support himself, much less his mama and five young siblings still at home. When SNCC folded up the Mississippi Summer Project for good, even his $38.56 monthly stipend stopped.

So he turned his eyes to the North.

MARY SUE'S OREGON PHONE number wasn't the only number stashed in Eddie's pocket the day he left Mississippi. The other was the address of his older sister, Jeansetta, who had moved north with her small children about the same time as their older brother, Ernest. Jeansetta had a special place in her warm heart for her enterprising little brother and had been urging him to join her in Chicago.

"Come on up, Eddie!" she told him over the phone. "I got room enough. You can stay here till you get on your feet."

So on a day in late August 1965, he gathered his few belongings, kissed his mama goodbye and promised to send money as soon as he found work, then turned toward the Truck Stop. He was leaving behind the bayous where he had caught buffalo fish, the train trestle where he had gone mud crawling against his mama's wishes, Club DeLisa where he had danced the funky chicken with Mary Sue, the cotton gins, the waterless swimming pool, the ashes of the theater.

At the Truck Stop, he met up with longtime pal James Givens, who had picked cotton with Eddie when they were in their early teens. Like Eddie, James had a sibling, a brother, who had settled in the Windy City. The two young men had found themselves in the same boat—a couple of twenty-somethings with no prospects in the Delta and not much to lose by pulling up stakes. "We decided, 'Let's go to Chicago,'" Eddie recalls.

Jeansetta's voice ("Come on up, Eddie!") nudged him forward. He imagined Chicago as a place of opportunity, a place of wider horizons, where black skin didn't instantly make you a magnet for hate or disdain. In his mind, Chicago was a sort of mythic city. A chance to start again, to reinvent himself. At the same time, stories about killings on Chicago's streets had made their way back to Shaw over the years.

"People said that someone would be killed on the street and people just walked around 'em and kept going," he remembers. Getting sideways with Chicago's gangs, like the notorious Black P. Stone Nation, could get you killed. In Mississippi, on the other hand, just looking crosswise at a white person could put you in the Klan's crosshairs.

Eddie was acquainted with danger, had been all his life. Bottom line, he needed a job. Weighing the possible risks against the probable rewards, he chose to take his chances in the industrial powerhouse up north.

Eddie and James climbed aboard the Greyhound as it idled beside the Truck Stop in a cloud of diesel fumes. Over his twenty-two years of life in Shaw, Eddie had mastered a posture of confidence, holding his shoulders back and his spine straight, a strategy for deflecting victimization by thugs and bullies who preyed on weakness. So it was that on that day, as he left behind everything and everyone that had defined him, his proud bearing showed nothing of the turmoil roiling in his gut.

As the bus pulled away from the Truck Stop, a song arose in Eddie's mind, frothing up from his mental playlist of jukebox tunes, church hymns, and freedom anthems. The song "Matchbox Blues," written by Blind Lemon Jefferson and later recorded by artists like Carl Perkins and Jerry Lee Lewis—even by the Beatles in the summer of 1964—started twanging through his memory, the rumbling of the bus adding syncopation.

Yeah, I'm sitting here wondering
Will a matchbox hold my clothes
Yeah, I'm sitting here wondering
Will a matchbox hold my clothes
I got no matches
Got a long way to go

Eddie thought about the ten dollars in his pocket and the handful of well-worn garments bundled in a brown paper bag on his lap and figured the answer was pretty close to yes.

As the long miles unrolled beneath him, he felt the tether to his old life stretch like a frayed rubber band. He closed his eyes and prayed.

THE CITY LIGHTS ARE what Eddie most remembers of the night he and James Givens rolled into the mythic city on the shores of Lake Michigan. The lights of Chicago—the nation's second largest metropolis with three and a half million souls—cast a yellow glow over the skyscrapers and factories and brownstones, bright even at midnight, blotting out the Milky Way that had swarmed over Shaw on clear nights, familiar and reassuring.

The bus pulled into the Greyhound station, a hubbub of confusion, buses rolling in and out, people milling around, babies crying, engines rumbling, horns honking. Holding tight to his brown paper bag with everything he owned, Eddie followed James as his friend scanned the crowd for his brother.

In the noise and the clamor and the glare, Eddie felt disoriented. One thought rose in his mind at that moment, one idea surfaced through the sensory overload like a diver coming up for a breath: his sister Jeansetta. Jeansetta was waiting for him with her arms open wide, something good to eat on the stove, a place to sleep. That idea—that someone from home, someone who loved him, was waiting for him—steadied him.

Eddie doesn't remember many details from that chaotic arrival, just climbing into the back of James's brother's car and gripping the seat as the brother pealed out, tires squealing on the pavement, and Eddie thinking he had come a long way just to die in a fiery car crash. As they drove toward Jeansetta's apartment, the glittering lights of downtown soon gave way to the dark streets of Chicago's west side, the neighborhoods where black migrants from Mississippi, Alabama, Georgia, and other southern states were settling by the tens of thousands.

The car turned off Roosevelt Road onto North Mozart Street. Just past Big Duke's Record Shop, the driver stopped. "Here y'are," said James's brother, pointing to a three-story brick building, shabby and dimly lit. Eddie's heart sunk a notch or two. Even Shaw looked better than this, Eddie thought as he said his goodbyes to the Givens brothers and stepped onto the street.

Eddie and James Givens were part of several waves of black workers leaving the South in the twentieth century. Longtime fieldworkers and sharecroppers were tossing their few belongings into burlap sacks or paper bags and scraping up bus fare to Chicago and other northern industrial cities in search of work. As Isabel Wilkerson wrote in her 2010 Pulitzer Prize–winning book, *The Warmth of Other Suns: The Epic Story of the Great Migration*:

> Over the course of six decades, some six million black southerners left the land of their forefathers and fanned out across the country for an uncertain existence in nearly every other corner of America. The Great Migration would become a turning point in history. It would transform urban America and recast the social and political order of every city it touched. It would force the South to search its soul and finally to lay aside a feudal caste system. It grew out of the unmet promises made after the Civil War

and, through the sheer weight of it, helped push the country toward the civil rights revolutions of the 1960s.

EDDIE'S FIRST NIGHT IN Chicago, as he tried to sleep in the back bedroom of Jeansetta's apartment, he heard gunfire coming from the direction of Big Duke's just down the street. The *pop-pop* of bullets ricocheted off the building. The next day he learned that someone had been shot and killed over on the next street.

He quickly landed a job at Shepherd's barbershop just around the corner on Roosevelt and North Francisco Avenue. He cut hair and shined shoes and fed nickels into the jukebox, the beat of R&B blending with the rasp of razor blades on whiskers, the *snip-snip* of shears, the *swoosh* of shaving cream foaming out of a can. Day after day, as he joked with the guys in the shop and played pool for whatever money he could win, he would punch the button for Percy Mayfield's hit song "Please Send Me Someone to Love" over and over. His mind kept turning to the girl from the North with whom he had canvassed and picketed, been arrested and jailed, petitioned officials and elected leaders, sung freedom songs in fulsome voice, stood up to cops carrying guns and batons, and stared down white supremacists prowling the streets in pickup trucks.

He landed a second job, this one at Aristocratic Glass and Mirror, where he cut, beveled, polished, and installed glass windows and mirrors with the owner, Dominic, for seventy-five cents an hour. Things were falling into place. He was earning some money, making some friends. Still, he felt the tug of regret, the ache of longing. Night after night in his bedroom at Jeansetta's as he tried to sleep, his mind kept turning toward Mary Sue with her steady gaze and resolute voice, the way she had held her head high when the sheriff arrested her, time and again, for her civil rights work. He remembered the way she had danced on Saturday nights, a little bit awkwardly, to the beats of Delta blues and rock 'n' roll when they would kick back at one of Shaw's black clubs after an exhausting week of activism.

When each of them had left Shaw for distant destinations, they had made no promises, voiced no expectations. There had been no talk of a shared future beyond Shaw. As it turned out, however, an unbreakable bond had linked their lives without their realizing it. Eddie still carried in his back pocket the rumpled scrap of paper with a scribbled phone number that could, in less than a minute, reconnect him to her.

One night in October, braced by a shot of the Canadian Club he kept in his room, Eddie walked through the small apartment toward the front door. "I'll be back soon," he said to Jeansetta, who was getting her children ready for sleep. He hurried down the block to the pay phone at the corner of Roosevelt and California, all the while praying that he wouldn't lose his nerve. Pulling from his pocket the scrap of paper and a handful of quarters, he dropped one of the coins into the slot and dialed.

As the phone rang, his heart was thumping like a catfish on a line. But the moment he heard Mary Sue's surprised voice and, across the miles, her laugh and obvious pleasure at getting his call, he was instantly at ease. An hour and a twenty-five-dollar long-distance charge from Bell Telephone later, he hung up.

Eddie stood there in the phonebooth looking out at the dark slums of West Chicago. Mary Sue had agreed to join him. The thrill of that promise waged war in his heart with the uncertainty of this new path he was treading. Would she really come? he wondered. What if she did? What then?

A couple of days after the phonebooth call, Mary Sue arrived in Chicago carrying her scuffed vinyl bag, the same blue-gray satchel she had slung over her shoulder and carried to South Korea in 1962, to Nashville in 1963, and to Mississippi in 1964. From the bus station, she hailed a cab and, double-checking the information she had scribbled down during her phone conversation with Eddie, gave the cabbie the address in the westside slums. "You sure about that, Miss?" the cabbie asked. "You sure you got the right address?" It was an unlikely destination for a young white woman.

When the cab pulled up to the old brick building, Mary Sue looked again at the scrawled address. As it had for Eddie, the rundown look of the crumbling structure made her uneasy. She paid the cabbie, climbed the steps to the second floor, and knocked.

Unaware that Mary Sue was coming to Chicago— unaware, even, that Eddie had asked her to come—Jeansetta opened the door to find a twenty-something white woman, six feet tall and skinny as a willow switch, standing on her stoop, a blue-gray vinyl bag slung over her shoulder.

"Hi, I'm Mary Sue, a friend of Eddie's," Mary Sue explained. Jean had heard about Mary Sue, of course, from

Eddie's other brothers and sisters back home. Her startled expression relaxed into a welcoming smile.

"Well, you come on in, then," Jean said. "You hungry? Let me fix you somethin' to eat. Sit on down, sit on down!"

Relieved by Jean's warm welcome, Mary Sue stepped into the apartment and looked around. She smiled at a tiny girl peeking out at her from behind a yellow floral-print sofa that was covered in clear plastic sheeting. The industrial-looking linoleum floor was softened a bit by the pink-and-cream floral pattern on the curtains, which were made of thin plastic. Plastic, it seemed, was a theme in Jean's décor. The hard, shiny polymers gave the place a brittle look. But she quickly learned the practicality of plastic in a district where coal-burning combustion shed black soot on every surface, every minute.

"The air was noticeably dirty," Mary Sue says of her first days in Chicago. "Jean had to work really hard to keep her place clean. She mopped her floors every day."

The toddler peeking out at Mary Sue was two-year-old Vivian, the youngest of Jeansetta's four children. Jean's three other kids—Charles, Gloria Jean, and Calvin, nicknamed "Little Calvin"—were old enough to be in school on the autumn day of Mary Sue's arrival. In the enterprising spirit of the Short family, twelve-year-old Charles was already earning money after school, carrying groceries for tips from folks around the neighborhood.

When Eddie walked into the apartment that evening after work and found Mary Sue sitting in Jeansetta's living room, he had the sensation that she was a vision, a figment of his longing. As he stood there, stunned, a wrestling match took hold in his heart. The dueling emotions were something like panic (What have I done?) and relief (My companion, my friend, my sweetheart is here at last—my dance partner, the woman who laughs at my jokes, the woman with oh-so-many opinions, the one who stood with me against the Boss Man, who respects my character and my skills and my restless ambition, the woman who sees the real me).

She stood up and smiled at him. There in his sister's apartment on the west side of Chicago, Eddie's momentary misgivings dissolved in the rightness of Mary Sue's embrace.

Mary Sue stayed at Jeansetta's for a couple of nights while Eddie scouted out a place for her. Meanwhile, she combed through the Help Wanted ads in the *Chicago Tribune* and quickly landed a job with a tutoring program on the South Side, which required her to take several buses and the el train to get back and forth.

"In the evening after work, we mostly hung out in the kitchen while Jean cooked," Mary Sue recalls. "We'd sit at her table—Formica top with steel legs—and play cards or dominoes or just talk and laugh and tease each other." Teasing wasn't something Mary Sue's family had engaged in, and it took a little getting used to.

Once in a while, when they could scrape together a few extra bucks, Mary Sue and Eddie went out. Chicago's nightlife was exponentially more exciting than the Club DeLisa and Arlena's Place back in Shaw. Near Jean's apartment was a bright, lively club where six-to-eight-piece black bands played live from midnight till four in the morning. So after the kids were asleep—Charles on the sofa and the three little ones tucked into Jean's bed—Mary Sue and Eddie headed to a nightclub for drinks and dancing, just as they had in Shaw.

"We'd go out about ten o'clock at night," Mary Sue says, adding, "That's when things started getting fun."

Dressing to the nines was standard attire for Chicago's black clubs—the customers, the staff, and especially the musicians who "looked sharp" in their suits and ties, according to Mary Sue. When Mary Sue had packed her satchel in Portland to join Eddie in Chicago, she had browsed her closet and seen the teal-green satin dress she had worn for her senior recital at the pipe organ. Taking the frock off the hanger, she stood before the bathroom mirror and held up the shimmery, scoop-necked dress to gauge the effect against her light-brown hair and creamy skin. She imagined Eddie's reaction, seeing her in satin for the first time. The thought made her smile. She folded the dress carefully and tucked it in the satchel. In Chicago, she wore the teal dress to dance with Eddie in his dark sharkskin suit and tie, clothes he had carried to Chicago carefully rolled up in the brown paper bag.

In the nighttime neighborhood of shabby brick walk-ups and storefronts of the westside slums, the club was an oasis of light and laughter. Its centerpiece was a big shiny wooden dance floor, which beckoned to the men and women gathered around the edges at small tables, drinking, flirting, tapping their best shoes to the rhythms of the band. It was a place where Mary Sue and Eddie could forget for a while that their incomes were meager, their circumstances tenuous, and their plans wholly unformed.

"The songs were all danceable," says Mary Sue, "both fast and slow"—songs like Little Richard's "Tutti Fruiti" and Otis Redding's "Mr. Pitiful." But it was a hit by Little Milton that Eddie, who so often drew upon his vast internal playlist for lessons on life, most took to heart. It spoke to the quandary of his future, a future that now seemed centered on the tall white girl from Oregon who had shown up in Chicago when he asked her to. Besides dancing to the song at the club, he played it over and over on the jukebox at the barbershop. Fifty years later, he sings these lyrics out loud from his mental soundtrack: "We're gonna make it. I know we will. May have to eat beans every day. But we're gonna make it. I know we will ... something, something, something ... peace of mind. I got your love. And I know you got mine."

The song he was remembering hit the R&B charts in 1965, just as Eddie was starting his new life in the North, working part-time for seventy-five cents an hour. It went like this:

We may not have a cent
To pay the rent
But we're gonna make it
We may have to eat beans every day
But we're gonna make it

We may not have a home to call our own
But we're gonna make it, I know we will
We may have to fight hardships alone
But we're gonna make it, I know we will
'Cause togetherness brings peace of mind

Eddie wasn't then, nor is he today, a poet or a lyricist. He was, and is, a man who speaks without embellishment. But the jukebox in his mind is packed with the blue-collar poetry of a thousand hits by a hundred R&B artists, melded with the gospel hymns and Negro spirituals he had sung in church since he was smaller than a cotton plant. All those notes, the sacred and the secular, were mingled in his mind with the freedom songs that had pulsed and powered his personal march to freedom in Bolivar County, Mississippi.

For Eddie, the songs said it all.

ONE DAY, HAVING SET aside a few extra dollars from his earnings, he walked four blocks down Roosevelt Road to a pawnshop he had noticed in the neighborhood. There in the window he saw a pair of matching fourteen-carat brushed-gold bands, handcrafted, each inlaid with tiny diamonds in a diagonal pattern. The clerk told him the rings could be his for fifteen dollars. Eddie, who had never bought a piece of jewelry before, paid for them with one-dollar bills and tucked the tiny box in his pocket, the same pocket where he had secreted the phone number of the woman he now hoped would be his wife.

By this time, the two sweethearts were spending much of their free time at Mrs. Julia Jackson's apartment across the street and down the block from Jeansetta's place. Mrs. Jackson, a short, stout, sixty-something black woman they called Mom, had rented her spare bedroom to Mary Sue for ten dollars a week to supplement her income cleaning white people's houses in wealthy suburbs. Even her long days of mopping and scrubbing and riding city buses for miles through the gritty streets of Chicago didn't siphon off any of Mrs. Jackson's energy for her church.

"I remember her cooking up a storm one weekend, getting

up very early to bake yeast rolls," Mary Sue recalls. "It was part of her church's fund-raiser called 'selling plates,' meaning selling paper plates loaded with food to make money for the church." Selling plates, Mary Sue explained, had long been a tradition in black churches, in the North just as in the South.

It was in Mrs. Jackson's rented room where one evening Eddie sat beside Mary Sue on the saggy single bed and pulled the tiny velveteen box from his pocket. Flipping open the lid to reveal the matching bands, he said, "Will you marry me?" Mary Sue looked at the gold rings with astonishment. "I hadn't seen it coming."

After her momentary shock, she felt a rush of delight as she tried on the ring, a perfect fit. She confesses now that marriage to Eddie had crossed her mind a few times in recent weeks as they sat at Jean's Formica table laughing and playing cards or as Eddie, wearing his dark-green sharkskin suit, whirled her around the dance floor at the nightclub. But until she saw him holding the ring box, his face as earnest as that of any supplicant, she hadn't guessed the depth of his feelings for her. His innate self-confidence—the survival skills, keen wit, and bottomless resilience that had served him so well—deserted him whenever he thought about revealing his feelings for her. Just as Mary Sue was clueless about Eddie's true feelings, Eddie was far from certain that she would accept his proposal.

This, then, was an act of extreme vulnerability for the proud young man. What if she said no? So, rather than struggling for the perfect words, he let the shiny rings in the tiny box speak for him. There was no ambiguity in the message. Nor was there any hesitation in her answer.

"I thought he was terrific, and by that time in our relationship I loved him, even though we hadn't said those words to each other. It was easy to say yes right away."

As for the conversation you might expect them to have as they looked ahead—the conversation about how difficult it might be for the two of them, a white woman and a black man, to be wed in a country where interracial marriage was still against the law in many states? Mary Sue doesn't remember either of them uttering more than a few cautionary words, words they quickly dismissed. The risks of being together were baked into their relationship, had been from day one. Even when they were just coworkers walking home after work at the Freedom Center, even when they danced together at Club DeLisa on Saturday nights or when they rode together in a donated car on Highway 61, they knew they were targets for slurs. Or worse. Society's scorn hadn't stopped them before. It wasn't going to stop them now.

"We weren't about to let possible harassment deter us," Mary Sue recalls.

It wasn't that they were naïve. They knew only too well that the taboo against interracial dating and marriage meant their union would draw scorn, even danger. That year, 1965, anti-miscegenation (race mixing) laws in at least sixteen states made marriage between a black person and a white person a crime punishable by incarceration. Mississippi, not surprisingly, was one of those states. Oregon, too, banned interracial marriage until 1951. The landmark U.S. Supreme Court decision *Loving v. Virginia* striking down such laws as unconstitutional was still two years away. They knew only too well the hurdles ahead. But by now there was an inevitability about the twining of their lives. And, in truth, they felt a bit invincible. They had survived Mississippi. What worse troubles might crop up?

It was only a few days later that the couple ran headlong into an obstacle that was not on the list of predictable problems. Mary Sue knew that Eddie had been married before. As an eighteen-year-old sharecropper in Shaw, he had married his eighteen-year-old girlfriend, Alice, who was expecting his baby. But Alice had died in childbirth, bleeding to death from a hemorrhage before she could get to the hospital in Cleveland. The baby had died, too. Eddie had been riven by grief. Plunging into Shaw's civil rights movement became, for him, one of his strategies for managing sorrow, pouring his energy into a life-affirming cause.

What Mary Sue didn't know was that Eddie had a child on the way. In fact, not even Eddie knew he had a child on the way until one day soon after his engagement to Mary Sue, when Jeansetta said, "There's a letter for you," and handed him an envelope.

Eddie, who was unaccustomed to getting mail, looked at the return address: Pasadena, California. Who did he know in Pasadena? he wondered.

Mystified, he opened the envelope and scanned the signature at the bottom of the page. The name written there, Barbara, jolted him. She was a young woman from Shaw, someone he had known for years and casually dated up until about the time he and Mary Sue became sweethearts. He knew she had moved to the West Coast. He didn't know, nor did she, that she was carrying Eddie's unborn child when she left Shaw. Eddie, she informed him in the letter, was about to be a daddy.

As soon as Mary Sue walked into the apartment after work

that evening, she knew by Eddie's stricken face that something had happened. He poured out the story as she listened. For the second time in a week, Mary Sue absorbed a message she hadn't seen coming. When she had gone off to work that morning, her life had seemed to be heading in a discernable direction, if not on a smooth glidepath. Now it felt like she was careening around a corner at full throttle.

She sat still for a few minutes. Then, drawing on the reasonable and practical aspects of her nature, she said she would understand if he broke off their engagement to be with his former girlfriend. He said, "No way," almost before she got the words out of her mouth. She looked into his eyes for signs of his sincerity and saw the same earnest supplication she had seen when he had produced the tiny ring box from his pocket days earlier.

Then it was his turn to offer *her* a way out. He told her he would understand if she wanted to drop their marriage plans and go back to Oregon. As he held his breath, she straightened her back and squared her shoulders. "No way," she said. The clarity in her eyes was the same clarity Eddie had seen time and again in Shaw as she stood her ground against injustice.

Eddie's implied message—no one will blame you if you walk away—was the same message Mary Sue had heard during her Freedom Summer training when the three civil rights workers had disappeared. She hadn't walked away then. She wouldn't walk away now. They would work out a way, together, to love and help support the child Eddie had fathered.

AT CHRISTMAS, EVERYBODY CHIPPED in their spare earnings, and Jeansetta got busy in the kitchen preparing a soul-food feast whose aromas smelled just like home in the Delta—a heaping platter of crispy fried chicken, cornbread warm from the oven, mac and cheese, collard and turnip greens cooked together with salt pork, and desserts, lots and lots of desserts: sweet potato pie, banana pudding, pound cake. Besides being a talented cook, Jeansetta was, like Mrs. Minley in Shaw, very "free-hearted," as black people from the Delta described a generous person. Friends stopped by to eat and laugh and share the season. Mary Sue felt warmed by the familial love and the hubbub of the holiday. Here with Eddie, she felt at home.

Eddie and Mary Sue wore their wedding rings for twenty-
five years, finally replacing them when the gold wore through.
(Photo courtesy of Eddie Short)

13

Passages

The uniqueness of Shaw, Mississippi, stems ... from its
place in the judicial records of the U.S. Court of Appeals
of the Fifth Circuit and its role in the history of a
continuing social and legal struggle for
equal municipal services.
—Charles Haar and Daniel Fessler,
The Wrong Side of the Tracks

Waukesha, Wisconsin, and Shaw, Mississippi, 1966 and beyond

Chicago, as it turned out, was only a momentary way station for Mary Sue and Eddie. In that teeming metropolis
of three and a half million people, a young white woman from
Oregon and a young black man from Mississippi might find
a way forward in the anonymity of the city. They could even
marry. In Illinois, marriage between a black person and a
white person had been legal since 1874. But another place
had opened its arms to them, a place they had never seen but
were connected to nonetheless. A place built on principles of
freedom and social justice—the principles the young couple
had worked so hard for in Mississippi.

That place was Waukesha, Wisconsin, then a verdant city of thirty-five thousand straddling the Fox River. Their quiet wedding ceremony was held in the home of Richard and Maxine Franz, who, like Ivan and Nissley Kaste, were pillars of the local social justice community. The Women's International League for Peace and Freedom—the organization that had adopted Shaw's freedom project and helped keep it solvent with donations of cash and goods—was a hub of this community. Richard was a graphic artist and mapmaker, Maxine an avid gardener and cook. They had devoted their lives to peace, equality, and environmental sustainability.

And so it was that the Franzes opened their home—a three-bedroom ranch-style in the quiet New Berlin suburb between the cities of Waukesha and Milwaukee—to the young black man and his white fiancée for the exchanging of holy vows and the tying of matrimonial knots. When Mary Sue and Eddie set the date, they were uncertain whether her parents, Harold and Verna, would make the trip from Oregon to be there. Mostly, it was a question of money. The household budget was and always had been squeaky tight for the Gellatlys.

Besides, Mary Sue wasn't certain they would endorse the union. Verna's main hesitation was not race but education. Would Mary Sue and Eddie, with such disparate educational backgrounds, be intellectually compatible? she wondered. She worried, too, about the hurdles their children would surely face growing up. As for Harold, it turned out that Eddie had made an end run around Mary Sue and called his future father-in-law—another slightly terrifying long-distance phone call to Oregon—to ask his permission to marry his daughter. Harold, conservative as he was, admired Eddie's old-fashioned deference to the father of the bride. The bottom line for Harold was the happiness of his only daughter. He said to Eddie, "If you love her, I'll support your marriage in any way I can."

In the end, Verna and Harold scraped up the plane fare to Milwaukee and then took a bus to New Berlin. It was Valentine's Day 1966. Their feelings as they walked the three or four blocks from the bus stop to the Franzes' house must have been a jumble, fretful and joyful in equal measure. When they knocked on the door, they stood at the threshold not only of their daughter's new life but also of their own uncertain future at a time when the country was seething with competing visions of race in America.

And then the door opened and there was Eddie, wearing his dark-green sharkskin suit and his trademark grin. Mary Sue held her breath as three of the people she loved most in the world—her mama, her dad, and her soon-to-be husband—shook hands and said their hellos. Standing there in a pink blouse and a wine-colored narrow-wale corduroy suit with black trim she had sewn in high school, Mary Sue exhaled as she saw Eddie draw in her parents and put them instantly at ease with his authentic and winning charm.

Also on hand that day, besides the Franzes, were Eddie's sister Jeansetta and the Franzes' daughter, Emily. Not attending was the other person Mary Sue loved best in the world, her younger brother, Bill, who by then was taking engineering courses at Portland State University and working as a drafter for Tektronix. When Bill heard about Mary Sue's plans to marry Eddie, he had called her and tried, forcefully, to talk her out of it. His political views at the time were in line with his conservative father's, and interracial marriage seemed to him like a recipe for trouble. Mary Sue, convinced that Bill's disapproval would prevent him from accepting an invitation to the wedding, had decided not to invite him—a decision she later regretted when Bill's attitudes softened as his father's had.

Eddie's uncle, the Reverend Ivory Short, came up from Chicago to perform the ceremony, alongside a local Baptist minister named Reverend Dwight Moody Bahr. After the couple kissed, the wedding party celebrated with a three-tiered angel food cake baked by one of the WILPF members.

Verna and Harold Gellatly, both tall and slender like their daughter, sat on the sofa with their plates of cake and cups of coffee. Harold was dapper in a dark-gray suit and crimson necktie in the Royal Stewart Tartan, a nod to his Scottish ancestry. Verna was quietly elegant in the only dress she owned, a lightweight black wool, and a silk scarf of blue and lavender. On her feet were black pumps, her only pair of dressy shoes. The coat that warmed her as she traveled to Wisconsin on this cool February day was her only coat, sewn for her by Mary Sue of gray-and-black wool tweed with black piping. Back home in her closet were two blouses, two pairs of slacks, and a cardigan sweater.

Verna's bare-bones wardrobe was not, as might be assumed, the result of the family's bare-bones budget. Harold's salary at Shell, while certainly not regal, was enough to cover the cost of new clothing now and then. Rather, Verna had made the choice to live simply, to own exactly what she needed and no more. Tied in with her voluntary simplicity was the parallel imperative to share what little she had with people less fortunate than she. She liked nonprofits with a "hand-up" rather than a "hand-out" focus—Frank Laubach's "Each One Teach One" literacy program, Habitat for Humanity, and the Heifer Project. And so, whether she fully realized it or not, she was among people who were as like-minded and free-hearted as she was that day in a place whose roots tapped into some of humanity's best instincts.

Even the modest earnings she made from a later-in-life enterprise, a sheet-music business she ran from her dining room table, she gave to others. Verna got the bug for vintage sheet music by American composers like Irving Berlin and George Gershwin one day when she and Harold were browsing garage sales in Portland. She picked up the music for the World War I hit "Over There," written by George M. Cohan. The striking red, white, and blue cover, a charming art-deco illustration that was patriotic with a touch of whimsy, struck her fancy. Here was an amalgam of two of her great interests—music and art—in a compact form that could be purchased for a few cents. Over the next couple of decades, her casual garage-sale Saturdays became a collector's obsession. She eventually built a base of two hundred customers, who received Verna's manually typed and mimeographed newsletter every quarter.

The Gellatlys flew home that evening.

Then the newlyweds, with ninety-four dollars between them, caught a bus back to Chicago. After giving notice to their employers and Mary Sue's landlady, Mrs. Jackson, they gathered their few belongings and set out for Wisconsin once again, this time to stay.

Wisconsin, like Mississippi, is a place carved by water. In the Delta, liquid water shaped the land, the Mississippi and Yazoo Rivers racing and twisting, surging and flooding, depositing rich alluvial soils across millions of acres, flat from horizon to horizon. In Wisconsin, it was frozen water that gouged and scoured and pocked the land over the millennia. Eddie and Mary Sue settled in Wisconsin's southeast corner, a region called the Southeast Glacial Plains. The landscape left behind there as the last ice age receded, the massive glaciers shrinking and melting over time, was a fantastical terrain testifying to the power of Earth's natural forces.

Waukesha lies between two metropolises: to the east, Milwaukee, perched on the shore of Lake Michigan, and to the west, Madison, Wisconsin's capital. Waukesha is the seat of government for Waukesha County, whose ancient glacial landscape now exists mainly in remnants—patches of oak forest and savanna, conifer swamps, shimmering lakes, and the undulating "kettle moraines," where slow-melting ice chunks formed kettle-shaped hollows in the earth.

For the young couple, Waukesha was a place of convergence. Before Freedom Summer, neither of them had heard of it. But by the time they said their marriage vows, Waukesha had taken on a kind of cosmic inevitability as their new hometown.

The accident of the rhyming place names—Waukesha and Shaw—was just a phonetic coincidence. The true linkage between the towns had to do with social justice. Not only had the Kastes and the Franzes and countless other townspeople reached out in compassion and generosity to the little Mississippi town in the mid-1960s, but Waukesha's early founders had staunchly opposed slavery. The *American Freeman*, an anti-slavery publication launched in 1844, was Waukesha's first newspaper. The *Waukesha Freeman*—where Ivan Kaste worked as a reporter when he and his family visited Mary Sue in Shaw—was originally "one of the state's most radical abolitionist newspapers," according to the Wisconsin Historical Society. Those early abolitionists had put their convictions into action, risking legal jeopardy as a way station on the Underground Railroad, a covert network that helped black slaves escape their captors.

In 1842, exactly one hundred years before Mary Sue Gellatly was born in Oregon, a sixteen-year-old girl named Caroline Quarlls took her destiny into her own hands when she ran away from an abusive slaveowner in Missouri. Her light skin and European facial features helped her blend in as she moved north with help from free blacks she met along the way. With slave hunters tracking her, she traveled by steamboat up the Mississippi to Illinois and then by stagecoach into Wisconsin. In Milwaukee, Quarlls was "hidden briefly by sympathetic allies," according to historical accounts. But "when authorities tracked her down, she was spirited away [by local abolitionists] to Waukesha, then called Prairieville, a town known for its anti-slavery radicals," the historical society reports.

The girl's harrowing escape is described in a memoir by Lyman Goodnow, the man who, at great risk to himself, concealed her in the back of his wagon and drove her to Detroit, where she crossed into Canada—a journey of more than five hundred miles, mostly at night, sometimes in drenching rain. He tells the gripping tale of Caroline's close calls and brave tactics to evade capture—climbing out a cellar window and hiding for hours in a cornfield, silently holding still in a dense thicket, riding on horseback through a dark wood, burrowing under piles of hay in the back of a wagon. Goodnow describes one of the last legs of the journey this way: "When night came on, we started, Caroline on the buffalo robe in the bottom of the buggy which covered her so that no one would know but that I had a sheep or a quarter of veal."

All along the way, a network of church elders, deacons, farmers, doctors, and Quakers kept young Caroline Quarlls one step ahead of the slave hunters, who were eager to pocket the three-hundred-dollar bounty for capturing the "colored girl," as she was described on reward posters tacked up as far away as Chicago. In one passage, Goodnow tells how Quarlls attained an outfit of disguise that freed her from hiding in prickly piles of hay and rough buffalo robes: "There were some young ladies [at Deacon Fowler's house] of about Caroline's size and they fitted her out with some clothes—a dress, some gloves, a thick veil, and a small reticule in which to put her jewelry.… Caroline, being well-dressed, after that sat in the seat."

Caroline Quarlls was the first fugitive slave whose journey through Wisconsin is recorded in historical documents. But she was far from the last. More than one hundred escaping slaves made it safely to Canada with the help of Wisconsin residents during the two decades before the Civil War.

The same courage that drove Caroline Quarlls's quest for freedom reverberated more than a century later when, in Shaw, Mississippi, black teenagers stood up, risking everything to take charge of their destiny and claim their rights as "first-class citizens," in the words of the inimitable Fannie Lou Hamer. When Ruby Richard and the other teenage freedom fighters confronted the white school board and the white cotton planters and the white city hall, the brave heart of Caroline Quarlls was beating again in their young chests. When the teenagers of Shaw marched to the school grounds, were poked with cattle prods, arrested and jailed—crunched together, hot and sticky in a tiny cell, eating baloney sandwiches and singing freedom songs—they were channeling Caroline Quarlls's urgency for freedom.

And just as Caroline Quarlls's bravery lived on in the indomitable spirits of Shaw's freedom fighters, so the nineteenth-century beliefs of Waukesha's abolitionists echoed into the next century, driving the Kastes and the Franzes and other citizens of the Wisconsin town when they wrapped their arms around the black citizens of Shaw.

So the newlyweds decided to stake their future in this place where acceptance seemed, if not guaranteed, at least possible, a place to raise children in an affordable neighborhood free of gangs and gunfire. But even in a town whose bedrock was solidly tolerant, racism had a foothold. To find an apartment, they scoured the "To Rent" ads in the Sunday newspaper. They made an appointment with a landlady to see a unit the following day. When they arrived, she took one look at them and suddenly remembered that she had already promised the unit to her son.

After that, Mary Sue went out alone to meet with landlords. She signed a lease agreement—eighty-five dollars a month for a one-bedroom furnished apartment in an old house. On moving day, she and Eddie showed up with their skimpy collection of belongings. While they were unloading, the landlord drove up and laid eyes on Eddie for the first time. In that moment, old memories welled up in the mind of this young black man from Mississippi. He braced for the worst. Whether the landlord was taken aback by Eddie's complexion is unknown. But he never said a negative word, and the couple moved in.

Mary Sue sewed curtains for their little place, just as she had sewed blue-and-white-striped curtains for the community center in Palmers Crossing during Freedom Summer. This time, though, the window coverings were sewn from love and homemaking, not from fear and self-preservation.

As MARY SUE AND Eddie were establishing their new life in Waukesha, events continued to unfold in Shaw. The Hawkins family, the most visible, vocal local leaders in Shaw's civil rights movement, had long lived in the crosshairs of the KKK. For a time, they were protected by the spotlight of public attention. When TV and newspaper reporters, northern activists, and civil rights lawyers were coming and going during the mid-sixties, the Klan laid low in Shaw. But when the last of the white volunteers left Mississippi in 1965, so did the national media.

The terrorism against the Hawkinses began one night in 1967. The family was awakened from their sleep by neighbors shouting. Stumbling out, half asleep in the dark, they were confronted with three wooden crosses burning hot and ominous in their front yard. Andrew and his son, Andrew Junior, doused the flames with buckets of water from the pump. The house and its inhabitants were unharmed. The terrorists, meanwhile, had withdrawn to their hideout to plan their next move.

Another attack under cover of darkness happened soon thereafter. The sleeping family was awakened by a neighbor pounding on their door and yelling, "Get out! Your house is on fire." Just moments after the Hawkinses stumbled out of the house, still dazed with sleep, their roof caved in. Once again, the family escaped injury. Still, they persisted.

IN OCTOBER 1967, EVEN as the Hawkins family braced for the next attack that surely would come, a legal milestone was reached in Mississippi. Seven men who had conspired to murder Michael Schwerner, James Chaney, and Andrew Goodman were convicted and sentenced to prison. The case had been making its way through the courts for three years. Oregon lawyer Jacob Tanzer played a key role in bringing indictments for conspiracy against Neshoba County's murderous gang of Klan thugs and corrupt officials under an obscure Reconstruction-era law. When the original grand jury in the case—eleven whites and one black woman—returned indictments against all the defendants, it was a historic moment. As Tanzer noted in his memoir, they were Mississippi's "first state or federal indictments since Reconstruction alleging crimes by white people against blacks."

Another historic moment was just around the corner, this one involving a high-profile lawsuit filed by Andrew Hawkins and twenty other black residents against the city of Shaw.

One morning after rain had deluged the Delta for days, Hawkins stepped off his front porch into muddy floodwaters.

These were common in his neighborhood of Promised Land. Unpaved roads, poor drainage, and poor storm water management systems were facts of life in Shaw's black districts. But on this particular morning, the fetid stench of human waste reached Andrew's nose, mixed with the familiar scent of wet Delta earth. Looking down, Andrew realized raw sewage was flowing through the open trench that carried storm water alongside the dirt road in front of his house.

Delta Hands for Hope, a nonprofit organization based in Shaw, described on its website what Andrew Hawkins did next:

> Disgusted by the putrid smell and worried about the health effects on his children, [Hawkins] took a walk around the town to assess the greater situation. He was struck by extreme differences in neighborhoods (black v. white). [He saw] deplorable living conditions in the black neighborhoods and modernized, upgraded living conditions in the white neighborhoods.... [He was] tired of the severely disparate living conditions and the "hard-core neglect" of municipal services (e.g., no access to sewer mains, street lighting, paved roads, etc.) in black neighborhoods by the city council. Instead of engaging in his usual routine of filing a complaint with City Hall, he wrote a letter to the U.S. District Court for the Northern District of Mississippi, which began the initial filing of the lawsuit, *Hawkins vs. Town of Shaw*.

The class-action suit filed in 1967, with Andrew and Mae Lou Hawkins among the plaintiffs, alleged what anybody could see with his or her own eyes: city services in Shaw's black neighborhoods were not equal to those in the town's white neighborhoods. White residents had all the modern amenities of mid-sixties America: paved streets brightly lit by streetlamps; fresh, clean water flowing through kitchen and bathroom faucets; flush toilets connected to underground sewer pipes. Black families, on the other hand, walked and drove on dirt or gravel roads that were lit—if at all—by bare bulbs that illuminated next to nothing. "You couldn't see your hand in front of your face," recalls Glory Hawkins-Scott, daughter of Andrew and Mae Lou, who was eighteen when the suit was filed. Black families, if they had access to water at all, typically used well water, pumped by hand outdoors into buckets, which they carried inside for bathing and dishwashing. And without flush toilets, folks were obliged to answer the call of nature in wooden outhouses.

Andrew and his fellow plaintiffs had plenty of legal firepower on their side. A team of lawyers from the NAACP Legal Defense Fund was handling the case.

The trial was held March 20–22, 1969, in the U.S. District Court for the Northern District of Mississippi. The plaintiffs presented mountains of evidence during the three-day trial, including photographs of sewage-filled rivulets of storm water running through shallow ditches just feet from the front doors of Shaw's black residents. The evidence, however, didn't persuade district court judge William Colbert Keady, who argued that if black citizens had a grievance with the city, they had recourse at the ballot box. The decision, which the judge apparently made with a straight face, dripped with irony, with a catch-22 mentality: If you don't like things the way they are, vote.

Andrew Hawkins must have seethed. He was the man who had tried to run for mayor of Shaw in 1964 but was told by elections officials, you can't run for mayor because you're not registered to vote. He was the man who had tried to register to vote but was told by the same elections officials, "You didn't pass the test."

But it was not in Andrew's nature to wallow in rage or resentment, nor was it in his nature to be deterred from his convictions. He and his lawyers appealed the case to the U.S. Court of Appeals for the Fifth District. Among the most seasoned of the lawyers representing Shaw's black citizens on appeal was Jack Greenberg, who had tried the landmark case *Brown v. Board of Education* in 1954. Also on the legal team was Melvyn R. Leventhal of New York, who had married acclaimed black author Alice Walker the same year Hawkins filed his lawsuit. Two legal scholars, Charles Haar of Harvard University and Daniel Fessler of the University of California, Davis, filed a friend-of-the-court brief in support of the appeal. Haar and Fessler noted, among other facts, that "in Shaw, ninety-seven percent of all housing facing on unpaved streets was black; three percent was white." This, they argued, was a prima facie case of discrimination—that is, the evidence showed discrimination on its face.

Years later, Haar and Fessler wrote a book called *The Wrong Side of the Tracks*, which they dedicated to "the Andrew Hawkinses of the world and the lawyers who defend them." Calling the inequities in Shaw "shameful," the authors noted that "even the name of Andrew Hawkins's neighbor-hood—Promised Land—seemed to mock the aspirations of its residents." (The Hawkins family later moved to Johnson's Addition.) In their highly erudite legal analysis, which is sprinkled with quotations from Chaucer, Aristotle, Nietzsche, Faulkner, and other giants of Western philosophy and litera-ture, Haar and Fessler use the *Hawkins* case as a launching pad for their argument that social justice has a longstanding basis in the common law.

Andrew and the other litigants won their appeal in 1971. Chief Judge Elbert Tuttle argued that "the discriminatory provision of municipal services based on race" cannot be accepted. He concluded that in the Shaw case, "a violation of equal protection has occurred."

The decision was reaffirmed by the full appellate court on March 27, 1972. Nearly five years had passed since he first filed the complaint against the city. Andrew's victory in court was a repudiation of a century's worth of exploitation, indignity, and neglect of Shaw's black citizens by their white landlords and civic leaders.

WHEN THE SUIT ENDED in a decisive win for Shaw's black neighborhoods, Shaw's ever-bubbling cauldron of white supremacy boiled over. To the white terrorists, the win in *Hawkins v. Town of Shaw* meant that their town's racial hierarchy was indeed crumbling. The ink was barely dry on the final appellate court ruling when the Klan served up its first shot of retribution against the Hawkinses.

On April 30, 1972, Mary "Mae" Lou Hawkins's life of resistance and activism ended. Glory Hawkins-Scott, who was married and living nearby in Johnson's Addition, got word that her mother was in some kind of dispute with the police. Glory hurried over to the family home just in time to see a police officer planting a big knife in the hand of her mother's lifeless body, which was slumped against a neighbor's house in a sitting position. "Mama was sittin' up by the house," Glory recalls. "I was shakin' her, 'Mama! Mama!' There was a hole straight through her heart. Mama sat dead next to the house all night. You could see the burns on her clothes. She was fifty-seven years old." Glory remembers in particular how her mother's body lay in the dust, her legs splayed so that her underwear was visible. That, Glory says, was an indignity too far.

The killing received coverage in the *Delta Democrat-Times* of Greenville, a town on the Mississippi River just south of the Bolivar County line. In an article headlined "Police Charged in Slaying" the day after the killing, Mae Lou was identified in the second paragraph as "the wife of Andrew Hawkins Sr. who initiated a federal court suit charging the city of Shaw with discrimination in provision of city services." Clearly, the lawsuit had made the Hawkins family particularly noteworthy in the Delta.

The story in the *Delta Democrat-Times* raised more questions than it answered. Drawing heavily from the police report, the reporter said that Mrs. Hawkins had gone to the home of black police officer Andrew Sharpe, presumably to talk to him about her son Junior, who had been in some trouble with the police the day before. Glory later described Officer Sharpe as a "white-controlled" black police officer, an assessment shared by other townspeople. The story went on to say that Mae Lou allegedly used abusive language toward the policeman.

> Sharpe told her she was under arrest. Mrs. Hawkins then ran from the house and Sharpe followed her in his car, according to Bolivar County Sheriff L. B. Williams. When Sharpe caught up with Mrs. Hawkins, he got out of his car and again told her she was under arrest. She allegedly pulled a knife and took a swing at Sharpe, he said. Williams said Sharpe jumped back, ran, and Mrs. Hawkins followed. Sharpe pulled his gun when Mrs. Hawkins came at him with the knife again, he said, and shot her near the heart.

The county held an inquest the following day, according to Glory. "When they went up to testify, everybody's memory failed," she recalls. Sharpe was tried for manslaughter and acquitted. "The case," Glory says, "was thrown out."

Seven years went by. It seemed that the bloodlust had been sated and the remaining family members would be allowed to live in peace.

On March 16, 1979, that hope was shattered.

It was late evening in the quiet town of Shaw. The sounds of the fertile Delta—the chirring and droning of insects—pulsed in the air as winter gave way to a new season. In Johnson's Addition, small children were tucked in for the night. Two of the children tucked in that night were Glory's little girls, Bernadette and Mary Yvette, the granddaughters of Andrew and Mae Lou. Glory's twenty-nine-year-old brother, Andrew Junior, was babysitting that night.

Beneath the seeming peace, a gang of white terrorists skulked in the shadows. That night as the family slept, the terrorists carried a wooden cross into the Hawkinses' yard and planted it in the earth just feet from the unpainted wooden house. They placed full cans of gasoline at intervals at the base of the rough siding, surrounding the house. Then they torched the gasoline-soaked cross and melted back into the night. By the time a neighbor saw the flames and ran to the Hawkinses' door, screaming for them to run, the house was nearly engulfed. As Andrew Junior ran to the back bedroom to rescue his two young nieces, the house exploded, unleashing a glowing orange fireball over Johnson's Addition.

Glory, who was twenty-eight then, had gone to downtown Shaw with friends that night. In the tiny town, residential neighborhoods were just blocks away from the commercial district. From the street, Glory saw the orange glow lighting the sky in the direction of her family's home. Alarmed, she grabbed a friend who had a car and they jumped in, barreling toward the Hawkinses' neighborhood. Smoke was billowing from the house, as neighbors looked on with helpless grief.

Glory bounded out of the car. She could feel the fire's heat radiating all around her. "My babies!" she screamed. "Where are my babies?" Learning that someone had driven one of the girls to the hospital in Cleveland, she again jumped into her friend's car and they raced north on Highway 61.

What she saw at the hospital were the remains of her nine-year-old daughter, Mary Yvette, who had suffered third-degree burns. "Her head was swollen, and you could see the bones in her shoulder," Glory says. As for her twelve-year-old daughter, Bernadette, "They didn't find nothin' but her heart."

The night of the fire, neighbors on the scene counted ten gasoline cans around the house. By the next morning, the cans were gone. "The police said they were investigating," Glory says. "Every ten to fifteen years, the FBI shows up. The case is in the *Harvard Law Review*—an unsolved case." She shakes her head in resignation. "I just turned it over to the Lord."

ONE MAN'S OUTRAGE AT seeing a river of human waste flowing through his neighborhood led to his subsequent fight with a city hall dedicated to keeping black neighbors down. The man's stance, planting his feet on the soil of justice for all people, set off a series of consequential events that played out for the better part of a decade.

Freedom Summer volunteer Heather Tobis Booth, who lived with the Hawkins family as a houseguest during Freedom Summer, summarized that unfolding at a 2014 conference on women's liberation in Boston:

> Their family challenged the town of Shaw in a lawsuit that some think is as significant as *Brown v Board of Education*—this one saying improvements in public services (in) the white part of town ... needed to reflect similar improvements in the black part of town.... In likely retribution for this suit, Mrs. Hawkins was killed by a policeman at her home and their home was firebombed twice killing her son and two grandchildren.

Congressman Bennie Thompson, who represents Bolivar County and the rest of Mississippi's Second District in the

U.S. House of Representatives, memorialized the heroism of the Hawkins family in a 2005 tribute on the floor of the House. As published in the Congressional Record, the tribute reads, in part: "They set out on an expedition against segregation and discrimination to improve life for black folks. Their stubborn will would not allow them to accept the unfair treatment imposed by white folks. In fact their willingness to lead and step out front brought death, alienation, house fires, and increased harassment upon the family. But that did not stop the Hawkins[es]."

Legal scholars still argue about the legacy of the case *Hawkins v. Town of Shaw* in the courts. But Representative Thompson echoed a widely held judgment about the importance of the case when he said it is "often equated with such paramount cases as *Brown v. Board of Education* for being one of the great pillars in African American history."

Heather Tobis Booth paid further tribute to Andrew Hawkins in a retrospective about Freedom Summer edited by historian Stewart Burns: "He believed in a society in which all people could live with dignity and respect," she wrote. "He treated people that way personally and organized to build a society that would act that way also."

The price the Hawkins family paid, as steep as it was, drew little notice beyond the Delta. In the history of Mississippi's white-on-black terrorism, the deaths of Mae Lou, Andrew Junior, Mary Yvette, and Bernadette Hawkins were only a footnote in the story of the civil rights struggle. That's because it was the same price paid by countless other men, women, and children born black in Mississippi's cauldron of racist hate. As Booth noted: "Four deaths in one family that was fighting for freedom and you probably never even heard about it. So it is with the many unrecognized heroines and heroes of the movement."

That might be the most shameful truth about the Hawkinses' fate.

Shaw's black neighborhoods were severely neglected by city officials before they were ordered to equalize services as a result of *Hawkins v. Town of Shaw*. (Photo by Professor Yale Rabin, University of Virginia)

Raw sewage running through open ditches in Andrew
Hawkins's neighborhood led to a successful class-action lawsuit. (Photo by Professor Yale Rabin, University of Virginia)

A dirt road in Shaw was named for the Hawkins family to honor their courage and sacrifice for civil rights. A much bigger sign was erected in 2019, officially naming a stretch of Highway 61 after the family. (Photo by Lee Anna Sherman)

14

Abiding

Blackbird singing in the dead of night
Take these broken wings and learn to fly
All your life
You were only waiting for this moment to arise
—Paul McCartney, from "Blackbird"*

Waukesha, Wisconsin, and Shaw, Mississippi, 1967 and beyond

One morning a year after Eddie and Mary Sue married and settled in Wisconsin, the phone rang at the apartment they were renting in Waukesha. It was Eddie's younger sister Bernice.

"Mama died last night," Bernice said.

And so Eddie packed a few things in a suitcase and boarded a jet for the sad duty of burying his mama, Janie Beatrice Phillips Short. Seven of Janie Bea's eight living children gathered in Shaw for her service at the Mount

---

* In 2002, Paul McCartney told interviewer Chris Douridas on KCRW radio that the song "Blackbird" came to him in Scotland in 1968 as a statement about "the black people's struggle in the southern states." The song debuted on *The Beatles* (the White Album).

Tabor Baptist Church across the street from the rented house where her weak heart had stopped beating. (Bernice, who was married by then, had just had her first child and was unable to attend.) Janie Bea was forty-six years old when she died.

Eddie's brother Freddie was fourteen. He remembers walking into the church and seeing his mother's body resting in a simple casket lined with satin. She was dressed in a pretty pastel frock—"I don't remember the exact color, but I think it was pink." Bernice recalls the color because she chose the dress for her mama's final rest. It was sky blue, the color of the firmament.

Freddie was struck by the peacefulness of her face, a peace he had rarely, if ever, seen on her countenance when she was alive. "I had seen her suffer so much," Freddie said many years later. "I had seen her lay in bed for three months at a time and couldn't get up. And I'd heard her wake up in the middle of the night vomiting. And that was an awful sound for us as little children, because it was as if she was gasping for breath, you know. She had prepared us, you know, for the fact that she might not live very long."

Janie Bea's favorite hymn was "Precious Lord, Take My Hand," a gospel tune written by the father of black gospel music, Thomas A. Dorsey, and a favorite of Dr. Martin Luther King Jr. King requested that the hymn be played at his own funeral, which came tragically just a year later. The hymn speaks of death in the loving, triumphant language of the Christian faithful:

When the darkness appears and the night draws near
And the day is past and gone

At the river I stand
Guide my feet, hold my hand
Take my hand precious Lord, lead me home

Freddie is almost certain the mourners in Shaw sang it at his mama's funeral, though he was so numb and shaken at the time he isn't sure. He loved his mama, but he shed no tears the day she was laid to rest at Mount Tabor Cemetery in her satiny casket. To Freddie, his mama's funeral didn't represent a departure so much as an arrival—a homecoming—for this woman of great faith.

Janie Bea had not seen her husband, Willie James—father of Jeansetta, Ernest, Eddie, Bernice, James, Lee Bertha, Freddie, and Calvin—since Calvin was in diapers. When she died, Calvin was twelve and in middle school.

In 1970, Eddie went to see his daddy in Chicago. He found Willie living alone in an abandoned warehouse on Chicago's west side.

"It was all black with coal soot, very dark with old tires lying around," Eddie recalled years later. "There were no windows, just bare lightbulbs." The roof leaked, and rainwater dripped from the ceiling, puddling on the concrete floor.

As Eddie stood there in the half-light of his daddy's makeshift home, his strongest emotion was sadness. As a child, he had loved and looked up to Willie James Short. Even after Willie fled from Shaw, Eddie clung to his filial love for the industrious man who led the church choir and was skilled in everything from butchering a hog to hanging wallpaper to sewing frilly dresses for his daughters and repairing radios.

As young as Eddie had been when his daddy left, he

fully grasped the threat his father had faced from white terrorists. Eddie got it. Far from blaming Willie for leaving, he hoped and prayed that Chicago would be a place of peace and prosperity for his daddy. It wasn't his daddy's departure but his father's broken promise—to send for Janie Bea and the children—that gnawed at Eddie as the months and then years went by.

"I always wanted to believe that his intention was to send for us," Eddie said, looking back. "When I saw his living conditions—they were atrocious—I understood why he couldn't do it."

Any lingering resentment Eddie harbored drained away. In that lonely, leaking, soot-filled warehouse on the west side of Chicago, the wayward father received the grace of his son's forgiveness.

MARY SUE AND EDDIE got wind of the Hawkins tragedies while building their life in Wisconsin. By then Eddie was working at Waukesha Bearings as a machinist trainee, a job he got through Manpower. Jim Crow was in their rearview mirror. Being black in Waukesha, Eddie says, was both better and worse than being black in Shaw. On the upside of the quality-of-life ledger, black citizens in Wisconsin didn't have to fight or risk their lives to exercise their constitutional rights. In Wisconsin, voting was not lethal. Drinking from a public water fountain, using a public restroom, eating in a public restaurant were everyday options for every citizen.

On the downside of the quality-of-life ledger were the missing ties of kinship, ties that ran deep in the black neighborhoods and churches and cottonfields of the South. Eddie reminisces about picking cotton with other black adolescents, their fingers flying over the prickly bolls so they could get ahead of their elders, joking and laughing as they worked. They had fun, Eddie says, even if the circumstances were dire. And they had each other, families lending a hand to their neighbors, people pitching in when they could. They gave to each other the respect that whites withheld. To Jacob Tanzer, the contrast in how black Mississippians acted with each other versus how they were forced to act around white people was as dramatic as midday versus midnight. "Among themselves," Tanzer wrote in his memoir, "they addressed each other respectfully as Reverend Smith or Deacon Brown or Sister Jones and tried to look out for each other.... Among themselves, they acted with a great dignity."

Eddie missed the warm support of an extended family and a tight community. In black-majority Mississippi, at least he blended in. In Wisconsin, he stuck out. When he started working at Waukesha Bearings in a suburb with big trees and big lawns surrounding ranch-style houses, he rode his bike to and from the nearby factory. One evening as he pedaled home, a cop pulled up beside him in his patrol car. "What're you doin' in this neighborhood?" the officer demanded. "I live here!" Eddie responded.

The second time it happened, Eddie's resentment nearly boiled over. He realized that tears were running down his face. How could he have moved nearly eight hundred miles to the north only to stare the same old bigotry in the eye? At work the next day, he talked to his boss about the incident. The boss dialed the police department and handed the phone to Eddie. After speaking to the officer in charge and giving him all his personal identifying information, Eddie ended the conversation by saying, "Now get your boys off my back!" Eddie was never harassed by cops again. But to this day, he still feels indignant, still feels the emotions of the fifty-year-old memory rising in his gut, when he tells the story.

EDDIE'S MAMA, JANIE BEA, hadn't embraced her son's relationship with Mary Sue at first. When she got word of their impending marriage, her response was, "I don't want no white grandbabies," a sentiment most certainly stemming from the lifelong oppression she and her family had endured. It also grew from her fears for biracial children, kids caught between two cultures—as Eddie puts it, "not black enough to be black or white enough to be white."

Janie Bea's death in July 1967 came just a few weeks before a trip to Waukesha she had planned to take. The "white grandbabies," the biological children of Mary Sue and Eddie, had not yet been conceived when she was laid to rest in her satiny casket. But had she lived to see those grandbabies—two beautiful little boys with light-brown skin—Janie Bea would no doubt have found it in her heart to love them.

She also would have felt sadness at the challenges they would encounter because of the color of their skin. Today, the City of Waukesha's official homepage features a smiling African-American child holding a basketball. But in the seventies and eighties when Eddie and Mary Sue's three sons were growing up, they ran into the racial stereotyping and animus that African-American and biracial kids still encounter all over America.

Eddie's child by the young woman from Shaw, Donald,

came to live with them as a toddler when his mother was unable to care for him properly in Pasadena. When Donald was five, Mary Sue gave birth to a child they named Luther Ellis. "Luther" jointly honored Fannie Lou Hamer and Dr. Martin Luther King Jr. "Ellis" was for pro football star Kenny Ellis, who played for the Green Bay Packers. When Luther was still an infant, the couple held a West African naming ceremony to add African names to both boys' birth names. Mary Sue sewed dashikis for Eddie, little Donald, and baby Luther—West African-style shirts printed in vivid colors and bold patterns that became fashionable among black Americans just about the time the Shorts settled in Waukesha. For Eddie, the dashiki symbolized his pride in his African roots.

To Donald's given name, his parents added Kofi Lumumba. "Kofi" is a West African name for a male child born on a Friday. "Lumumba," meaning "gifted," was chosen to honor Patrice Lumumba, the independence leader and first democratically elected prime minister of the Democratic Republic of the Congo. To Luther's given name was added Yao Damani. "Yao" is a male child born on a Thursday, and "Damani" means "thoughtful."

"We told the children they could use whichever name they wanted," Mary Sue says. "They always used their African names."

When their next son was born eighteen months later, he received his full name right away: Julian Frederick Kofi Babatu—"Julian" for famed black leader Julian Bond (whose notable role in the civil rights movement included communications director for SNCC, member of the Georgia House of Representatives, and chair of the NAACP), "Frederick" for the great statesman and abolitionist Frederick Douglass, and "Kofi" for a baby boy's Friday birth. "Babatu" means "peacemaker."

The children were raised to take pride in their heritage. In the house the family bought in a quiet neighborhood on the outskirts of Waukesha, the three little boys were immersed in positive images of black leaders. The walls of their bedroom were hung with photos from *Ebony* magazine as they applied their Crayolas to coloring books depicting black people, played a black-history board game, and read comic books with themes from black culture.

In a town that was more than ninety percent white—with a sizeable Hispanic community but only a handful of African Americans—the Short family's black-pride stance helped gird the boys against the racism that sometimes came their way. In school, they heard the term *zebra* hurled their way, a crude reference to their biracial genetic makeup. One time, when Babatu was a seventh-grader, one of his classmates tossed the word *nigger* at him. Babatu lashed back, giving the boy a thumping. Babatu got suspended from school, but for the other boy, there were no consequences. Eddie, strongly muscled from lifting weights and sporting a big Afro, went to see the principal. "I guess I looked pretty mean," he says. "I had a large cast on my arm, and I looked like a guy who had seen a hundred fights and could win a hundred more, which wasn't too far from the truth." Standing in the office of the white principal, Eddie asked him why the slur-slinger had not been punished.

"Aren't you going to do anything about this racism?" Eddie demanded.

"Well," the principal retorted huffily, "is your son going to beat up anybody who calls him a bad word?"

"Yeah!" Eddie shot back. "And if you call him that, I'll come down and beat you up, too."

The blood drained out of the principal's face, and his hands were noticeably trembling as he asked his secretary to show Mr. Short out. Babatu was back in school the next day.

The boys looked out for each other. One day at school, Damani heard another kid make a cutting remark to his younger brother, Babatu, in the hallway. Worse yet, the guy making the remark was Jeff, a white buddy of Damani's. "It was hurtful," Damani says, the sting of it not altogether gone after twenty-some years. "I grabbed him and slammed him up against the lockers. His feet were off the ground, and he was gasping." Jeff managed to sputter, "What're you doin'?" And I said, "What're *you* doin'!"

Then there was a time when the boys were in their teens and a three-hundred-pound kid named Tommy sat on top of Babatu in a neighbor's backyard. Once again, it was Damani to the rescue, wrestling Tommy off his younger brother. About the same time, Babatu was working at Burger King, and Damani got wind that a twenty-one-year-old, six-foot-three-inch supervisor had belittled Babatu. The next night, Damani showed up at closing time and gave the supervisor a severe piece of his mind. Babatu's harassers left him alone after that.

After a career in musical theatre as a singer, dancer, and actor in New York City, Lumumba—who now goes mostly by Kofi—became prevention program manager for Diverse and Resilient, a Wisconsin nonprofit dedicated to achieving health equity and improving the safety and well-being of LGBTQ people. In 2019, Lumumba was named to the Wisconsin governor's Health Policy Advisory Council.

Damani says now that his "overarching feeling" as a kid growing up was "fairly fine and comfortable." But in comparison to the school experiences of white classmates, the Short brothers took more than their share of verbal and physical attacks. He learned to compartmentalize his emotions—to "park it"—but "it grinds on you," he admits. After earning a bachelor's degree at the University of Wisconsin, Damani rose up the corporate ladder at GE Healthcare. In 2016, he launched a firm called Lexico Consulting to guide companies in technological and business strategies.

Babatu, like his brothers, takes pride in his ancestry. As a human-resources professional in the business world, he spends a lot of time meeting and greeting potential employees and clients in industries from consumer goods to manufacturing to healthcare, often with an international scope. When he meets someone new and introduces himself as Babatu, the other person sometimes pauses, maybe looks a little puzzled, and then, as if a light turns on, says, "Can I call you Bob?"

"No, it's Babatu," he insists, gently but firmly. Nobody calls him Bob.

LIKE SOLDIERS COMING HOME from war, Mary Sue and Eddie were dogged by trauma for many years after leaving Shaw. Whether it was full-blown post-traumatic stress disorder or not, it had eerie echoes of PTSD. One night, soon after little Lumumba came to live with them, Eddie was working the graveyard shift down at the plant. Mary Sue was sound asleep when a loud thump jolted her awake. She sat up in bed, her heart racing. The noise had come from the front of the house. It instantly brought up the terrorism of Mississippi, of firebombs and Klansmen and cattle prods, which she thought she had left behind. Still suspicious of police officers after her many run-ins with cops in Shaw and Bolivar County, she called Eddie at work. He told her the cops in Waukesha were a different breed from those down south. When the officers came to the house a few minutes later, they found that someone had thrown a beer bottle on the Shorts' front porch, nothing more. Still, Eddie and Mary Sue carried the PTSD for years to come, and their sleep often was troubled by nightmares.

A few years after the beer bottle scare, Mary Sue landed a job with a job-training program for the County of Waukesha. The same day she got the offer, a deputy sheriff strode into the county office building and asked for the personnel director. The deputy clutched in his hand a thick folder stuffed with papers. His face was a study in fury. "Here's what you just hired!" he bellowed, slamming the folder on the director's desk. "You better withdraw that offer, now!"

The personnel director opened the folder and thumbed through page after page of FBI reports with the subject name Mary Susan Gellatly. The reports were filled with details about Mary Sue's civil rights activities in Mississippi—her arrests, voter registration campaigns, public protests, union organizing, even her relationship with Eddie. It felt to Mary Sue like the FBI was surveilling her still. The personnel director, however, was already fully aware of Mary Sue's record because she had written down every one of her arrests on her job application. He refused to withdraw the offer, and Mary

Sue worked for the county for the next decade, moving up to become deputy director of the Employment and Training Department.

Eventually, Mary Sue and Eddie launched a start-up firm of their own—a recruiting business that took special care that women and diverse candidates got equal consideration from employers, especially for managerial positions. At the same time, Eddie spent most of his career, some forty years, at Wisconsin Centrifugal, now a division of MetalTek, machining metal parts for jets, ships, cars, and other products. At his retirement party, the company president stood up and told the gathering: "If you're looking for an example to follow, follow the example of Eddie Short."

MEANWHILE, BACK IN MISSISSIPPI the town of Shaw sat on the fulcrum of a seesaw. On one end was the economy. On the other end was equality. As equality rose, the economy sank.

When black residents rose up and claimed their constitutional rights to eat in public places, swim in public pools, vote in elections, and send their children to good schools, white residents shut down their businesses, drained the pool, and sent their children to private schools, all to dodge integration. The white school board in Shaw went so far as to sell a school to white residents for one dollar, thus making it private. And so the seesaw tipped. A town long bereft of equality became in the late 1960s a town where black citizens took the helm of local government—not so they could take revenge on whites for centuries of abuse, as many white people feared, but so they could improve their lives through the ballot box.

The downside of the seesaw was the economy. The once-booming cotton town slumped economically when "white flight" emptied out the storefronts downtown and planters pulled up stakes or abandoned black labor in favor of machines. It was the same impulse that was driving northern white families from inner-city neighborhoods to sprawling suburbs.

In June 1981, two years after the Hawkins home was firebombed, the *New York Times* ran a story about Shaw titled "From 1932, a Reminder on a Mississippi Main Street," that was picked up by the Associated Press and run in the New Orleans *Times-Picayune* under the headline, "Integration Isn't on Menu in a 1-Room Cafe." The story began by capturing the town's visage fifteen years after Mary Sue and Eddie left. "At 6 a.m., the town looks more ghostly than usual," the reporter wrote. "The business district, once a booming cotton-trading center, now a single block of tattered storefronts where old wooden awnings tilt like pictures imperfectly hung, is nearly deserted."

The *Times* described the seesaw effect on Shaw that began in the early 1960s: "In that decade, a flood of civil rights activity came and went. Another tidal wave hit at the same time: mechanized farming, which swept jobs and money out of Shaw. When the waters receded, Shaw was a different place, formally integrated, economically sapped."

The *Times* story focused on an old white man, owner of a small diner in downtown Shaw, where the menu featured traditional southern fare, dishes like barbecued pig ribs, turnips and greens, fresh okra. The old man, Dinty Moore, had felt the rumblings of a rising: rumors of secret meetings of black activists, reports of charismatic young organizers huddling with black citizens across the Delta, news of agitation for integration in Washington, D.C., stories of demonstrations and boycotts and sit-ins across the South. Dinty Moore wasn't about to open his greasy-spoon diner to black folks. So in 1962 his diner became a private club. To get into the Shady Nook Key Club, customers needed their own key. Only white people were given keys. It's no coincidence that 1962 was the same year Andrew Hawkins took the helm of Shaw's NAACP chapter.

This private club/personal key strategy to keep Jim Crow alive had a solid toehold in the mid-sixties, as noted in a collection of Mississippi freedom school writings. A restaurant owner in the Delta town of Indianola, not far from Ruleville in Sunflower County, offered several white civil rights workers a key to his eatery. "The keys were supposed to prevent integration of the restaurant," reported the freedom school newspaper, the *Ruleville Freedom Fighter*. But when the man learned that the young white people were Freedom Summer volunteers, he angrily rescinded the offer. Key clubs exemplified the creativity of white supremacists as they scrambled to fend off equality. They were a soft form of terrorism. Firebombs and burning crosses weren't the only road of racism in Mississippi.

The story of Shaw's rising can be bookended, like a parable, by two old men, one black, the other white. The black man, Miller Lark, opened the door of his rough-hewn home to welcome white volunteers that summer of 1964, offering to them the only thing he had, songs and prayers. The white man, Dinty Moore, began locking the door of his diner in 1962 to keep his black neighbors out. It was still locked in 1981 when the *New York Times* reporter showed up and knocked. Moore's door was fitted with a tiny window, a one-way peephole, where he could peer out to appraise the skin color of any would-be customer. If you're white, come on in, belly up to a plate of barbecued pig ribs and okra. If you're black, no one's home. Keep on goin' down the road.

By then, 1981, Shaw had its first black mayor, a thirty-year-old named Gregory Flippins. Most of the town's elected officials and two-thirds of its residents were black. None were welcome in Moore's tiny diner.

Still, aspects of the town were undergoing a transformation. The impact of the Federal Housing Administration (FHA), which had become part of the Department of Housing and Urban Development in 1965, was huge. The FHA allowed low-income citizens to buy homes with low down payments, low interest rates, and affordable monthly mortgage payments based on income. Eddie's sister Bernice and her husband, Jake Shaw, were among the many Shaw residents who took out home loans through the FHA. During the twenty or thirty years after Freedom Summer, the shacks in Shaw's black neighborhoods gradually disappeared as small homey-looking brick houses took their place—houses that met building codes and included such basics as electric lights, baseboard heating, insulation, and indoor plumbing.

Andrew Hawkins, had he remained in Shaw, would have seen at least partial fulfillment of his dream of equal city services for black families. But after the police shooting that killed his wife and the firebombing that took the lives of his son and two granddaughters, Andrew moved away from the town and the community he had led with such conviction. He made a new home for himself in Kansas City.

Willie James Short (seated) and some of his adult children gathered for Christmas in 1970 at Jeansetta's home in Chicago. Also pictured are (from left): Jeansetta, Ernest, James, Lee Bertha, Calvin, and Eddie. (Photo by Mary Sue Short)

Eddie took this snapshot of Fannie Lou Hamer with her granddaughters, Lenora and Jacqueline, when he and his son Lumumba, a toddler, visited Mrs. Hamer in Ruleville in about 1968. (Photo by Eddie Short)

In Ruleville, Fannie Lou Hamer and her husband, "Pap," are buried side by side in a memorial park honoring her singular voice and steadfast stand against racism. (Photo by Lee Anna Sherman)

The Short brothers, (counterclockwise, back to front) Damani, Babatu, and Kofi Lumumba, posed for this photo in 2011. (Photo by Diverse & Resilient, Milwaukee, Wisconsin)

Downtown Shaw fell into ruin after white business owners
closed their stores in the aftermath of federal integration
laws. (Photo by Lee Anna Sherman)

Mary Sue and Eddie returned to the Bolivar County Courthouse in 2016 to find their arrest records from five decades
earlier. (Photo by Lee Anna Sherman)

Epilogue

A late-summer squall pounds the windshield as Eddie steers his gray Chrysler south down Highway 61. Fields fly by, one after another, corn, rice, soy. Once upon a time, it was all cotton here in Bolivar County, Eddie says. Now cotton grows only "here and there." The last cotton gin in the small town of Shaw closed not long ago. Once there were four or five.

The year is 2016. A half century has passed since Eddie Short and Mary Sue Gellatly first encountered one another in this forlorn corner of the Mississippi Delta. They have brought me and my husband, Bill Gellatly—Mary Sue's brother—to Bolivar County to see it for ourselves.

On our way to Shaw from Cleveland, we stop for lunch at The Senator's Place. It's noon, and the place is humming. We line up at the buffet and ogle the steaming trays of stewed okra, of meat so tender it falls from the bone, of yams roasted in nutmeg and cinnamon, of cornbread and collard greens. Eddie whispers to the manager, a striking young woman named Sarita, and soon Democratic state senator Willie Simmons emerges from a back room to clap Eddie on the back and hug Mary Sue like the longtime acquaintances they are. It turns out that Sarita runs the place for Senator Simmons, who is her daddy.*

---

* In 2019, when Senator Willie Simmons stepped down

When we sit down to our plates piled with soul food, the senator takes a seat at our table to talk. "My biggest frustration in the legislature is voting on measures that spend $20 billion, $30 billion, and then coming back to my local community and not seeing any impact," says Simmons, who sits on the appropriations committee and chairs the transportation committee for District 13, which includes Bolivar, Sunflower, and Tallahatchie Counties. Still, he relishes his connection to Delta culture. "I'm the only senator in the world that can say B.B. King—King of the Blues—is buried in my district." Simmons is proud, and it shows. He talks about other icons of the Mississippi Delta: Charley Patton, who fathered the Delta Blues; Muddy Waters, who transplanted the Delta Blues to Chicago; and Fannie Lou Hamer, the sharecropper-turned-activist who told her truths to the nation in the unembellished words of a woman who was "sick and tired of being sick and tired."

"Mrs. Hamer brought about inclusion," Simmons says. "She's buried in my district."

Fast-forwarding to today, he mentions an icon of a new era, Morgan Freeman, an Academy Award–winning actor and film narrator whose voice resonates in the minds of most Americans through movies like *Driving Miss Daisy*, *The Shawshank Redemption*, and *Invictus*. Freeman's childhood was spent, in part, in the Delta, and now he splits his time between New York and his Mississippi ranch—a sanctuary for honeybees—in Clarksdale, just a few miles northeast of the Bolivar County line. Clarksdale is the site, too, of the actor's

---

after a quarter century representing District 13, his daughter Sarita ran for and won the seat.

Ground Zero Blues Club, a juke-joint style venue featuring artists like Super Chikan and Bill "Howling-Madd" Perry. "Morgan Freeman lives in one of the counties I represent," Simmons notes. He adds that GRAMMY Museum Mississippi in Cleveland is another of his district's shining stars. "These are things to be proud of as a state senator."

The history of Bolivar County—the notorious as well as the notable—has too often gone untold, he says. Take Freedom Summer, for example. "Sheriff Charlie Capps felt he had a relationship with both the NAACP and the grand wizard of the KKK," the senator muses. "He didn't want any uproar. So he went to the editor of the *Bolivar Commercial* and said, 'Don't cover the Freedom Summer movement.' It was on ABC, NBC, CBS. But it wasn't in the local paper." It's true that the newspaper ran no fact-based accounts of the extraordinarily newsworthy events of Freedom Summer. Instead, readers got only racist rantings in the opinion pages. Despite his efforts at news suppression, Sheriff Capps failed to stifle the "uproar."

Black citizens viewed 1964's influx of white volunteers as a mixed blessing, at best. "We were glad to see them, but we were fearful of the reactions of the (white) locals—that they would take it out on us. Your parents wanted to make sure you were a 'boy'—be deferential to whites, don't be seen with a white female, etcetera."

We get back on the road to Shaw. By the time we turn off the highway, the rain has stopped. Dusk is gathering over the Delta. On the edge of downtown Shaw, we step out of the air-conditioned Chrysler into a blanket of hot air, still wet and heavy from the deluge. Steam rises from the pavement.

The shadowed cypresses along the bayou pulse with the vibration of an invisible life-form, cicadas, so loud we raise our voices a notch to hear each other.

It's a Friday evening. The streets are mostly deserted. On a wire above the street sits a cardinal, its ruby plumage at odds with the graying town. The red bird calls into the dusk.

I follow along behind Eddie and Mary Sue, holding Bill's arm and watching my footing. The sidewalks are buckled and crumbling. Weeds grow in the cracks. Everywhere are boarded-up storefronts, loose bricks, granular mortar. We pass Doc Peeler's old office, where once upon a time black patients were required to use a separate entrance marked "Colored." On the long-ago threshold of a dry goods store, blue and white ceramic tiles that once spelled RUBENSTEIN's are cracked and missing.

The day fades into twilight. The old train depot and Liar's Park seem to hold the ghosts of white men who once loitered there, swapping stories. There are the usual institutions of any municipality: city hall, police station, post office. On the street level of the First National Bank building, dated 1904, a neon sign glows "Open" at the Cozy Corner barbershop, one of a handful of enterprises still holding on in downtown Shaw. Across the street, Deb's Beauty Salon is fronted by a thicket of lawn signs advertising everything from hand-dipped ice cream to chicken wings for fourteen dollars a bag.

You can still get your hair done in Shaw. But you can't check out a book. A sign tacked on the door of the Field Memorial Library reads, CLOSED UNTIL FURTHER NOTICE.

A food truck hawking snow cones rolls by, its tinkly music

momentarily breaking the stillness. A pickup truck hauling a 350-gallon cast-iron smoker pulls up and parks at the curb. We chat with the owner, Charlie Jackson, a black man in a green apron selling white-oak-smoked sausages, which, he tells us, are lower in fat than other sausages. He uses real honey in his barbecue sauce, he adds. As we listen to Mr. Jackson's sales pitch, there is a sudden commotion: a gimpy dog races by "like a shootin' star!" as a barefoot boy wearing black-framed glasses exclaims. The boy and his sister, thin and bashful in a green dress—Mr. Jackson's grandkids, we learn—stand watchfully on the sidewalk as the dusk deepens. Another little girl walks up to the truck and gives the peddler two dollars for a bottle of water. Hardly anyone drinks the tap water in Shaw, I later learn. "You can't drink the water now," laments Glory Hawkins-Scott when we meet her the next day. "You have to buy bottled water." She tells us, too, that the town flooded in April. "There was water up the walls eleven or twelve inches," she says, shaking her head. "They had to pick up some people in boats."

We walk across the bayou and ramble through the residential section of Johnson's Addition. The roads are pitted and pocked with potholes. Back in Eddie's day, most houses were built of wood. Now the few old wooden homes that have survived fires and floods and firebombs are mixed with small brick houses built with low-interest loans from the FHA. Skinny dogs sniff under the shrubbery. Cats watch from low rock walls. There are shade trees. There are crape myrtles, whose flamboyant blooms in purples and pink seem oddly garish against the dusty tones of the neighborhood.

As we walk, Eddie points out this house and that house,

recalling the neighbors whose lives peopled his childhood and whose abodes were, and clearly still are, the most significant landmarks in his mental map of his hometown. He sees the neighborhood as it was back then. At the unlocking of these long-ago recollections, his demeanor brightens. "The lady who took the tickets at the theater lived here," he says. "I used to cut her lawn." He indicates the home of Daisy Greenwood, who once hosted a freedom school in her living room. Then he gestures toward an empty lot, overgrown, where his family lived after moving into town from the plantation. "The house is gone now."

He points out the onetime grocery store of Joe Canonici, the Italian grocer who served black customers and civil rights workers, cashing their checks when others wouldn't. For these kindnesses, Mr. Canonici became the target of a hate flier circulated by local white supremacists. He points to Mrs. Evie Nola's boardinghouse that also took in old folks. Memories of the 1960s, of Freedom Summer, of being an agent of change in a place where change once seemed illusory, unthinkable, crowd into Eddie's consciousness. "There's the Church of God in Christ where we had the mass meetings," he says. "There's where the Bartley house was," he says, pointing to the ashy remains of a recent fire. Velma Bartley and her husband, T. S., operated Club DeLisa out back, where Mary Sue and Eddie and the other activists had kicked back to jukebox tunes on Saturday nights. "Her sons, Thomas and Charles, were two of the people who integrated the white school." The nightclub now is just a concrete slab.

As we head back to the car with night full upon us, Eddie remarks, mostly to himself, "Shaw's not what it used to be."

ON SUNDAY MORNING, WE once again climb into the Chrysler. This time Eddie steers toward the countryside. We pass the churchyard where Eddie's first wife, Alice, and the couple's unborn baby are buried. "There were no permanent markers in those days," Eddie remarks. We pass a white-folks-only cemetery. Even in death, white Mississippians imposed segregation on their black brethren.

A gray shroud of rain hangs on the horizon as we drive toward our destination, a black church called Pilgrim Rest Missionary Baptist. We cross Bitter Creek, pass a pecan orchard, see long, straight irrigation channels from horizon to horizon. Metal grain storage bins stand like sentinels in the fields. A sign hanging on a shed says PRECINCT. Telephone poles, heavy with vines, lean at odd angles along the road. Now and then, we pass a big plantation house. "There used to be little houses for workers," Eddie notes. Those little houses—those plantation shacks like the ones Eddie lived in as a small child—have long since rotted into the fertile Delta soil.

At the intersection of two quiet roads among corn and bean fields stands a small church. Outside, there's not a breath of wind or an audible decibel of sound. But inside, hallelujah! After Shaw's spectral silences, the cemeteries and churchyards, the pastoral quiet of planted acres, I feel like I've found the life force of Bolivar County. The parishioners welcome us warmly, with smiles and open arms. Mary Sue, Bill, and I are the only white folks in the lovely sanctuary. After meeting some of the people and sharing a bit of the story of Mary Sue and Eddie's activism, we take our seats in the rows of polished wooden pews. "Sunday best" is the dress code here. Teenage girls with long braided cornrows wear pretty cotton frocks in pastels of blue and pink and yellow. In an alcove at the right front of the church sit the church mothers—dignified ladies in feathered hats, pearls, navy-blue suits. In the mass meetings of Freedom Summer, the church mothers always sat in the first few rows and started the first song.

I glance at Eddie and notice a difference. The muscles in his face have relaxed. He looks completely at ease for the first time since I've known him. The Shaw of his boyhood has mostly dissolved into the past, existing in the gray matter of yesterday. But his true home, the rock upon which he has staked his adult life, is, to him, immoveable. Paradoxically, it is also portable, outlasting all earthly places yet carried in the mortal heart. Here in this humble church, its steeple rising at a country crossroads on the outskirts of the Mississippi Delta, Eddie Short lets down his guard.

The pastor reads from Matthew 5:5. "Blessed are the meek, for they shall inherit the earth ..." People follow along in their Bibles, worn and frayed, bristling with bookmarks. One deacon reads the passage on a Kindle. A man plays an electric bass guitar. I can feel the sonic vibrations in the floorboards under my feet. The singing of the people reverberates off the walls and ceiling. The Reverend Harold Wilson reminds the congregation that you can be the "town scoundrel" or the "low-downest" person around and still be redeemed by the Lord.

He introduces Eddie and Mary Sue as civil rights workers from the sixties, asking them to stand. Everyone claps. He reminds the worshippers that "back in the day," blacks had to sit at the back of the bus, had no central air conditioning to relieve the oppressive Delta humidity, and often had nothing to eat for dinner but cornbread and buttermilk. "Now you can go to any college you want," he tells them. "That's why I don't go around hating white people—you never know who's going to help you. Y'all say 'Amen'!"

IN THE SPRING OF 2018, Bill and I visit Shaw again with Mary Sue and Eddie. Since our first visit two years earlier, Shaw's citizens have given the town a kind of facelift, hand painting murals—colorful images crelebratory of the town's history—on the ruined facade of the downtown commercial district. The facelift reflects the pride of a community that lacks the resources to rebuild yet lovingly retains the dignity of a cherished hometown. It reflects a steely resilience that abounds in the town of Shaw—a gritty tenacity that springs, most certainly, from the people's unshakeable faith in the Lord and buttressed by the bonds of kinship that wrap around them. Everyone knows everyone else, and chances are they have cousins in common. They are as tightly knit as a handmade sweater.

Shaw's resilient spirit pervades the town's two public schools, McEvans Elementary and Shaw High, which are housed together on the same schoolgrounds where Eddie and Mary Sue were arrested in 1965. All but one of the students enrolled here are black. Meanwhile, on the other side of town, the old brick school that was once the pride of Shaw's white community sags and crumbles, its windows boarded up with plywood, a monument to white flight, when families pulled their kids out of public education and enrolled them in private institutions after integration became inevitable in the 1960s.

A palpable sense of mission wraps around the cinderblock

building, refurbished to rid it of mold and asbestos. Principal Daphne Young welcomes us. Black students, once forced to make do with frayed textbooks handed down from the white school, still don't have many books, Young admits. But curriculum materials are abundant and available on the school's sixty Google Chromebooks, laptop computers that students can check out. Nearly 95 percent of the high school students graduate, the principal boasts, and most of them aspire to college. State assessments, however, show that fewer than 15 percent of Shaw's graduates are proficient in college readiness. Whether headed for college or not, they likely will move away from Shaw, where jobs are as scarce as ivory-billed woodpeckers, limited mostly to a Dollar General store and a couple of gas stations.

When American history teacher Tikisha Latham strides in to meet us, she brims with the Shaw spirit. She tells us she couldn't wait to return to her hometown and put her teaching certification and master's degree from Delta State University to use. Her strategy is simple: teach not just to students' heads, but to their senses, all of them. Her unit on civil rights, for example, locates racial history squarely in the realm of personal experience, of hometown lore, of family ancestry, of real life. Dry, pedantic, and faded her material is not. Rather, she teaches in three dimensions, animating the lessons, literally, out on the landscape, out on the Mississippi Delta where most of her students first opened their eyes upon the world.

"I sell it to them like it's a story," the young teacher says, her tone suggesting the moral conscience she brings to her teaching. "We talk about the Voting Rights Act, the march on Selma. About MLK and Malcom X, how they paved the way. I tell them to think about the blood, sweat, and tears. They become emotional. I tell them, 'Just imagine going to the movies and you can't sit where you want.' I say, 'We live in a town where African-American kids couldn't go to the white school. People mocked them and spit on them.'" She takes her students on a tour of the Delta, shows them the Mississippi Blues Trail, the Amzie Moore memorial park, Fannie Lou Hamer's hometown of Ruleville. They go to Dockery Plantation, the cotton farm in Sunflower County where the Delta blues sprang up. They go to Parchman Farm, the notorious prison farm where black prisoners worked the fields and were leased to landowners for their labor. They watch the movie *The Butler*, a historical drama about a black butler working in the White House.

"I pass these stories down to our kids," she says. "I let them know what happened in the sixties. It gets them thinking about current policies. My prayer every morning is, I want to impact someone's life."

At The Senator's Place in the summer of 2016, we top off our beans and greens with bowls of rhubarb crisp. The senator talks with feeling about the unintended consequences of integration and the subsequent white flight that pulled the rug out from under the town.

"Shaw lost its financial base," he says. "The high school is in very bad shape. There are little to no resources because business and industry left. There's no tax base. Since fifty years ago, the county has shifted politically. Municipal leaders are mostly black now. Politics has shifted, but economics has not. Blacks are still the have-nots."

In 1960, the population of Bolivar County was fifty-four thousand, Simmons says. Now, it's thirty-four thousand. Fifty years ago, there were five hospitals. Now there's one. Head Start had twenty-one centers in 1966. Now there are seven. The nearby town of Merigold, he says, "has a good tax base, a magnet school, a nationally recognized elementary school." He attributes these assets to Merigold's thriving business scene, which boasted wildly popular enterprises like Crawdad's seafood restaurant, McCarty's pottery gallery, and an iconic place called Po' Monkey's. In a 2007 article in the *New York Times*, Erik Eckholm described Po' Monkey's as "a patched-up sharecropper shack," one of the Delta's "last authentic juke joints." Simmons sings its praises. "It attracts folks from all over the world, blacks and whites, New York and Japan, everybody loves each other. It's the most diverse place in Mississippi."

In Eddie's day, blues joints like Po' Monkey's gave black citizens respite from the aches of hard labor and the bitterness of racism. In later decades, this living relic of a bygone era seemed like a time machine, where people could step into yesterday for a few hours, feel the pulse of a world that had come to embrace the richness of Delta history and culture, if only in the rearview mirror. Now even this shred of an era is gone. Po' Monkey's closed when owner Willie Seaberry died in his sleep the very summer Simmons waxed nostalgic about the place. The artifacts of the juke joint were sold at auction in 2018.

Every year when October rolls around, Shaw calls its

citizens home. The Shaw diaspora returns. Hundreds of residents, current and former, gather for the town's annual reunion. In 2019, that reunion was particularly meaningful—a commemoration of the fiftieth anniversary of *Hawkins v. Town of Shaw*, organized by the nonprofit organization Delta Hands for Hope and sponsored by Delta State University, the Mississippi Humanities Council, the National Parks Conservation Association, Veterans of the Mississippi Civil Rights Movement, and U.S. Congressman Bennie Thompson, among others. Mary Sue spoke as part of a panel on the civil rights movement in Shaw. A segment of Highway 61 was renamed Andrew and Mary Lou Hawkins Memorial Highway.

This tribute, so long in coming, brings honor to the small town of Shaw and its rise against bigotry. The plantation shacks have sunk into the soil. The back-of-the-bus, end-of-the-line, whites-only access to public services are the subjects of museum exhibits and the remembered burden of black citizens old enough to have lived them.

Yet, just eleven miles up Highway 61, a statue towers upon the grounds of the Bolivar County Courthouse, a monument to the Confederate soldiers—the "dead upon the field of glory, hero fit for song and story"—who fought and died for the right to enslave black people, to buy and sell the ancestors of these citizens of Shaw. Dedicated in 1908 and sponsored by the United Daughters of the Confederacy, the statue is one of 1,747 monuments pinpointed on a "hate map" by the Southern Poverty Law Center in its 2019 publication *Whose Heritage: Public Symbols of the Confederacy*. It is in the shadow of this statue that Bolivar County conducts official business, the business of the people, in the year 2020. And so the stain remains.

Author's Note

This story has been pieced together from many sources. The unpublished memoir of Eddie and Mary Sue Short formed the scaffolding upon which I layered information gleaned from multiple interviews with the Shorts, their children, their fellow Freedom Summer volunteers, Eddie's sister and brothers, and citizens of Shaw who participated in the events described here. Other primary sources included FBI reports of surveillance activities and contemporaneous newspaper accounts of civil rights activities in the Delta, including editorials in the *Bolivar Commercial*, which I read on microfiche at the Bolivar County Library in Cleveland, Mississippi. Secondary sources included the richly researched books by many authors documenting the tumultuous times during which this account takes place.

Naturally, after more than fifty years, people's memories of events fade. To fill in some of the gaps in personal recollections, I have worked closely with the Shorts, weaving together their still-vivid memories of events with my writer's "empathetic imagination" to give readers a rich, nuanced sense of the human drama that played out in Shaw during the civil rights movement. Any errors in this account are mine alone.

Lee Anna Sherman

Bibliography

Abbott, Carl. "Vanport," in *The Oregon Encyclopedia*. Portland, Oregon: Oregon Historical Society, 2019.

Ackerman, Kenneth D. *The Young J. Edgar Hoover: Hoover and the Red Scare, 1919–1920*. Falls Church, Virginia: Viral History Press, 2011.

———. "Five Myths About J. Edgar Hoover." *Washington Post*, November 9, 2011.

"African-American Families." *International Encyclopedia of Marriage and Family*. Encyclopedia.com, 16 March, 2019.

"Alabama Prisoners Are Accusing Police of Using 60's Cattle Prods." *New York Times*, August 30, 1981.

Angelou, Maya. *And Still I Rise*. New York: Random House, 1978.

Ardery, Philip. "Revolution in the Delta: Farm Hands Go on Strike." Atlanta, Georgia, *Southern Courier*, July 16, 1965.

Atwater, James. "'If We Can Crack Mississippi'." *Saturday Evening Post*, July 25, 1964.

Belfrage, Sally. *Freedom Summer*. New York: Viking, 1965.

Blackmon, Douglas A. *Slavery by Another Name: The Reenslavement of Black Americans from the Civil War to World War II*. New York: Anchor Books, 2009.

Bond, Julian. Introduction to Elizabeth Martinez, ed., *Letters from Mississippi: Reports from Civil Rights Volunteers and Poetry of the 1964 Freedom Summer*. Brookline, Massachusetts: Zephyr Press, 2007.

Booker, Simeon, with Carol McCabe Booker. *Shocking the Conscience: A Reporter's Account of the Civil Rights Movement*. Jackson, Mississippi: University Press of Mississippi, 2013.

Booth, Heather Tobis. "Foreword," in Stewart Burns, ed., *Freedom Summer: Citizenship Supreme: Testimony of Participants*. Bloomington, Indiana: AuthorHouse, 2014.

———. "Some Civil Rights and Student Movement Origins to Women's Liberation." Paper presented at "A Revolutionary Moment: Women's Liberation in the Late 1960s and Early 1970s," Boston University, March 27–29, 2014. Available at www.bu.edu/wgs/files/2013/10/Booth-Some-Civil-Rights-and-Student-Movement-Origins-to-Women's-LIberation.pdf.

Bragg, Rick. "Memories of a Deadly Assault in 1966 Are Reawakened at Klan Trial." *New York Times*, August 19, 1998.

Brown, Luther, Lee Aylward, and Henry Outlaw. *War Comes to the Delta: World War II and the Mississippi Delta, as Told by the People Who Lived It*. Cleveland, Mississippi: Delta Center for Culture and Learning at Delta State University, 2002.

Carmichael, Stokely, with Ekwueme Michael Thelwell. *Ready for Revolution: The Life and Struggles of Stokely Carmichael (Kwame Ture)*. New York: Scribner, 2003.

CBS News. "The Search in Mississippi." Special report broadcast June 25, 1964.

Crevar, Alex. "Driving the Juke Joint Trail." *New York Times*, May 17, 2013.

Dees, Morris, with Fiffer, Steve. *A Lawyer's Journey: The Morris Dees Story*. Chicago: American Bar Association, 2001.

"Delta CR Worker Linked to Reds: State Agency Brands Shaw Woman." *Jackson Daily News*, June 28, 1965.

Delta Hands for Hope. "Background of the Case." Available at www.deltahandsforhope.org/casebackground.

deShazo, Richard D., ed. *The Racial Divide in American Medicine: Black Physicians and the Struggle for Justice in Health Care*. Jackson, Mississippi: University Press of Mississippi, 2018.

Dretzin, Rachel, and Phil Bertelsen, directors. *Hope and Fury: MLK, the Movement and the Media*. National Broadcasting Company, March 24, 2018.

Eckholm, Erik. "At Night, Farmer Trades His Tractor for the Blues." *New York Times*, March 7, 2007.

Estes, Steve. "Engendering Movement Memories: Remembering Race and Gender in the Mississippi Movement," in Renee C. Romano and Leigh Raiford, eds., *The Civil Rights Movement in American Memory*. Athens, Georgia: University of Georgia Press, 2006.

Forman, James. *The Making of Black Revolutionaries*. New York: Macmillan, 1972.

Gonzales, Laurence. *Deep Survival: Who Lives, Who Dies, and Why*. New York: Norton, 2003.

"From 1932, a Reminder on a Mississippi Main Street." *New York Times*, June 1, 1981.

Goodnow, Lyman. "Recollections of Lyman Goodnow." Manuscript in the Milwaukie Area Research Center, Gold Meir Library, University of Wisconsin-Milwaukee (Milwaukee SC 19). Online facsimile at digital.library. wisc.edu/1711.dl/wipionexp.Goodnow2e.

Gray, William F. *Imperial Bolivar*. Cleveland, Mississippi: Bolivar County, 1923.

Haar, Charles M., and Daniel Wm. Fessler. *The Wrong Side of the Tracks: A Revolutionary Rediscovery of the Common Law Tradition of Fairness in the Struggle Against Inequality*. New York: Simon and Schuster, 1986.

"'Happy' Negroes Dispute Sheriff; Mississippians Write of Life in Letters to The Times." *New York Times*, August 9, 1964.

Harrington, Michael. *The Other America: Poverty in the United States*. New York: Scribner, 1962.

Huie, William Bradford. *Three Lives for Mississippi*. Jackson, Mississippi: University Press of Mississippi, 1965.

Jones, Lucy. *The Big Ones: How Natural Disasters Have Shaped Us (and What We Can Do About Them)*. New York: Doubleday, 2018.

Kaiser, Robert G. "Eastland Going, but His Era Is Long Gone." *Washington Post*, March 23, 1978.

Kaste, Ivan. "Southern Travels Destroy Stereotypes." *Waukesha Freeman*, May 7, 1965.

Ku Klux Klan. *Kloran. Klan in Action. Constitution.* Tuscaloosa, Alabama: Imperial Press, 1968.

Lee, Chana Kai. *For Freedom's Sake: The Life of Fannie Lou Hamer.* Urbana and Chicago: University of Illinois Press, 1999.

Martin, E. L. Journal of the Proceedings of the Constitutional Convention, of the State of Mississippi: Begun at the City of Jackson on August 12, 1890, and Concluded November 1, 1890. Jackson, Mississippi: State of Mississippi, 1890.

Martin, Gordon A. Jr. *Count Them One by One: Black Mississippians Fighting for the Right to Vote.* Jackson, Mississippi: University Press of Mississippi, 2010.

Martinez, Elizabeth, ed. *Letters from Mississippi: Reports from Civil Rights Volunteers and Poetry of the 1964 Freedom Summer.* Brookline, Massachusetts: Zephyr Press, 2007.

McAdam, Doug. *Freedom Summer.* New York: Oxford University Press, 1988.

McCain, Franklin. Interview with Michele Norris. "The Woolworth Sit-In That Launched a Movement." NPR, February 1, 2008.

McCartney, Paul. Interview with Chris Douridas. KCRW, Los Angeles, May 25, 2002.

Mendelsohn, Ink. "The Jukebox Still Rocks." *Chicago Tribune*, February 26, 1989.

Miller, R. Robin, and Sandra Lee Browning. "Sharing a Man: Insights from Research." *Journal of Comparative Family Studies* 31 (Summer 2000): 339–346.

Mills, Kay. *This Little Light of Mine: The Life of Fannie Lou Hamer*. Lexington, Kentucky: University Press of Kentucky, 2007.

"Mississippi Freedom Labor Union." Memo to FBI director from Special Agent in Charge, FBI, U.S. Department of Justice, Jackson, Mississippi, June 3, 1965.

Moody, Anne. *Coming of Age in Mississippi*. New York: Dial Press, 1968.

Moses, Robert P. "Speech on Freedom Summer at Stanford University," Palo Alto, California, April 24, 1964. Available at americanradioworks.publicradio.org/features/blackspeech/bmoses.html.

"Negroes Holding a Mock Election in Mississippi." *New York Times*, November 1, 1964.

Nevins, Buddy. "Bruce Rogow Rocks the Boat." *South Florida Sun-Sentinel*, September 18, 1988.

Nokes, R. Gregory. *Breaking Chains: Slavery on Trial in the Oregon Territory*. Corvallis, Oregon: Oregon State University Press, 2013.

Nossiter, Adam. "Unearthing a Town Pool, and Not for Whites Only." *New York Times*, September 18, 2006.

Patch, Penny. "Sweet Tea at Shoney's." In Constance Curry et al., *Deep in Our Hearts: Nine White Women in the Freedom*

Movement. Athens, Georgia: University of Georgia Press, 2000.

Pauley, Garth E. "John Lewis, 'Speech at the March on Washington' (28 August 1963)." *Voices of Democracy* 5 (2010): 18–36.

"Police Charged in Slaying." Greenville, Mississippi, *Delta Democrat-Times*, May 1, 1972.

"Portland Girl Tells of Terrorism in Mississippi." *Oregonian*, November 13, 1964.

Roberts, Wallace. July 13, 1964, letter from Shaw, Mississippi, available in the Civil Rights Movement Archive at www. crmvet.org/lets/640713_roberts-let.pdf.

Roberts, Wally. "Sheriff Capps and the Shaw Freedom School" (2014), available in the Civil Rights Movement Archive at www.crmvet.org/nars/shawfs64.htm.

Robinson, Jessica. "Honorary Degree: What's It Good For?" NPR, May 10, 2012.

Sack, Kevin. "Mississippi Reveals Dark Secrets of a Racist Time." *New York Times*, March 18, 1998.

Scarbrough, Tom. "Bolivar County (Supplemental Report)." Mississippi Sovereignty Commission, June 18, 1965.

Short, Eddie, and Mary Sue Short. *Fireproof Freedom*. Unpublished memoir.

Sklar, Kathryn Kish, and Elaine DeLott Baker. "How and Why Did Women in SNCC Author a Pathbreaking Feminist Manifesto, 1964–1965?" In *Women and Social Movements in the United States, 1600 to 2000*. Alexandria, Virginia: Alexander Street, March 2015.

Stevenson, Bryan. *Just Mercy: A Story of Justice and Redemption.* New York: Spiegel and Gau, 2014.

Student Nonviolent Coordinating Committee. *The General Condition of the Mississippi Negro.* Atlanta, Georgia: Student Nonviolent Coordinating Committee, 1963.

Sturkey, William, and Jon N. Hale, eds. *To Write in the Light of Freedom: The Newspapers of the 1964 Mississippi Freedom Schools.* Jackson, Mississippi: University Press of Mississippi, 2015.

Tanzer, Jacob. *1964, My Story of Life and Death in Mississippi.* Unpublished memoir.

Tyson, Timothy B. *The Blood of Emmett Till.* New York: Simon and Schuster, 2017.

"Unofficial Vote." *Memphis World*, November 14, 1964. Available at dp.la/primary-source-sets/fannie-lou-hamer-and-the-civil-rights-movement-in-rural-mississippi/sources/857.

von Hoffman, Nicholas. "A Bitter Cotton-Chopping Strike: The Delta Negroes' Poverty Fight." *Chicago Daily News*, July 27, 1965.

Watson, Bruce. *Freedom Summer: The Savage Season That Made Mississippi Burn and Made America a Democracy.* New York: Viking, 2010.

Weiner, Tim. Interview with Terry Gross. "The History of the FBI's Secret 'Enemies' List." NPR, February 14, 2012.

"Whose Heritage? Public Symbols of the Confederacy." Montgomery, Alabama: Southern Poverty Law Center, 2019.

Wilkerson, Isabel. *The Warmth of Other Suns: The Epic Story of the Great Migration*. New York: Vintage Books, 2010.

Wiltse, Jeff. *Contested Waters: A Social History of Swimming in America*. Chapel Hill: University of North Carolina Press, 2007.

Wiltse, Jeff. Interview with Michel Martin. "Public Swimming Pools' Divisive Past." NPR, May 28, 2007.

Wisconsin Historical Society. "The Underground Railroad in Wisconsin." Available at www.wisconsinhistory.org/Records/Article/CS566.

Wren, Christopher S. "Mississippi: The Attack on Bigotry." *Look* magazine, September 8, 1964.

Wright, Richard. *Black Boy (American Hunger): A Record of Childhood and Youth*. New York: Harper and Brothers, 1945.

Acknowledgments

I am grateful beyond measure to Mary Sue and Eddie Short for entrusting me with the telling of their story. It has been one of the great privileges of my life not only to write about their remarkable journey but also to travel with them in Mississippi, twice, doing research for this book. They have enriched my understanding of history and humanity in immeasurable ways.

Deepest gratitude, also, to the many residents of Shaw who offered up their memories for this book. In particular, Bernice Short Shaw, Freddie Short, James Short, Glory Hawkins-Scott, Bernice Watts, Ruby Richard Brown, Peyton Brown, and Gregory Flippins, Shaw's first black mayor, contributed invaluable recollections and insights. Freedom Summer volunteers Dennis Flannigan and Robert Weil gave generously of their time to share details of their work in Shaw and their motivations for joining the struggle.

Sheridan McCarthy and Stanton Nelson of Meadowlark Publishing Services in Corvallis, Oregon, made this indie book possible with their wealth of knowledge and practical experience. I thank them, particularly, for sticking with the project through an especially thin spot in the thick-and-thin. Monica Drost, mapmaker extraordinaire, was a delight to work with and showed grace under pressure through countless revisions. It is my good fortune to have as a dear friend

Lorraine Anderson, book editor par excellence. Lorraine brought her impeccable judgment to the editing of this book, which is vastly improved by her attention both to the finest details and to the storyteller's art. She is the best. As for the women of my beloved writing group—Lorraine Anderson, Carol Savonen, and Carla Wise—their feedback and moral support made bringing this project along infinitely more enjoyable.

Many thanks to Bill Blakney for reading an early draft of the manuscript and vouching for its cultural authenticity from his viewpoint as a Mississippi native. And thanks to my mother, Molly, my sister, Teri, and my brother, James, for enthusiastically reading early chapters and giving over-the-top familial praise. Teri also brought her lifetime of graphic design talent to refinements of the cover design. Kudos also to Cynthia Short for bringing her abundant talents to creating our website and designing marketing materials. Reference librarian Tamara Blackwell gave generously of her time and expertise in the Mississippi Collection at the Bolivar County Library in Cleveland.

Finally, to my husband, Bill Gellatly, younger brother of Mary Sue, I offer my loving thanks, first for bringing me into his amazing family, and second for his invaluable help and support throughout the book project. Beyond his hands-on endeavors to organize photos and seek permissions, beyond the grilled-cheese sandwiches that sustained me through many working lunches, beyond his diligence digging into archives and libraries with me in Mississippi, it was his believing in me that made all the difference.

Credits

Grateful acknowledgment is made for permission to reprint excerpts from the following copyrighted works. Unless noted here, lyrics are from songs in the public domain, and quotes are within the realm of fair use doctrines.

Maya Angelou, "Still I Rise," from *And Still I Rise*. Copyright © 1978 by Maya Angelou. Used with permission of Random House.

Nina Simone, lyrics to "Mississippi Goddam." Copyright © 1964 by Nina Simone. Used with permission of Alfred Music Publishing.

Photo of Mary Sue playing the guitar at the July 4 party at the Dahmer farm is used with permission of the curators of the Herbert Randell Collection at the University of Southern Mississippi.

Photo of George Shelton is used with permission of the *Southern Courier* with the cooperation of the Alabama State Archives.

Three photos of street scenes showing substandard and hazardous sewers and drainage ditches in Shaw are by Yale

Rabin and were published in Charles M. Haar and Daniel Wm. Fessler, *The Wrong Side of the Tracks* (New York: Simon and Schuster, 1986) and submitted as evidentiary records in the *Hawkins v. Town of Shaw* lawsuit.

Photos by Wallace Roberts are used with permission granted in writing to the Shorts.

Every effort has been made to trace copyright holders and to obtain their permission for the use of copyrighted material. The author apologizes for any errors or omissions in the above list and would be grateful if notified of any corrections that should be incorporated in future reprints or editions of this book.

About the Author

A native northwesterner, Lee Anna Sherman worked as a reporter, feature writer, and editor for various publications after earning a master's degree from the School of Journalism at the University of Oregon. In the late 1990s, she helped launch the nationally recognized magazine *Northwest Education,* which she edited for eight years. Most recently, she was a founding staff member of *Terra* magazine, Oregon State University's award-winning research magazine, serving as research writer and associate editor for more than a decade. She is co-author with Betsy Ramsey of *The Reading Glitch: How the Culture Wars Have Hijacked Reading Instruction* (Lanham, Maryland: Roman and Littlefield, 2006). Her work has received recognition from the Oregon Newspaper Publishers Association, the Oregon Society of Professional Journalists, the Alliance of Area Business Publications, the Association of Educational Publishers (EdPress), and the Council for Advancement and Support of Education. She lives in Corvallis, Oregon, with her husband, Bill Gellatly.

CPSIA information can be obtained
at www.ICGtesting.com
Printed in the USA
LVHW081018210420
654181LV00001B/91